THE AUTHOR

Muhammad Zafrulla Khan, a distinguished scholar in world religions, is a member of the Ahmadiyyah Movement, a missionary branch of Islam. He has served as Vice-President and Judge of the International Court of Justice in The Hague. He became Foreign Minister of Pakistan in 1947 and for many years has led the Pakistan Delegation to the General Assembly of the United Nations. He is now President of the Seventeenth Session of the General Assembly.

ISLAM
Its Meaning for Modern Man

RELIGIOUS PERSPECTIVES
Planned and Edited by
RUTH NANDA ANSHEN

RELIGIOUS PERSPECTIVES · VOLUME SEVEN

ISLAM

Its Meaning for Modern Man

by Muhammad Zafrulla Khan

LONDON

ROUTLEDGE AND KEGAN PAUL

First published 1962
by Routledge & Kegan Paul Limited
Broadway House, 68–74, Carter Lane,
London, E.C.4

Printed in Great Britain
by Richard Clay & Company Ltd.
Bungay, Suffolk

CONTENTS

RELIGIOUS PERSPECTIVES

VOLUMES ALREADY PUBLISHED

RELIGIOUS PERSPECTIVES
Its Meaning and Purpose

RELIGIOUS PERSPECTIVES represents a quest for the rediscovery of man. It constitutes an effort to define man's search for the essence of being in order that he may have a knowledge of goals. It is an endeavor to show that there is no possibility of achieving an understanding of man's total nature on the basis of phenomena known by the analytical method alone. It hopes to point to the false antinomy between revelation and reason, faith and knowledge, grace and nature, courage and anxiety. Mathematics, physics, philosophy, biology and religion, in spite of their almost complete independence, have begun to sense their interrelatedness and to become aware of that mode of cognition which teaches that "the light is not without but within me, and I myself am the light."

Modern man is threatened by a world created by himself. He is faced with the conversion of mind to naturalism, a dogmatic secularism, and an opposition to a belief in the transcendent. He begins to see, however, that the universe is given not as one existing and one perceived but as the unity of subject and object; that the barrier between them cannot be said to have been dissolved as the result of recent experience in the physical sciences, since this barrier has never existed. Confronted with the question of meaning, he is summoned to rediscover and scrutinize the immutable and the permanent which constitute the dynamic, unifying aspect of life as well as the principle of differentiation; to reconcile identity and diversity, immutability and unrest. He begins to recognize that just as every person descends by his particular path, so he is able to ascend, and this ascent aims at a return to the source of creation, an inward home from which he has become estranged.

It is the hope of RELIGIOUS PERSPECTIVES that the rediscovery of man will point the way to the rediscovery of God. To this end a rediscovery of first principles should constitute part of the quest. These principles, not to be superseded by new discoveries, are not those of historical worlds that come to be and perish. They are to be sought in the heart and spirit of man, and no interpretation of a merely historical or scientific universe can

7

guide the search. RELIGIOUS PERSPECTIVES attempts not only to ask dispassionately what the nature of God is, but also to restore to human life at least the hypothesis of God and the symbols that relate to him. It endeavors to show that man is faced with the metaphysical question of the truth of religion while he encounters the empirical question of its effects on the life of humanity and its meaning for society. Religion is here distinguished from theology and its doctrinal forms and is intended to denote the feelings, aspirations, and acts of men, as they relate to total reality.

RELIGIOUS PERSPECTIVES is nourished by the spiritual and intellectual energy of world thought, by those religious and ethical leaders who are not merely spectators but scholars deeply involved in the critical problems common to all religions. These thinkers recognize that human morality and human ideals thrive only when set in a context of a transcendent attitude toward religion and that by pointing to the ground of identity and the common nature of being in the religious experience of man, the essential nature of religion may be defined. Thus, they are committed to re-evaluate the meaning of everlastingness, an experience which has been lost and which is the content of that *visio Dei* constituting the structure of all religions. It is the many absorbed everlastingly into the ultimate unity, a unity subsuming what Whitehead calls the fluency of God and the everlastingness of passing experience.

These volumes seek to show that the unity of which we speak consists in a certitude emanating from the nature of man who seeks God and the nature of God who seeks man. Such certitude bathes in an intuitive act of cognition, participating in the divine essence and is related to the natural spirituality of intelligence. This is not by any means to say that there is an equivalence of all faiths in the traditional religions of human history. It is, however, to emphasize the distinction between the spiritual and the temporal which all religions acknowledge. For duration of thought is composed of instants superior to time, and is an intuition of the permanence of existence and its metahistorical reality. In fact, the symbol* itself found on cover and jacket of each volume of RELIGIOUS PERSPECTIVES is the visible sign or representation of the essence, immediacy, and timelessness of religious experience; the one immutable center, which may be analogically related to Being in pure act, moving with centrifugal and ecumenical necessity outward into the manifold modes, yet simultaneously, with dynamic centripetal power and with full intentional energy, returning to the source. Through the very diversity of its authors,

---

* From the original design by Leo Katz.

the Series shows that the basic and poignant concern of every faith is to point to, and overcome, the crisis in our apocalyptic epoch—the crisis of man's separation from man and of man's separation from God—the failure of love. The authors endeavor, moreover, to illustrate the truth that the human heart is able, and even yearns, to go to the very lengths of God; that the darkness and cold, the frozen spiritual misery of recent time, are breaking, cracking, and beginning to move, yielding to efforts to overcome spiritual muteness and moral paralysis. In this way, it is hoped, the immediacy of pain and sorrow, the primacy of tragedy and suffering in human life, may be transmuted into a spiritual and moral triumph.

RELIGIOUS PERSPECTIVES is therefore an effort to explore the *meaning* of God, an exploration which constitutes an aspect of man's intrinsic nature, part of his ontological substance. The Series grows out of an abiding concern that in spite of the release of man's creative energy which science has in part accomplished, this very science has overturned man's conception of the essential order of nature. Shrewd as man's calculations have become concerning his means, his choice of ends, which was formerly correlated with belief in God, with absolute criteria of conduct, has become witless. God is not to be treated as an exception to metaphysical principles, invoked to prevent their collapse. He is rather their chief exemplification, the source of all potentiality. The personal reality of freedom and providence, of will and conscience, may demonstrate that "he who knows" commands a depth of consciousness inaccessible to the profane man, and is capable of that transfiguration which prevents the twisting of all good to ignominy. This religious content of experience is not within the province of science to bestow; it corrects the error of treating the scientific account as if it were itself metaphysical or religious; it challenges the tendency to make a religion of science —or a science of religion—a dogmatic act which destroys the moral dynamic of man. Indeed, many men of science are confronted with unexpected implications of their own thought and are beginning to accept, for instance, the trans-spatial and transtemporal nature of events and of matter itself.

RELIGIOUS PERSPECTIVES attempts to show the fallacy of the apparent irrelevance of God in history. The Series submits that no convincing image of man can arise, in spite of the many ways in which human thought has tried to reach it, without a philosophy of human nature and human freedom which does not exclude God. This image of *Homo cum Deo* implies the highest conceivable freedom, the freedom to step into the very fabric of the universe, a new formula for man's collaboration with the creative process and the only one which is able to protect man from the terror of existence. This image implies further that the mind and conscience are capable of making genuine discriminations and thereby may reconcile the serious tensions between the secular and religious, the profane and sacred. The idea of the sacred lies in what it *is*, timeless existence. By emphasizing timeless existence against reason as a reality, we are liberated, in our communion with the eternal, from the otherwise unbreakable rule of "before and after." Then we are able to admit that all forms, all symbols in religions, by their negation of error and their affirmation of the actuality of truth, make it possible to experience that *knowing* which is above knowledge, and that dynamic passage of the universe to unending unity.

The volumes in this Series seek to challenge the crisis which separates, the crisis born out of a rationalism that has left no spiritual heirs, to make reasonable a religion that binds and to present the numinous reality within the experience of man. Insofar as the Series succeeds in this quest, it will direct mankind toward a reality that is eternal and away from a preoccupation with that which is illusory and ephemeral.

For man is now confronted with his burden and his greatness: "He calleth to me, Watchman, what of the night? Watchman, what of the night?"[1] Perhaps the anguish in the human soul may be assuaged by the answer, by the *assimilation* of the person in God: "The morning cometh, and also the night: if ye will inquire, inquire ye: return, come."[2]

RUTH NANDA ANSHEN

---

[1] Isaiah 21:11.

[2] Isaiah 21:12.

ISLAM
Its Meaning for Modern Man

Explanatory Note

THIS BRIEF EXPOSITION OF THE PRINCIPLES AND teachings of Islam is based upon the Quran, the Scripture of Islam. The explanations and illustrations furnished by the Prophet of Islam have also been drawn upon. Together these constitute the most authentic source material on Islam.

Except when otherwise indicated, all references are to the Quran. Every chapter of the Quran, with the exception of chapter 9, which is considered a continuation of chapter 8, opens with the verse: "In the name of Allah, Ever Gracious, Most Merciful." The verse is, in each case, part of the revelation. In most translations, however, this opening verse is not counted in the numbering of the verses of any given chapter. This incorrect method of numbering has not been followed in this volume. The system of numbering used herein starts with the opening verse and proceeds accordingly.

There are several English translations of the Quran. No particular translation has been uniformly followed in this volume. As Professor Arthur J. Arberry of Cambridge, England, has pointed out in the Preface to his *The Koran Interpreted*, the Islamic Scripture is, strictly speaking, untranslatable. Each verse, indeed each phrase, is rich in meaning, has several facets, and must be construed with reference to the context. A faithful paraphrase in keeping with the context is the best that can be attempted. In rendering the Arabic text into English, the author has kept closest to the English translation by Maulawi Sher Ali published by the Oriental and Religious Publishing Corporation Ltd., Rabwah, West Pakistan, under the title *The Holy Quran*. Incidentally, that translation follows the correct method of numbering the verses. It should be noted that in the Quran, references to Allah often change abruptly from first to third person, but the context makes the meaning clear.

The events of the Prophet's life and his exposition of Islamic values and principles are based upon authentic and well-recognized original sources. As, however, English translations of these are not easily available to the average Western reader, it has not been considered necessary to add references which could serve no useful purpose. Orientalists and scholars of Islam will have no difficulty in locating the references in the original biographical works and the six authoritative collections of Traditions.

In most instances, modern place names have been used, e.g., Ethiopia, not Abyssinia.

In the author's treatment of the subject, care has been taken to avoid doctrinal differences and controversies. The writer is a member of the Ahmadiyya Movement, the most active missionary movement in Islam today. It is anticipated, however, that the broad perspective of Islamic teachings here attempted will be generally endorsed by Muslim scholars. There is, indeed, little scope for difference or exception on the topics touched upon. Any such difference or exception can relate only to matters of detail or result from niceties of juristic or scholastic interpretation which would leave the main thesis unaffected.

M. Z. K.

I

Background

WHEN MUHAMMAD, THE PROPHET OF ISLAM, WAS
born in August, 570, of the Christian era, at Mecca, the principal
town of Arabia, the civilizations associated with the names of
Egypt, Babylon, and Greece were already matters of history.
They awaited the researches of the archaeologist, the antiquary,
and the scholar to be rescued from oblivion.

Europe was still largely pagan, devoted to the worship of
Nordic, Teuton, and a host of other gods. In South Asia, Brah-
manism and Buddhism had long passed their prime and had
entered upon a placid and prolonged old age.

In the Far East, the homely philosophy of Confucius and the
"way" of Lao-Tze pursued a sluggish and somnolent course. They
had earlier been stirred by the advent of Buddhism into China,
but had fallen back into passivity, along with Buddhism. Chinese
scholars, feeling that a period of decline and decay had set in,
made sporadic efforts at revival.

The two great empires of Iran and Byzantium were interlocked
in a struggle which ultimately resulted in death for both. The
sudden end of one and the slow expiration of the other followed
in due course, though the final blows in each case proceeded from
a quarter entirely unexpected.

Religion, philosophy, and learning were at a low ebb. The
spirit, the mind, and the intellect languished. Mankind had entered upon a decline. The earth seemed to be dying. It was the
darkest period of the Dark Ages. There was only an occasional
glimmer of light here and there. As the Quran says: "Corruption
had overtaken both land and water, in consequence of that
which the hands of men had wrought" (30:42).*

* "Land" here signifies peoples who did not profess belief in any Divine
revelation, while "water" refers to peoples who professed belief in such revelation.

15

In Arabia the gloom was almost unrelieved. The peninsula was an outlying and neglected region, its inhabitants innocent of learning, philosophy, and science. Although indifferent toward both the arts of peace and the regulations of war, the Arabs were good fighters. The hard and unrelenting struggle for existence in a waste and arid region left little margin for any other pursuit.

The need of water to sustain human and animal existence was urgent and insistent, and largely determined the pattern of life. With the exception of a few townships, Arab life throughout the peninsula was tribal and nomadic. Each tribe moved with its few belongings, its camels and sheep, in search of water and pasture, within a roughly defined area, according to the season of the year and the vagaries of the rainfall.

Mecca, forty miles from the Red Sea, enjoyed a degree of pre-eminence on account of the Sanctuary attached to the Ka'aba, the House of God, a pilgrim resort traditionally built or rebuilt by Abraham and his son Ishmael. Meccans claimed descent from Abraham through Ishmael. They revered Abraham as patriarch and prophet, and had vague notions of a Supreme God. They believed, however, that it was not possible for ordinary mortals to obtain access to Him save through intercessors. Abraham, being a Holy Man, had direct access to God, they conceived, but for themselves they sought the aid of gods and goddesses, whom they worshiped in the form of idols (39:4). For such intercession, it is related, they had installed as many as three hundred and sixty idols in the Ka'aba itself. Other towns had their own major and minor gods and goddesses. Such idolatry was prevalent throughout Arabia.

The Arabs possessed certain types of virtue. They had a lively sense of honor, and were very sensitive about anything that they deemed touched this honor. The virtue of hospitality was practiced to an exaggerated degree. A guest was entertained and protected to the utmost limit of the host's capacity. Notions of chivalry were sometimes carried to fantastic lengths. Courage and bravery were called for and were displayed in every exigency of their stern and austere life.

Fighting broke out frequently and tribal raids were common. Brutal and savage deeds, such as cutting off the ears and noses of the enemy dead and tearing out their hearts and livers, were not only practiced, but were gloried in.

Little was known of art. The main channels of artistic and

emotional outlet were furnished by poetry and oratory. In consequence, though writing was little known, spoken Arabic had been developed to a very high degree of excellence.

The Arabs were not familiar with any of the then known sciences, but being a people under the necessity of traveling at night —particularly during the hot season—across pathless deserts, they were interested in the elements of astronomy and had acquired a certain degree of proficiency in them.

Their principal vices were indulgence in liquor and gambling, and promiscuity in sexual relations. Woman was held in little honor, and among certain families who prided themselves on their status, the practice of infanticide of females was common. In fact, woman was regarded more as a chattel than as a companion or helpmeet, occupying a position only slightly above that of a slave. When a man died his sons inherited all his wives, except the mothers of the sons. Each son, however, was responsible for the welfare of his own mother.

Slavery was a familiar and widespread institution, and there was no limit to the hardship and indignity to which a slave might be exposed. The condition of slaves was a cycle of wretchedness and misery, terminated only by death.

The wealth and substance of the nomadic tribes consisted of horses, camels, sheep, and goats, all of which were highly valued on account of their useful qualities. They served as means of transport and sustenance, and they provided protection in the form of tents and clothing fashioned from their wool, hair, and hide.

The town dwellers carried on considerable trade through caravans, which plied not only between the townships of Arabia proper, but as far north as Syria, including Palestine, and also to the countries immediately to the east and west of the northern part of the peninsula. There was a certain amount of trade with India; Indian swords were highly prized.

Dates and liquor were among the products of Arabia, of which the former were much appreciated outside Arabia also. A certain amount of sericulture was carried on in Yemen and other parts of the peninsula, and silk cloth and stuffs were manufactured.

The political situation was confused and unstable. At the time of the birth of the Prophet, control over Yemen was exercised by Ethiopia, from across the Red Sea. Only that year—A.D. 570— Abraha, Ethiopia's Viceroy in Yemen, had led an expedition against Mecca, with the declared intention of destroying the

B

Ka'aba. The expedition proved an utter failure. Abraha's forces, which included some elephants, were struck by a virulent epidemic that destroyed large numbers of them during their encampment in a valley a few miles outside Mecca. The remainder of the group retired in confusion and terror. The year of that expedition is still known as the Year of the Elephant. The event is the subject matter of a brief chapter in the Quran (ch. 105).

Some years later Yemen appears to have passed under the suzerainty of Iran. It was the Iranian Viceroy of Yemen who was directed by the then Emperor of Iran to arrest the Prophet (who by then had migrated to Medina) and to forward him under guard to the Emperor. For this purpose the Viceroy sent emissaries to Medina. When the Prophet was apprised of their mission, he—wishing time for prayer and reflection—asked them to wait a day or two. During that time the assassination of the Emperor of Iran was revealed to the Prophet. When he informed the emissaries of his revelation and pointed out that the Emperor's orders could no longer have effect, the astonished men hastened back to Yemen to communicate to the Viceroy the Prophet's words—words soon confirmed by dispatches from the Ethiopian capital. This incident led the Viceroy and his court as well as large numbers of the people of Yemen to embrace Islam.

The Christian tribes in the north of the peninsula were in treaty relations with Byzantium, and enjoyed the protection of the Byzantine Emperor.

Mecca itself was a sort of republic. Its affairs were administered by a Council of Elders, composed of the heads of the leading families of the Qureish, the principal tribe inhabiting Mecca. The Council met as occasion demanded within the precincts of the Ka'aba, in a structure known as the House of Consultation, for the transaction of business relating to the affairs of the town. Different families of the Qureish had been assigned various functions in connection with the service of the Ka'aba, the regulation of the pilgrimage, and the administration of the city (9:19).

The Ka'aba and its enclosure were then, as they are now, the center of life in Mecca.

The prosperity of Mecca depended upon the veneration accorded throughout Arabia to the Ka'aba, which was a center of pilgrimage, and upon the profits derived from the trade caravans plying regularly to Yemen in the south, to Syria in the north, and even farther afield on occasion (106:2–3.),

2

Muhammad: Early Years

MUHAMMAD WAS BORN AN ORPHAN. HIS FATHER, Abdullah, had died some time before his birth. Abdullah had been the favorite son of Abdul Muttalib, and the latter was delighted at the news of the birth of Abdullah's son, whom he took under his care and protection. In conformity with a practice followed by urban families, Abdul Muttalib entrusted the young Muhammad to the care of Haleema, a member of a desert-dwelling tribe, to be nurtured and brought up in the fresh air of the desert. Haleema's little charge spent three or four years in the desert with his foster parents, being taken at intervals into town so that his mother and grandfather could be reassured with regard to his health and well-being.

Muhammad entertained grateful memories of Haleema's care, and always accorded her the respect and affection due to a well-loved mother. In Muhammad's case these sentiments may have been deepened by the sad bereavement he suffered shortly after his return to his mother's care, for his mother died while on a journey to Mecca from Medina, where she had gone with Muhammad to visit some of her relatives. The little boy was thus deprived of the love and care of his mother during his early boyhood. Not long afterward, the death of his grandfather, Abdul Muttalib, removed not only the head of the family but also the person who had been in the place of a father to him since birth.

Muhammad now passed under the care of his uncle, Abu Talib, who had several children of his own and was by no means well-off. Muhammad shared whatever was available with the rest of the family, and was accorded a mother's care and affection by his aunt. He had affectionate recollections of all that his aunt had done for him and had meant to him. Many years later, when she died at a ripe old age, the Prophet himself lowered her body into the grave, and said of her: "Thou wert ever an affectionate mother to me."

Enough is known of the youth and early manhood of Muhammad to indicate that he was gentle, patient, and obedient, respectful toward his elders, affectionate with his companions, and full of compassion for those who, on account of age, infirmity, or adversity, stood in need of help. As he grew to manhood, his good qualities were recognized by his contemporaries. They were impressed by his complete integrity, in word and deed, and he became generally known among them as "*El-Ameen*," meaning "the Trusty," or "the Faithful."

At home he helped with the household chores, and outside he assisted his uncle by carrying out such tasks and duties as pertained to him or were assigned to him. On one occasion, at least, he accompanied his uncle in a trade caravan to Syria. During the course of this journey, Abu Talib observed that his young nephew possessed a reserved and retiring disposition, betrayed no inclination toward levity or indulgence, and was indeed a person of modesty and good sense—a sharp contrast to the behavior of other young men of similar situation whom Abu Talib knew.

While still a young man, Muhammad was employed as a trade agent by Khadeeja, a wealthy, middle-aged widow of Mecca in business on her own, and he proceeded in that capacity on one or two journeys with a trade caravan. He acquitted himself so well in the discharge of his duties that each venture brought considerable profit to his employer. She received favorable reports of his deportment, habits, and behavior. This must have confirmed the good impression that she had herself conceived of the young man's person and character, and she made up her mind to send him an offer of marriage. When the offer was communicated to Muhammad through his uncle, he took counsel with the latter, who advised acceptance, and the match was concluded.

Muhammad was twenty-five when he married Khadeeja, who was forty, had been twice widowed, and had had children. In making his own decision Muhammad must have been principally influenced by the kindly treatment Khadeeja had accorded him while he worked for her, and the good impression her other qualities had made on him. It is true Khadeeja was wealthy, but this could not have influenced Muhammad, for it is well known that when Khadeeja placed all her resources at her husband's disposal, he distributed the greater part of her goods and property among the poor, the needy, and the afflicted, and set free all her slaves. He thus voluntarily chose a life of poverty for himself and his wife, and it speaks highly of Khadeeja's deep affection for her husband and of her lofty character that she accepted his choice cheerfully.

The marriage, despite the disparity in age and affluence, proved a very happy one. Khadeeja bore Muhammad several children; of these, the sons died in infancy, but the daughters grew to womanhood and in due course married. The descendants of only one daughter, Fatima, who was married to the Prophet's cousin Ali, son of his uncle Abu Talib, have survived. All those who today claim direct descent from the Prophet are descended through Fatima and her two sons, Hasan and Husain. The latter suffered martyrdom near Kerbala in Iraq, where he is buried.

When at home Muhammad occupied himself, as was his wont, in helping with the household tasks and taking care of his wife and children. He took no prominent part in the life of the city, but did not withdraw himself altogether from it.

Muhammad was a loving and affectionate husband, showing tender regard and consideration for Khadeeja; she, on her part, was so devoted a wife that when, fifteen years after their marriage, her husband received the Divine Call, she responded to it immediately, and was a constant source of comfort and support to him throughout the remaining ten years of their life together.

We have, in the previous chapter, attempted an outline of the conditions that prevailed in Arabia at the time of Muhammad's birth and during his youth and early manhood. The preoccupations and pursuits of an average young man of Mecca at that period would comprise a routine of trade, hunting, gambling, participation in drinking bouts (to which those who could afford it invited their friends as often as five times a day), and the indulgences attendant thereupon. This routine was, of course, diversified in individual cases under stress of personal needs and inclinations, family circumstances, or tribal emergencies. Life was subject to many hazards, and resort to arms was had at the slightest provocation. Long-pursued vendettas, often originating in slight incidents, exacted a heavy toll.

From his earliest youth Muhammad kept aloof from all this. He possessed a sensitive mind and a grave and serene disposition. He felt keenly the distress of his fellow beings and reacted very sharply to it, affording such relief and assistance as were within his power.

On one occasion he observed an old slave laboring hard to fulfill his task of drawing water in a heavy bucket for tending his master's garden. Muhammad went to his assistance and drew up a quantity of water, which gave relief to the old man for a short while, so that he could rest and husband his failing strength. Muhammad spoke cheering and comforting words to him, and on leaving him said: "Whenever you feel you are in need of help you can call on Muhammad." Many such incidents are on record.

That which affected his mind most deeply and painfully, however, was the moral and spiritual decline into which his people had fallen, and from which he could see no way of rescuing them, save through Divine guidance and help. He himself had never bowed to an idol or indulged in any idolatrous practices. On the physical side, he had preserved complete purity; he had never gambled or taken liquor, and had led an absolutely chaste life. He enjoyed the trust of his fellow townsmen, and was held in respect by them. An illustration of both the position which he occupied even as a young man in Mecca, and the wise understanding that was characteristic of him is furnished by the story about the Black Stone.

As already observed, the Ka'aba and its precincts were the center of Meccan life, and a great part of the prosperity of the town was connected with the Ka'aba, as the principal resort of pilgrimage in Arabia. The structure of the Ka'aba had fallen into disrepair, and it was decided to rebuild it. The famous Black Stone —a cornerstone, probably of meteoric origin—had to be replaced in position in the southeastern angle of the walls. Several leading families of the Qureish coveted the honor of placing the stone in position, and vehemently pressed their claim. The controversy became heated, tempers rose, and threats were uttered that the sword would be the arbiter. Someone suggested that the matter might be settled peacefully through arbitration. Muhammad chanced to enter the enclosure of the Ka'aba at that moment, and it was agreed that the dispute should be referred to him, and that his decision should be accepted. After ascertaining the cause of the argument, Muhammad spread out his cloak on the ground and placed the Black Stone on it. He then invited the leading members of the families that desired to have the honor of placing the stone in position to lift the cloak and carry the stone in this manner next to the angle of the wall where it had to be placed. Muhammad then lifted the stone and placed it in position. This satisfied every-body, and resolved a situation that had threatened to become grave to the point of possible bloodshed.

Though ever ready to promote justice and orderliness, and to soften, so far as it lay in his power, the hardships of life for those in distress, Muhammad continued to be tormented by the spectacle of the moral and spiritual degradation of his people, and his mind and soul were in constant travail over it. At the invitation of three young men—each named Fadhal—Muhammad entered into a mutual pledge to go to the assistance of any person who was oppressed by another, to obtain justice for him. That Muhammad did not regard the pledge lightly will appear later.

For the purpose of communing with himself and imploring the light and guidance of the Supreme Being concerning the problems that troubled his mind and soul, he formed the habit of retiring, for several days at a time, to a cave on one of the hills a few miles out of Mecca. There he occupied himself in prayer and contem-plation. Taking with him a quantity of dates and a little water by way of provisions, he would spend his days and nights in self-examination, in reflecting on the problems that troubled him, and in prayer and supplication to God. There is no record of the struggle that went on in his soul during these periods of retreat. Muhammad was not a man who talked much about himself. Indeed, he spoke only when the need for speaking arose, and then as briefly as the occasion would permit. With regard to his mental processes and his spiritual reactions during the years between his marriage to Khadeeja and his receipt of, and response to, the Divine Call, we can only speculate. In the nature of things it is not granted to any of us to probe into the depths of another's soul, to appraise accurately and completely its travail and its ecstasies. That is a holy secret between each individual and his Maker. Those years were, however, years of preparation, when Muham-mad's soul was being deepened and proved and made ready for the heavy responsibility that the Divine Will had decreed should be placed on him.

In the Quran we read God's word concerning Moses: "I wrapped thee with love from Me, and this I did that thou mightst be reared before My eye. . . . We proved thee in various ways. . . . Then thou camest up to the standard, O Moses, and I chose thee for Myself" (20:40–42).

As with Moses, so with Muhammad.

Muhammad is reminded of this in the Quran: "Did He not find thee an orphan and take thee under His protection? He found thee perplexed in search of Him and guided thee unto Himself. He found thee in want and provided thee with abundance" (93:7–9).

3

The Prophet at Mecca

MUHAMMAD WAS FORTY YEARS OLD—IN THE YEAR
610 of the Christian era—when the Divine Call came to him in
his retreat in Hira, the cave to which he was in the habit of repair-
ing for prayer and contemplation. He beheld a gracious Presence,
who asked him to recite. Muhammad answered that he knew not
how to recite. The Presence insisted: "Recite in the name of thy
Lord Who created: Created man from a clot of blood. Recite! Thy
Lord is the Most Beneficent, Who taught man by the pen, taught
him what he knew not" (96:2–6).

Muhammad repeated the words as commanded. The Angel
then vanished. Muhammad, overpowered by the experience,
immediately made his way home, all atremble. He told
Khadeeja what had happened. He expressed fearful apprehension
whether a frail human being like himself could prove equal to the
heavy responsibility that the incident portended God was about
to lay upon him.

"Surely, God will never suffer thee to fail," was Khadeeja's
comforting response. "Thou art kind and considerate toward thy
kin. Thou helpest the poor and forlorn and bearest their burdens.
Thou strivest to restore the high moral qualities that thy people
have lost. Thou honorest the guest and goest to the assistance of
those in distress."

Khadeeja's observations on this occasion throw a flood of light
on the Prophet's character as observed by his closest and most
intimate companion. The honest testimony of husband or wife
with regard to the character and disposition of the other is of the
utmost value, for no other person has the opportunity to make so
accurate an estimate based upon close observation and personal
experience.

Khadeeja suggested that Muhammad go with her to her aged

cousin Waraqa, who was a Christian hermit, and relate the experience to him. When Waraqa heard the account of the incident he observed: "The Angel that descended on Moses has
descended on thee. I wish I would be alive to give thee my support when thy people turn thee out."

"And will they turn me out?" Muhammad exclaimed in surprise.

"Never has that come to any which has come to thee but that
his people have turned against him," Waraqa replied.

Waraqa's reference to Moses was probably based upon the
prophecy contained in the words: "I will raise them up a Prophet
from among their brethren, like unto thee, and will put My words
in his mouth; and he shall speak unto them all that I shall command him. And it shall come to pass, that whosoever will not
hearken unto My words which he shall speak in My name, I will
require it of him" (Deut. 18:18–19).

It is striking that the first revelation that came to the Prophet
commanded him: "Recite in the name of thy Lord." Every
chapter of the Quran opens with: "In the name of God, Ever
Gracious, Most Merciful."

The call was Muhammad's first experience of verbal revelation.
A tremendous concept is conveyed by the verses revealed to him
on this occasion. Muhammad is warned that God has chosen him
as the instrument for conveying His message to mankind. The
Arabic word "*iqra*" connotes both recitation and conveying by
word of mouth. This message is to be conveyed to mankind in the
name of God who is the Creator of the Universe. Attention is
drawn to the insignificant origin of man, but the comforting
assurance follows that man's progress and development are under
the fostering care of the Most Beneficent, that God's beneficence
has decreed that many and varied avenues of knowledge shall
be thrown open to man, and that all this increase and accession
of knowledge shall be promoted through writing. One should
remember in this connection that the Prophet himself was not able
to read or write (29:49), and that proficiency in reading and writing was the privilege of only a few at that time in Arabia.

For a while there was no further experience of the same kind;
and then the Prophet began to receive revelation at brief intervals.
He has described the experience vividly, in this way: "Revelation
comes to me in different ways. Sometimes the words strike directly
at my heart, like the ringing of a bell, and this is physically hard

on me. Sometimes I hear the words as if spoken from behind a veil. Sometimes I see a Presence that speaks the words to me." This is confirmed by the Quran (42:52–53).

Thus it is clear that revelation in this context meant direct verbal revelation, conveyed in any one of the forms just mentioned. There are other forms of revelation also, which will be referred to later in the chapter dealing with that subject.

Soon the Prophet was commanded to proclaim widely and openly that which was being conveyed to him, and to turn aside from those who ascribed associates to God (15:95). His attempts to convey God's message to those around him in Mecca at first drew only ridicule upon him. Four persons, however, believed in him from the very outset: his wife, Khadeeja; his young cousin, Ali, son of Abu Talib, a lad only eleven years of age; his freedman, Zaid; and his friend, Abu Bakr.

Zaid was a well-born, intelligent young man, who had been captured while in his teens in a tribal raid, and was sold from one person to another until finally he was purchased by Khadeeja. Zaid was given his freedom by Muhammad after his marriage to Khadeeja, but he chose voluntarily to stay on with Muhammad. Some time later, his father and uncle traced him to Mecca and came with the purpose of ransoming him from Muhammad. The Prophet told them that Zaid was already a free man and that there was no question of any ransom. Pleased with this news, the father invited his son to accompany them home. Zaid had naturally been overcome with emotion on meeting his father and uncle, more particularly at their reminder that his mother had remained grief-stricken all through the period of separation from him and was impatiently awaiting his restoration to the family. He acknowledged the force of all this, but said his devotion to Muhammad had grown so deep that he could not bear the idea of parting from him. He sent loving messages to his mother, but was firm in his resolve not to leave Muhammad. When Muhammad found that Zaid was determined to remain with him, he took Zaid to the Ka'aba and, in the presence of his father and his uncle, announced that not only was Zaid a free man, but that henceforth he would be treated like a son.

Abu Bakr, who had been away from Mecca when the Prophet proclaimed his mission, returned to hear reports that his friend Muhammad must have become afflicted with madness, inasmuch as he had announced that God had commanded him to proclaim

His Unity and to denounce idols. Abu Bakr on hearing this exclaimed: "That mouth utters no lies!" He then sought out the
Prophet and inquired whether what he had heard was true. The
Prophet tried to explain, but Abu Bakr was insistent that his
question be answered Yes or No. The Prophet then affirmed that
what Abu Bakr had heard was true. Said Abu Bakr: "I believe."
He added that he had not wished to hear any explanation at this
stage because of his firm conviction that the Prophet was in-
capable of uttering an untruth, let alone inventing a lie against
God.

These four joined the Prophet and undertook to help him
spread the Divine Light. When this became known to the
Meccans, they laughed in derision. But they did not laugh long.
Verse by verse the revelation proceeded, "precept upon precept,
precept upon precept; line upon line, line upon line; here a little
there a little" (Isa. 28:13) until many wondered, and some began
to be drawn to it.

Among those who still resisted, mockery gave way to active
concern. They awakened to the fact that the message Muhammad
proclaimed threatened their whole way of life and their very
means of subsistence. If the worship of idols were abandoned, they
reasoned, Mecca would cease to be a resort for pilgrims, would
lose its position as a leading town, and would see its main industry
wither. Even the trade caravans might be altogether diverted
from Mecca. It was, therefore, resolved to suppress by use of
force this threat to their established way of life and to their
prosperity.

The new doctrine made a strong appeal to the weak and the
oppressed. The slaves, who suffered extreme hardship and indignity, began to hope that the Prophet's message might bring
deliverance to them. Women, who were in some respects treated
worse than animals, began to look up, and felt that the time was
nigh when they might gain a position of dignity and honor beside
their fathers, husbands, and sons. Young men were inspired with
visions of a noble and dignified existence. The early converts
came from the ranks of such as these. As the little band grew in
number, the Meccans embarked upon a course of persecution
which grew more cruel and savage as time passed, but their
efforts failed to arrest the progress of the new doctrine of the
Unity of God, the dignity and equality of man, and the lofty and
noble goal of human existence.

None was secure against persecution, not even the Prophet himself, who was continuously subjected to all kinds of indignities and molestations. But the worst affected were the slaves who accepted Islam, and whose masters inflicted unbearable torments upon them in vain attempts to force them to recant. They were taken out during the scorching heat of the midday sun and were made to lie down on their bare backs on the burning sands and rocks, while sun-heated rocks and pebbles were heaped upon their bare bodies. Even inside the town, boys were incited to make them victims of their cruel sport. They would tie ropes to the ankles of a slave and drag him through the streets paved with rough, jagged stones, leaving him a lacerated mass of bruises and bleeding cuts. Some succumbed under such tortures. Nor were women spared, some of them being subjected to shameless and unmentionable torture.

The Prophet's soul was tormented by the sufferings thus inflicted upon his helpless followers for no reason save that they said: "God alone is our Lord." He could do nothing to alleviate his own or their lot. He counseled patience and steadfastness, and assured them that God would open a way for them.

The Qureish, becoming more and more apprehensive of the inroads being made by the new doctrine, sent a delegation to Abu Talib, the Prophet's uncle. They asserted that though his nephew's denunciation of idol worship was intolerable to them, they had so far refrained from taking any extreme measures out of respect for Abu Talib, who was a revered chief and whose protection Muhammad enjoyed. Could not Abu Talib persuade his nephew to give up the preaching of the new doctrine, perhaps on pain of being disowned? They made it plain that if Abu Talib did not adopt this course, they would be compelled to disown their chief.

Abu Talib agreed to do what he could. But when he gravely spoke to his nephew, conveying what the delegation had said, Muhammad firmly replied that, while he lamented his uncle's dilemma, he was under Divine orders and could not disobey.

"Do not give up your people, Uncle," Muhammad said. "I do not ask you to stand by me. You may disown me as they have suggested. As for me, the One and Only God is my witness when I say that if they were to place the sun on my right and the moon on my left I would not desist from preaching the truth that God commands. I must go on doing so until the end."

Abu Talib plunged into deep thought. He had not himself

declared his belief in the Prophet's message, but he was very fond of his nephew and must have felt a surge of pride at Muhammad's firm and noble resolve, which he had expressed, to carry out his mission as commanded by God. Finally he raised his head, saying:

"Son of my brother, go thy way: do thy duty as thou seest it; my people may disown me but I shall stand by thee."

As the tempo of bitter persecution continued to mount, the Prophet advised some of his followers to leave Mecca and migrate across the Red Sea to Ethiopia, where they would find conditions more bearable under the rule of the Christian Emperor. A small band under the leadership of a cousin of the Prophet departed for Ethiopia. A delegation of the Qureish followed them, demanding of the Emperor that the fugitives be delivered to them. The Emperor heard both sides and rejected the demand of the Meccans.

The Qureish delegation then adopted a clever stratagem. Seeking out the bishops and other dignitaries of the Christian Church, they charged that the followers of the Prophet were adherents of a new creed which did not hold Jesus in honor. They hoped that this would set the Emperor and his Court against the fugitives and that the Muslims would be expelled from the country in disgrace. When the Emperor summoned both sides to his presence again, the bishops and nobles urged that the Meccan fugitives deserved no sympathy on account of what the Qureish had alleged against them. The Emperor made inquiry concerning this from the Muslims, who replied that far from this allegation being true, they held both Jesus and his mother Mary in great honor and believed in Jesus as a righteous prophet of God. Their leader, the cousin of the Prophet, recited relevant verses from the Quran in support of their statement (19:17–41). The Emperor, deeply affected by the recitation, affirmed the truth of these verses and stated flatly that he believed neither more nor less concerning Jesus than that which had been recited. He dismissed the Qureish and told the Muslims that they could dwell in the land without fear of molestation.

About this time, the persecuted and harassed Muslims in Mecca received some support and encouragement by the adherence of Umar to Islam. Umar was a leading Meccan whose courage and prowess were well known. Much troubled by the strife agitating Mecca as a result of the preaching of the new doctrine by Muhammad, he made up his mind to put an end to it all by putting an end to Muhammad. On the way to search out the Prophet, he was stopped by a friend who inquired whither he was bent. Umar explained his design; the friend retorted that he should look nearer home first, inasmuch as his sister and brother-in-law had already embraced Islam. In a rage, Umar stormed into his brother-in-law's house and by his violent entry interrupted a recitation of the Quran to which his sister and her husband had been listening. Umar drew his sword to attack his brother-in-law, but his sister parried the blow, and received a slight injury which drew blood.

This served to check further violence on the part of Umar, and in the end he asked that he might also hear what was being recited to them.

Umar listened to the recitation (20:15-17) and marveled at it. "Surely this is the truth," he exclaimed. Proceeding immediately to the Prophet, he made his submission to Islam.

Umar's acceptance of Islam was fervently welcomed by the Muslims, who had hitherto always congregated in secret and had performed their worship five times a day behind closed doors. They now felt that with a man of Umar's standing among them, they could worship God openly.

Umar's conversion did not, however, bring about any change in the attitude of the Meccans. Umar was treated in the same manner as the rest of the Muslims. Persecution grew more bitter and intense. Aiming to starve them out, a complete boycott of the Muslims and those who sided with them was put into effect. The small band of Muslims, together with some members of the Prophet's family who, though they did not believe in his mission nevertheless stood by him against Meccan persecution, were completely blockaded within a narrow enclosure belonging to Abu Talib. Contact with them for any purpose whatever was forbidden.

However, this measure also failed. The Prophet and his companions, refusing to entertain any thought of surrender or compromise on so transcendent a matter, steadfastly endured extremes of privation. At night some of them managed to slip out to procure meager provisions from people who were known to be sympathetic but dared not openly show their sympathy. Often, however, there was nothing but hunger and attempts to assuage its pangs with grass and leaves.

This state of affairs continued for nearly three years, until

finally five leading Meccans reacted against the savagery and in-
humanity of their fellow citizens, and let it be known that they
would invite the Prophet and his companions to come out of
their place of retreat and to go about their business as before. Thus
was the blockade lifted. But the privations and hardships endured
by the Muslims had gravely affected the health of both Khadeeja
and Abu Talib. Khadeeja died within a few days, and Abu
Talib's end came a month thereafter.

Though the boycott was lifted, every obstruction was placed in
the way of the Prophet to prevent him from establishing contact
with his fellow townsmen. The death of his faithful and beloved
wife left him bereft of his principal source of earthly comfort and
consolation, and the death of his uncle exposed him to greater
ill-treatment and persecution. In dozens of ways his opponents
made it almost impossible for him to leave his house to carry his
message to any section of the people of Mecca or to those who
might be on a visit there. Because of these circumstances Muhammad decided to go to Ta'if, a town about sixty miles southeast of
Mecca, which was also a resort of pilgrimage and was more
pleasantly situated than Mecca itself. The people of Ta'if had
close trade relations with the people of Mecca. They carried on
agriculture and fruit-growing in addition to their trade activities.
On his journey to Ta'if, the Prophet was accompanied by Zaid,
his freedman.

In Ta'if the leading townsmen received Muhammad and freely
let him have his say—but paid little heed to his message. After
a while they even showed signs of apprehension lest his welcome
in Ta'if might embroil them with the Meccans. So they left him
to be dealt with by street urchins and the riff-raff of the town.
The Prophet and his companion were finally turned out by mock-
ing and jeering crowds who pelted them with stones. Both were
wounded and bleeding as they left Ta'if behind them.

Weary and sore, they dragged themselves along a short distance, and when quite clear of the town, stopped in a vineyard
belonging to two Meccans. The owners, who happened to be in
the vineyard at the time, had been among Muhammad's perse-
cutors in Mecca, but on this occasion they felt some sympathy
toward their fellow townsman and permitted him to rest there a
while. Presently they sent him a tray of grapes by the hand of a
Christian slave. This slave, Addas by name, belonged to Nineveh.
The Prophet took up a grape, and before putting it into his mouth

he recited what has become the Muslim grace: "In the name of God, Ever Gracious, Ever Merciful." This excited the curiosity of Addas who inquired the identity of the stranger. The Prophet told him, and the conversation that ensued led Addas to declare his acceptance of Islam, so that Muhammad's journey to Ta'if did not prove entirely fruitless.

He had now a difficult problem to resolve. He had left Mecca and he had been rejected by Ta'if. Under Meccan custom, he could not go back there unless his re-entry was sponsored by some leading Meccan. There was nowhere else to go. He prayed earnestly for light, guidance, and help, and then set out with Zaid on the return journey to Mecca. He stopped on the way at a place called Nakhla for a few days and sent word to Mut'im bin 'Adi, a leading Meccan, asking whether he could be permitted to return to Mecca. Mut'im replied that he was prepared to sponsor his re-entry into Mecca, and when the Prophet approached Mecca Mut'im and his sons met him in the outskirts and escorted him back into the town.

But on the whole Mecca was as hostile as before, and the Meccans were determined that the doctrine preached by Muhammad should gain no footing among them. They resorted to every device to make life impossible for the Prophet and his followers in Mecca.

Muhammad's prayers and the revelations that came to him steadily were his only sources of consolation and strength. The latest revelations began to hint at the necessity for him to leave Mecca. Mecca was the town of his birth, where he had spent the whole of his life, had married, where his children had been born, and where the Divine Call had come to him. Despite the bitter and cruel persecution that he and his followers continued to suffer, its people were very dear to his heart and he knew that the parting, whenever it came, would be hard for him to bear. But his life was completely dedicated to his mission and he was ready to carry out in good spirit whatever might be God's pleasure concerning him. The painful prospect of having to leave Mecca was, however, softened by the Divine assurance that God would surely bring him back to it (28:86).

The determination of his next move came about as a result of a long-followed custom of the Prophet, namely, to try to make contact with parties from other parts of the country who visited Mecca on the occasion of the annual pilgrimage, and to make an

C

effort to interest them in his mission and message. On one such occasion he met a party of six or seven pilgrims from Medina, then known as Yathrib, who were encamped in a valley outside Mecca. At that time Medina was inhabited by two Arab and three Jewish tribes. The Arab tribes—Aus and Khazraj—were pagan idol worshipers, but had to some degree become familiar with Jewish traditions. They had heard from their Jewish fellow townsmen that the latter were expecting the advent of a Prophet which had been foretold in their Scriptures (Deut. 18:18).

The men whom the Prophet encountered on this occasion belonged to the Khazraj tribe. When he told them that God had appointed him as Messenger and had charged him with a message for mankind, they gave him a ready and eager hearing. In the end they declared their faith in him and his message, agreeing to convey it to their fellow townsmen on their return to Medina.

The following year twelve men of Medina, representing both the Khazraj and Aus tribes, came to the pilgrimage and met the Prophet in secret. It was necessary to take precautions lest the Meccans learn of their adherence to Islam and try to create difficulties for the people of Medina performing the pilgrimage. When the Prophet explained his mission in greater detail to them, they announced their own acceptance of Islam, and also the readiness of many people in Medina to accept it. The Prophet asked them to ascertain from their fellow Muslims and their fellow tribesmen whether they would be willing to give shelter to the harassed and persecuted Muslims of Mecca. They promised to bring back a reply the following year. But before the year was up, the Prophet had to send someone to Medina to answer the many eager inquiries about Islam provoked by the tribesmen as they reported their meeting with the Prophet. Mus'ab, the Meccan Muslim sent to Medina, instructed the new converts in the teachings and commandments of the faith.

In the meantime, mounting persecution in Mecca made life increasingly unbearable for the Muslims. When the season of the pilgrimage came round again, a large and representative delegation from Medina, including two women, met the Prophet and assured him that not only were their people in Medina ready to receive and give shelter to their brethren in faith from Mecca, but that they were very eager and would be greatly honored to receive the Prophet himself if he decided to go to Medina.

On this occasion the Prophet was accompanied by his uncle,

Abbas, who, though he had not yet accepted Islam, was fond of the Prophet and was anxious for his safety. He warned the Medina delegation that they were undertaking a heavy responsibility in inviting the Prophet to Medina. The Qureish would pursue him with their rancor and would rouse other tribes against him and his adherents in Medina. He asked them to pause and reflect before they incurred the risk involved in their offer. He pointed out to them that though Mecca was bitterly hostile to the Prophet, his own family stood by him and would give him their protection as far as they were able. In Medina, he would be exposed to every danger and hazard.

The leader of the Medina delegation replied that they and their people had carefully considered the hazards and believed any risk involved to be of little account. They would guard the Prophet with their lives, and no harm would come to him so long as any one of them was alive to prevent it.

Abbas also tried to dissuade the Prophet from accepting the invitation extended to him by the Medina delegation. The Prophet, however, decided that the Muslims of Mecca would migrate to Medina and that for himself he would await God's command. The Prophet then admonished the members of the delegation to order their lives in full conformity with God's command and His will, and to carry the message of Islam to all and sundry.

He then returned to Mecca.

The Muslims in Mecca were told that their brethren in Medina were ready to receive them and that those who were able to leave Mecca should proceed to Medina quietly and without creating a stir. Family after family made their preparations and departed in silence. The Meccans found that house after house occupied by the Muslims was being evacuated so that sometimes in the course of a week a whole row of houses would become empty. And so it came about that after a short period the only adult male Muslims left in Mecca were the Prophet, Abu Bakr, and Ali, and a handful of slaves, who had no choice in the matter. The Meccans took alarm that the Prophet might soon move beyond their reach, and they decided to put a violent end to him on a particular night. At this point, the Prophet received God's command to leave Mecca, and it so happened that the night fixed for his departure was the one that his opponents had chosen for their murderous designs. Abu Bakr, having learned from the Prophet of the decision to leave Mecca, asked whether he would be permitted to come along, and the Prophet gave his assent.

The following evening the Prophet left his house as soon as it was dark while those who had designs upon his life were collecting round the house in ones and twos, and proceeded to the rendez-vous with Abu Bakr. The two then made their way out of Mecca and went up one of the surrounding hills, there to take shelter in a cave called "*Thaur*," which had an entrance so narrow that a person had to lie flat and crawl into it. It was not a very safe place to spend much time in, as there was considerable danger from poisonous snakes and vipers. But perhaps for that very reason it afforded a chance of security against pursuit and discovery.

During the course of the night the Prophet's would-be assailants discovered that he was no longer in the house. At daybreak they took counsel together and decided to follow his tracks, which, they found, were soon joined by those of Abu Bakr. The tracker led them up the hill to the mouth of the cave, and there the tracks disappeared.

"The fugitives have not gone any farther; they have either sunk into the earth or ascended into the sky!" exclaimed the tracker, puzzled. The others ridiculed him, as there was nowhere for any-body to go except inside the cave; and this possibility they ruled out. Who would take the risk of serious bodily harm, and possibly death, from the vipers that abounded inside and around the cave?

Inside, Abu Bakr heard the voices of the men, and through the narrow opening of the cave he could observe some of them moving about. He was much afraid, knowing that if their hiding place were discovered, serious harm would come to the Prophet. When he mentioned his fear, the Prophet replied: "Grieve not. We are not two only; there is a third with us, even God" (9:40).

The pursuers returned to Mecca foiled in their immediate ob-jective, but still firm in their purpose. They announced that any-body who brought back the fugitives alive or dead would receive a reward of one hundred camels. This was widely proclaimed around Mecca.

The Prophet and Abu Bakr spent two nights and two days in the cave. Each night a shepherd in the employ of Abu Bakr, who had been instructed to graze his goats near the cave, brought a she-goat to the entrance of the cave and milked it for the benefit of his master and his friend. Some provisions were also sent from Mecca by Abu Bakr's daughter, Asma. On the second night, Abu

Bakr sent a message to a servant in Mecca, asking him to bring to the cave the following evening the two camels which Abu Bakr had specially reserved for this occasion, along with a trusted guide who could lead them to Medina. The party of four then started on the journey to Medina.

They had not proceeded far from Mecca when a Bedouin chief, Suraqa, attempted to intercept them, hoping to turn them over to the Meccans and thus earn the proffered reward. He was dissuaded from his purpose, made his submission to the Prophet, and then the party proceeded on their journey.

Ten days after leaving Mecca, the small party arrived within sight of Medina, where they were joyfully welcomed by the Muslims from Medina and those from Mecca who had preceded them. The Prophet decided to stop for a few days in Quba, a suburb of Medina, and then proceed to Medina. On arrival in Medina his first act was to purchase the site where his camel had stopped, for the purpose of building a mosque thereon. He then accepted the offer of a Muslim whose house was nearest to the selected site to put him up temporarily, while the mosque and his own quarters next to it were being built.

4

The Prophet at Medina

WITH THE ARRIVAL OF THE PROPHET IN MEDINA (in the year 622 of the Christian era), Islam began to spread rapidly among the two Arab tribes of the town. But, as often happens in a mass movement, not all who declared their adherence to the faith were inspired by sincerity and high ideals.

Some time before the Emigration, as it has since been called, the Aus and Khazraj, wearied by their long, drawn-out mutual hostility, which had often erupted into fighting and had exacted a heavy toll of life, had decided to put an end to this state of affairs and to set up a form of administration in Medina which should have the support of both tribes and should also be acceptable to the three Jewish tribes. For this purpose it had been agreed that Abdullah bin Ubayy ibn Salul, chief of the Khazraj, should be elected king of Medina. This plan had not yet been put into effect when the Prophet was invited to come to Medina. When he arrived it was generally felt that he was the most appropriate person to take on the responsibility of administering the affairs of Medina. Under his direction a covenant was drawn up which was accepted by both Arabs and Jews. A common citizenship of Medina was established and conditions were prescribed for the regulation of the affairs of the town as well as for organizing its internal order and external security.

The principal conditions were that the internal affairs of each section would be regulated according to its own laws and customs, but that if the security of Medina were threatened from outside all sections would co-operate with each other in its defense. No section would enter into any separate treaty relations with any outside tribe, nor would any section be compelled to join in any fighting which should take place outside Medina. The final determination of disputes would be referred to the Prophet, and his decision would be accepted and carried out. This became, as it were, the Charter of Medina. Thus was the Republic of Medina set up.

Abdullah bin Ubayy was deeply chagrined at the loss of a crown, which, before the arrival of the Prophet, he had thought was assured for him. He became the leader of the disaffected party in Medina. This party was a source of constant worry and insecurity for the Prophet and the Muslims. It is referred to in the Quran, at various places, as "the hypocrites." *

The Jews, on their part, were not disposed to let the Prophet remain in peace at Medina. They were, it is true, eagerly awaiting the advent of a Prophet foretold in their Scriptures (Deut. 18:18), but they felt that to accept an Arab as the fulfillment of that prophecy would raise the prestige of the Arabs above that of the Jews in the religious and spiritual spheres and this, as Jehovah's chosen people, they were not prepared to tolerate.† While not daring to oppose the Prophet openly, they let no opportunity pass of conspiring and intriguing against him and the Muslims both inside Medina and outside it.

The Meccan Muslims had found a place of refuge in Medina, and they could now openly perform their daily worship of God, together with their brethren of Medina, without hindrance. They appreciated this as a great boon, but in Medina also the Muslims were exposed to many hazards and had to keep constantly on the alert. The Prophet himself, who was responsible for the security not only of the Muslims but of the whole of Medina, and had many more cares added to the discharge of his mission as a Prophet, found little time for sleep or rest. When this became known, the Muslims arranged to mount guard by turns outside his quarters at night so that he could have a few hours of sleep. To the

---

* See, for instance, chap. 63.

† The Quran states that the Beni Israel, i.e., the descendants of Jacob, were the recipients of God's favors (2:48, 123), but it also recites some of the causes that had led to their fall from grace, e.g., their breaking of their covenant with God, their denial of the Signs of God, their seeking to kill the prophets who were sent to them, their disbelief in Jesus, their uttering against Mary a grievous calumny, their claim that they had put Jesus to death on the cross, their taking interest though they had been forbidden it, their devouring people's wealth wrongfully, their transgression in respect of the observance of the Sabbath, etc. It also holds out a promise of redemption: "But those among them who are firmly grounded in knowledge . . . believe in what has been sent down to thee and what was sent down before thee, and those who observe Prayer and those who pay the Zakat, and those who believe in God and the Last Day: Upon these will We surely bestow a great reward" (4:156–163).

internal problems of Medina and the dangers and hazards con-
fronting the Muslims, and most of all the Prophet himself, a
formidable threat was soon added from Mecca.

When the Meccans learned that the Prophet had arrived safely
at Medina and had been joyfully received there by the Muslims
and that Islam was making progress among the two Arab tribes
there, they resolved to adopt coercive measures to secure his
expulsion from Medina. They addressed a letter to Abdullah bin
Ubayy, warning him and the people of Medina that if they did
not expel the Prophet from the city—or, failing that, did not take
up arms against him and the Muslims, jointly with the Meccans—
the Meccans would come with a mighty force and put to the
sword all the male adults and enslave all the women.

On receipt of this letter, Abdullah held a secret council of his
supporters and proposed that, in view of the Meccan ultimatum,
the only course open to them was to force the Prophet and his
followers to leave Medina. When news of this reached the Prophet,
he went to see Abdullah and tried to dissuade him from embark-
ing on such a course, pointing out that any such adventure could
lead only to his own ruin. For the time being Abdullah forbore,
but he never abandoned the hope that an opportunity might
arise when he could take measures to rid Medina of the Prophet
and the Muslims, and thus secure his own recognition as the chief
and ruler of Medina.

Saad bin Muaz, chief of the Aus and a brave and sincere Muslim, visited Mecca about this time to perform the customary circuit of the Ka'aba. He was noticed by Abu Jahl, a Meccan chief
and a sworn enemy of the Prophet, who accosted him, asking how
he dared come to Mecca to perform the circuit when it was well
known that he had once sheltered the Prophet in Medina. Did he
not realize that by giving shelter to Muhammad, the people of
Medina had earned the enmity of the Meccans and could no
longer be permitted to perform the rites and ceremonies connected with the Ka'aba? Saad retorted that if this were the attitude of the Meccans, their caravans plying between Mecca and
Syria would no longer enjoy the right of free passage between
Medina and the coast.

And so the stage was set for open warfare between the Meccans
and the Muslims in Medina.

Meanwhile the Prophet was organizing the Muslims as a religious community who should put into effect all the command-

ments and values inculcated by Islam. His undertaking involved tremendous responsibility. To weld into a homogeneous whole a community made up of Meccan refugees and Medina Arabs drawn from tribes which had till lately been sworn enemies, and to instruct them in ways which would make their individual and communal lives wholly beneficent for themselves as well as for those who came in contact with them demanded unremitting attention and every moment of available time. It was a monumental task even for a man with the capacity of the Prophet, strengthened and reinforced by Divine revelation. The administration of the affairs of Medina and its people was an onerous addition to this main purpose. The threat of invasion from Mecca greatly multiplied the Prophet's responsibilities and preoccupations, and taxed his capacities to the utmost. Yet he set about doing whatever was needful in a serene and steadfast spirit, putting his complete trust in God and exhorting the Muslims in their turn to be patient and steadfast, and constantly to foster their communion with God, so as to make it a rich and living experience.

All due precautions were taken. For, though God's promise of succor for, and ultimate triumph of, Islam was wholly true and completely to be depended upon, God required that every effort be put forth in support of the cause. Therein lies the secret of the strength of Islam as a faith. The fullest confidence in, and reliance upon, God's grace and help and the putting forth of the utmost effort that man is capable of—both these in combination, as taught by God Himself, help achieve the goal (53:39–40). All success in every beneficent endeavor comes from God, but it follows upon sincere and steadfast effort combined with perfect trust and humble supplication to God (2:46–47, 145).

It was necessary to know what plans and preparations were afoot in Mecca. The Prophet, therefore, sent out small parties from time to time to reconnoiter along the routes to and from Mecca and the surrounding area. He learned that the Meccans were seeking to incite other tribes against the Muslims and to strengthen their own position with alliances. The Prophet made efforts to establish friendly relations with outside tribes whenever the opportunity offered itself, the purpose being to organize resistance to aggression and to secure freedom of conscience and belief for everyone. This was the beginning of the Pax Islamica.

A reconnoitering party was sometimes involved in an incident or minor skirmish, but this was unavoidable in view of the hostile designs and activities of the Qureish. It was felt on both sides, however, that matters could not continue as they were and that a clash was inevitable inasmuch as the Qureish were determined to stamp out the faith preached by the Prophet before its adherents gained enough support and strength to resist successfully any force that might be mustered against them.

One of the devices of the Meccans was to use their trade caravans plying between Mecca and Syria to incite the tribes on their route against the Muslims. They even diverted these caravans from their regular route so that these activities could be spread out as widely as possible. Everybody in Mecca had a direct interest in these caravans, which were substantial affairs, as practically all the savings of the Meccans were invested in them. Each caravan was accompanied by an armed guard, which might consist of a force of from one hundred to five hundred men, depending upon the size of the caravan and the value of the merchandise it carried—a formidable threat to the security of Medina.

About a year after the Emigration, intelligence began to reach the Prophet that the Meccans were preparing a strong force to advance upon Medina. Their pretext was that one of their large caravans returning from Syria was likely to be attacked by the Muslims at a point near Medina, and that an adequate force had to proceed north to secure its safe passage. And they may well have been genuinely apprehensive concerning the safe passage of the caravan, in view of their behavior toward the Prophet and the Muslims over the years in Mecca and Medina. It was a large caravan, carrying valuable merchandise; but it was accompanied by an adequate armed force which has been estimated at four to five hundred men. Although the Meccans knew that the Muslims could not possibly muster a force strong enough to constitute a real threat to the safety of the caravan, they went ahead with their warlike preparations. By the time the Meccan army set out on its march north, news arrived that the caravan had passed safely through the danger zone, and that no attempt had been made to interfere with it. Nevertheless, the Meccan army continued its march in the direction of Medina.

In the meantime, the Prophet was taking stock of his own position. Permission to take up arms in defense had been accorded in Divine revelation (22:40-42). The Prophet assembled a force of about three hundred Muslims from Mecca and Medina, and marched out with them.* This heterogeneous body—it scarcely deserved the designation "force"—was united only by the common bond of faith and the determination to die in defense of that faith. Although it included some of the older Meccan Muslims who were experienced fighters, the greater number were young men, some still in their teens, who had had little, if any, combat experience. Their devotion to their faith and their zeal in its support were their only qualifications. Ill-armed, in poor physical condition because of the privations they had been enduring, and with but two horses and a few camels, they presented a pitiful contrast to the Meccan army, which consisted of at least a thousand tried warriors who were well-armed and well-mounted.

Those who accompanied the Prophet as he set forth from Medina knew that they had been called out to take up arms in defense of their faith, but they were not aware of their exact objective. There had been rumors both of the trade caravan with its armed escort passing near Medina, and of the Meccan army marching north, but the Prophet had said nothing about them. Some of those with the Prophet hoped that if there were to be a clash it would be with the caravan rather than with the army (8:8). Not till the party was two days' march out of Medina did the Prophet disclose that they would have to face the strong, well-equipped force advancing from Mecca. On the next day the Muslims, having arrived at a place called Badr, took up their position near a well. The Prophet had been advised by one of the Muslims to make camp there on account of the supply of water which was available, although the ground underfoot was sandy and the few experienced fighters in the group were apprehensive that this would be a serious handicap during battle because the sand would not permit easy and rapid movement. The Meccan force on its arrival took up a position opposite on firm clay soil.

Night set in. The Prophet spent the greater part of it in earnest prayer and supplication. He knew, none better, that the revelation being vouchsafed through him to mankind was the guarantee and the source of man's honor, dignity, and welfare both here and in the Hereafter. He had firm faith in every Divine promise, but he also realized fully the complete supremacy of the Divine Being and the many weaknesses that beset mortals. He prayed for succor; he prayed for strength; he prayed for steadfastness for

* The exact number was 313.

himself as well as for those with him. Part of his prayer and supplication during that fateful night has been preserved and has come down to us. It reveals the core of his anxiety: "O Lord, if Thou wilt suffer this little band to perish, Thy Holy Name will no more be glorified on earth and there will be none left to worship Thy Glorious Majesty in true sincerity."

Morning approached. The Prophet and the Muslims beheld the dawn of the day which was to decide the issue of one of the most fateful contests ever waged in the history of man between the forces of truth and righteousness, and those of falsehood and ignorance. There was a shower of rain which firmed the sand underfoot while turning the clay into slippery mud, and the Muslims were comforted and encouraged. The Prophet drew up his men in battle array and gave them instructions, but he repeatedly went back to prayer under a hastily improvised shelter. When the fighting began, the Prophet was prostrate before his Lord in an agony of supplication. Abu Bakr approached him and put a gentle hand upon his shoulder, saying: "Messenger of God, thou hast prayed enough." The Prophet raised himself and announced to the people that God had given him to understand that the time had arrived for the fulfillment of the Prophecy revealed several years earlier at Mecca: "Do they say, 'We are a victorious host?' The hosts shall soon be routed and will turn their backs in flight. Aye, the Hour is their appointed time; and the Hour will be most calamitous and most bitter" (54:45–47).

The issue did not remain long in doubt. The flower of the Qureish was left upon the field, dead and dying (Isa. 21:16–17). Abu Jahl, the bitterest enemy of the Prophet and the commander of the Meccan forces, was mortally wounded at the commencement of the battle. As he lay dying, he lamented his fate, not so much that he was about to die, but that his death should have been compassed by two striplings, twelve and thirteen years old, of the non-warrior tribes of Medina. Several prisoners were taken, among them the Prophet's uncle, Abbas, who had been coerced into joining the Meccan forces, and one of his sons-in-law.

The Prophet, while giving thanks to God for the great deliverance which He had vouchsafed, was grieved that so many of the Meccans had perished in pursuit of their vain purpose. On beholding the prisoners bound and held fast, tears coursed down his cheeks. When Umar inquired why, in the midst of victory, he felt so grieved, the Prophet pointed to the prisoners and said: "Behold what disobedience to, and defiance of, the will of God leads to."

There was much debate as to the fate of the prisoners. According to Arab custom they could have been dispatched immediately, but the Prophet determined otherwise. It was decided that those who could offer suitable ransom would be released on payment of the ransom, and those who could not offer ransom would be released as an act of grace. The ransom of such of the prisoners as were literate was fixed at teaching ten Muslim boys to read and write.

When the news of the catastrophe reached Mecca, there was mourning in every house. But all customary lamentations and other expressions and exhibitions of grief were forbidden by the Elders till the Meccans had had time to reorganize their forces and to avenge the disastrous defeat.

On returning to Medina, the Prophet resumed his main task of instructing the Muslims in the tenets, doctrines, and commandments of the faith, and in organizing them into a society such as Islam was designed to establish. All this had to be carried on under the constant threat of attack and aggression. The Prophet was aware, and indeed the Meccans fleeing from the battle of Badr had announced, that they would soon return to avenge their defeat. In Mecca, preparations toward that end proceeded briskly. Among other measures it was resolved that all profits derived from commercial ventures should be paid into a war fund, to be used for equipping an army strong enough to march against Medina. In a year's time the Meccans were ready, and a well-armed force, three thousand strong, took the road to Medina.

When the news reached the Prophet, he held a council to determine how this new threat should be met. He had had a dream, part of which he interpreted as meaning that it would be better for them to stay in Medina and await the enemy's attack. However, the younger men, particularly those who had not taken part in the previous battle, were eager to meet the foe before they could enter the town. Finding that a majority of those present were in favor of meeting the enemy outside Medina, the Prophet adopted their suggestion and marched out of the town at the head of approximately one thousand men.

The Muslims took up their position at the foot of a range of hills a few miles east of Medina. The Meccan army coming up from the south had veered to the east, intending to attack the town from that direction. The Prophet discovered that a certain number of Jews from Medina had also joined his following, and asked them to go back, saying that they had no obligation in respect of the defense of Medina that involved fighting outside the town. Abdullah bin Ubayy took umbrage at this, and announcing that the Muslims were no match for the force the Meccans had brought up, withdrew with three hundred of his supporters, leaving seven hundred men at the Prophet's disposal. Of these, the Prophet posted fifty to guard a gap in the range of hills at the rear, with instructions that they were not to leave their post until ordered to do so.

The disparity between the opposing forces was even more strik-ing now than it had been the previous year. Against three thou-sand well-armed Meccan warriors, seven hundred of whom were in armor and two hundred mounted on horses, there were only six hundred and fifty Muslims (excluding those guarding the pass at the rear), of whom only one hundred were in armor, and they had only two horses. Yet, when battle was joined, the Meccans were soon put to flight. Seeing this, the men guarding the pass became eager to join in the pursuit, and despite the remonstrances of their captain, the majority of them left their post, contrary to their instructions. One of the Meccan commanders, Khalid, drew the attention of another commander, 'Amr, to the sparsely guarded pass, and the two of them, having collected a number of their followers, veered round behind the hill, slew the remaining men at their post, and fell upon the rearguard of the Muslims, by now scattered over the field, some in pursuit of the Meccans and others withdrawing from the battle under the impression that no further fighting was called for. Hearing the cries of their fellow fighters who had attacked the Muslims from the rear, the fleeing Meccans in front rallied and returned to the fray. In a moment all was confusion, and the Prophet, the target of the Meccan attack, was left with only a handful of Muslims to guard him. Most of these were killed by the arrows that rained down thick and fast upon them. Even as this took place, the Prophet prayed for his enemies: "Lord, grant guidance to my people, for they know not what they do." Hardly had he uttered the prayer when he himself was hit in the cheek by a stone that drove two of the rings of his helmet into the flesh. He fell down, unconscious, among the heap of Muslim dead, others falling on top of him.

The Meccans, thinking that the Prophet had been killed and that their main purpose had been achieved, withdrew from the field, content with the victory that they believed to be theirs. The scattered Muslims gathered round the spot where the Prophet had fallen, and finding him still alive though unconscious, raised him up. One of them pulled out with his teeth the rings of the Prophet's helmet which were embedded in his cheek, losing two of his teeth in the effort. The Muslims were heartened. Despite the losses and the reverse they had suffered, they were happy that the enemy had retired without having achieved his main purpose.

Various incidents during the battle of Uhud, named from one of the hills at the foot of which it was waged, confirmed the interpretation which the Prophet had put on his dream. It was realized by all that the Prophet's judgment had been correct, and that the complete victory which the Muslims had achieved in the early part of the day had almost been converted into defeat by disregard of the Prophet's instructions to the fifty men who had been assigned to guard the pass at the rear (3:153-155).

The women and children remaining in Medina during the battle were sorely grieved by reports that the Muslims had been defeated and the Prophet killed. Many of them streamed out of the town in the direction of Uhud, but when they were reassured that the Prophet was alive, all other considerations gave way to joy and relief. If the Prophet was safe, all had been gained and nothing lost. However, to the disaffected among both the Jews and the weaker Muslims in Medina, the course of the battle gave great encouragement. The Meccans, on their side, who had begun to suspect before retiring from the field of battle that the Prophet was alive, renewed their efforts at inciting the tribes in the central and southern parts of the peninsula against the Muslims.

In Medina the behavior of two of the Jewish tribes became increasingly arrogant and mischievous. As they had become a serious menace to the security of the town, they had to be expelled from it eventually. One tribe settled in Syria; the other, partly in Syria and partly in Khaibar, a Jewish stronghold to the north of Medina. Thus Khaibar also became a center of anti-Muslim intrigue, and the Jews of Khaibar in concert with the Meccans started a campaign directed mainly toward inciting the northern tribes against the Muslims.

In the meantime, Muslim society was rapidly taking shape and the foundation was being laid for the social and economic organization of the Muslims. The commandment prohibiting the use of liquor and indulgence in gambling was revealed about this time, and was instantly and eagerly put into effect by the people, many of whom had been addicted to these vices all their lives (2:220; 5:91–92).

Shortly after the battle of Uhud, the Meccans were afflicted with a severe famine. When the Prophet learned of their distress, he raised a relief fund and sent it to Mecca. But this gracious and generous gesture of goodwill did not soften the implacable hostilities of the Meccans. Their persistent incitement of the tribes against the Muslims soon began to bear fruit.

To the other devices employed by the enemies of Islam, treachery was now added. Two tribes, one after the other, pretended interest in, and sympathy toward, the new faith, and begged the Prophet to send them persons who could instruct them in its tenets and practices. To the first tribe, the Prophet sent ten selected instructors, who were treacherously and cruelly murdered. When the request for instruction came from the second tribe, the Prophet hesitated to comply, but yielded on a guarantee being furnished by one of the tribal chiefs. He sent seventy instructors, each having learned by heart the Quran, so far as it had then been revealed. They met with a similar fate.

This and other incidents convinced the Prophet that if peace were ever to be established and freedom of conscience were to be won for all, he would have to take more active steps than had hitherto been possible, to secure law and order and the observance of treaties and agreements. Henceforth, trying to stem the evil at its source, he would lead an expedition whenever he received intimation that hostile forces were gathering for an attack against him. He moved so rapidly in each case that he took his opponents by surprise, and on several occasions their designs were frustrated and peace was restored, even though only temporarily and precariously, without recourse to fighting. When fighting did have to be resorted to, the issue was determined without serious loss of life. All that the Prophet asked was that his opponents lay down their arms and bind themselves to keep the peace.

This made the Meccans and their Jewish allies more desperate, and they redoubled their efforts to put an end to the Prophet and all that he stood for. By the fifth year after the Emigration, about two years after the battle of Uhud, they succeeded in arousing general hostility against the Muslims throughout Arabia, and laid most of the tribes under contribution to raise an army against the Muslims. This army, known as the Confederates, was estimated at eighteen to twenty thousand men. Their preparations were on a proportionate scale. They advanced in all their might against Medina, confident that this time there could be no escape for the Muslims.

When the Prophet was apprised of this, he held a council, as was his wont. This time there was no question of the Muslims being able to offer resistance outside Medina. They had to defend the town as best they could with such means as came to hand. Among the Prophet's companions at the time was Salman, an Iranian. Asked by the Prophet what Iranians would do in a similar situation, Salman replied that a township in the position of Medina would defend itself from behind a trench. The Prophet, approving of this suggestion, ordered a deep and wide trench to be dug on the side of Medina which was open to the plain, and thus was the most probable side for attack. On the other sides some security was offered by a range of hills, by the strongholds of the remaining Jewish tribe, and by stone houses and groves which lay thickly together. The Jewish tribe was in alliance with the Muslims and was bound by the terms of the Charter of Medina to co-operate in the defense of the town.

The Muslim population of Medina at that time comprised approximately three thousand males of all ages. With the exception of infants and very small children, they all flocked to the lines marked out for the digging of the trench and were divided into groups for digging and clearing the trench in sections. Even the women co-operated and helped relieve the men of such tasks as they could suitably perform. The total length of the trench was about a mile. It was scarcely ready before the Confederate army arrived in front of Medina. They were amazed to find their entry into the town barred by the trench, which was for them a new spectacle.

The Meccans made camp short of the trench and a state of siege began. Continuous attempts to cross the trench were repulsed. The fighting was not severe and there was little loss of life, though the strain on the Muslims was heavy and sustained. The Prophet had ordered the women and children under fifteen years of age away from the trench. This left him with about twelve hundred men to guard the trench and to oppose the entry of the

D

Confederates into the town. The Muslims' desperate resistance
was based on the realization that once the enemy gained a footing
on their side of the trench it would mean the end of everything:
neither man, woman, nor child would be spared and the Muslim
quarters of Medina would be utterly destroyed.

The Confederates, finding the trench a formidable obstacle to
their advance into the town, began to consider other means of
gaining their objective. Through Huyai bin Akhtab, chief of one
of the Jewish tribes which had been expelled from Medina, they
tried to win over to their side the remaining Jewish tribe in
Medina. At first their approaches were repulsed, but in the end
Huyai succeeded in convincing the Jewish leaders that this time
there was no escape for the Muslims and that it would be wise
and prudent for the Jews to cast in their lot with the Confederates.
It was agreed that as soon as the Confederates were able to force
a passage across the trench, the Jews would rise and attack the
Muslim quarters, so that the Muslims would be caught between
the Confederates in front and the Jews in the rear.

Relying on the loyalty of the Jews and their duty in respect of
the defense of Medina, the Prophet had posted no forces for the
purpose of guarding the Muslim quarters of the town, and had
left only a handful of watchmen to supervise the security of the
women and children. When it became known to the Prophet that
the Confederates had won over the Jews to their side, he assigned
two bodies of men, three hundred and two hundred strong re-
spectively, to the Muslim quarters of the town to take measures
for their defense against the Jews should they attempt an attack.
This reduced the forces at his disposal at the trench facing the
Confederate army to seven hundred and fifty men. Again, the disparity in numbers and in every other respect between the opposing forces was not only striking but pitiful.

The Confederate army now pressed their attack across the
trench, and there was continuous and desperate fighting. The
plight of the Muslims is graphically described in the Quran
(33: 11–24).

During one of the attacks, when a party of the Confederates
had crossed the trench and were repulsed, a noted tribal chief
was left dead on the Muslim side. His people, fearing that the
Muslims would mutilate his dead body, as would have been their
own procedure, offered a sum of ten thousand dirhems for the recovery of his body. They did not know that the Prophet had

abolished all barbarous customs and that their fears were un-
founded. When their offer was conveyed to the Prophet he declined to receive any payment, saying, "A corpse has no value for
us. They can remove it whenever they like."

Before the day decided upon for the joint assault by the Confederates and the Jews, relief came from an unexpected source:
the weather. It was a stormy and turbulent night. The fierce wind
caused great confusion in the Confederate camp. Further con-
sternation arose when one of the tribal chiefs observed that the
fire in front of his tent had gone out; according to Arab super-
stition, this portended death or defeat for him in the next day's
battle. To avoid this, the chief told his people to strike camp so
that they could withdraw quietly into the desert for a day or two.
This move was interpreted by both Jew and Confederate as a device to secure safety against a feared night sortie by the Muslims.
The alarm spread and there was general panic. Tents were hastily
pulled down, and a disorderly retreat ensued. When morning
came, the whole plain in front of the trench was empty. There was
no trace of the Confederate forces (33:10).

The Muslims, who had been suffering extremes of privation and
fatigue, and had considered themselves at the end of their tether,
rejoiced greatly at this sudden deliverance. But respite was not yet
to be. The treachery of the Jewish tribe in Medina had to be dealt
with. The Prophet told his men to be ready to march against the
Jewish strongholds, and he sent his cousin, Ali, to demand from
the Jews an explanation of their conduct. Far from furnishing any
explanation or offering any excuse, the Jews behaved most
arrogantly toward Ali, repudiated their covenant, and uttered
vile abuse of the Prophet and his family. Manning their fortified
strongholds, they dared the Muslims to do their worst. Ali, returning to the Muslim quarters, was met by the Prophet, who was
advancing toward the Jewish sector with his men. When Ali
described the situation to the Prophet and begged him not to proceed farther himself, but to entrust the mission to somebody else,
the Prophet said: "Ali, are you afraid that I might hear abuse
from our opponents? Moses was of their own kith and kin, and
they treated him far worse than they have treated me. I can
expect nothing better at their hands."

The Jewish strongholds were surrounded by the Prophet's
forces, and the Jews soon found that they had no alternative but
to surrender. Instead of throwing themselves on the Prophet's

mercy, however, they asked for arbitration by Saad bin Muaz,
the chief of the Aus, who had been their ally before the Emigration. Saad had been wounded during the battle of the Trench,
and was being tended in the mosque at Medina. Brought before
the Prophet and the leaders of the Jewish tribe, Saad was informed
why his presence was desired. After making sure that his decision
would be accepted by both sides and would be carried out, Saad
pronounced sentence in accordance with the Jewish law applicable
in such a case (Deut. 20:10–18).

It was a terrible sentence: death to all males, and all property
to be taken as booty. But the Jews had brought it upon themselves,
first by their treachery, next by their resistance to the Muslims
after they had been caught in their treachery, and finally by pre-
ferring the judgment of Saad, who had been their ally, rather than
throwing themselves upon the well-known and oft-experienced
mercy of the Prophet. The sentence was carried out, but the
Prophet invited intercession on behalf of the condemned, and in
response to every plea of intercession, he remitted the sentence.
When it was pointed out to him that he was bound to carry out
Saad's decision and that there was no room for either intercession
or mercy, he replied that he was bound by the award, but as
head of state he nevertheless possessed the prerogative of mercy,
which he could exercise freely. Some of the Jews who had dissoci-
ated themselves from their people before the matter was submitted to the arbitration of Saad were permitted to go free, without need for intercession.

Despite the desperate nature of the encounters that had taken
place in the course of the siege of Medina by the Confederates and
the continuous and heavy strain which the situation had imposed
upon the Muslims during the terrible three weeks that it endured,
there was little loss of life in battle on either side. The Prophet was
convinced that the siege of Medina had been the highwater mark
of the Meccan effort to subdue the city by force. There was no
respite in the intensity of Meccan hostility toward the Prophet
and the faith, but the Meccans were beginning to entertain doubts
whether further efforts to destroy the Muslims and their faith by
the use of aggressive force would meet with success. They were,
however, determined not to entertain any suggestion of what in
terms of today might be described as peaceful co-existence. Every
type of harassment, including plunder and murder, was resorted
to, and the incitement of the tribes throughout Arabia against the

Muslims was actively pursued, both by the Meccans and by the Jews. This left the Prophet no choice but to maintain the utmost vigilance and to be always ready to lead in person or to dispatch forces wherever preparations for active assault might be under way.

A state of alarums and excursions obtained in Medina and everybody was kept on the *qui vive*. A companion of the Prophet subsequently said: "In those days we could only obtain snatches of sleep at fitful intervals and had to keep our arms close by us, and we often prayed, 'O Lord, wilt Thou, by Thy Grace vouch-safe us such security that we may go to sleep at night without any fear in our hearts save only the fear of Thy Majesty.' "

5

The Concluding Years

IN THE SIXTH YEAR AFTER THE EMIGRATION, THE
Prophet saw in a vision that he was performing the circuit of the
Ka'aba with a party of Muslims (48:28). Relating this vision to
his companions, he asked them to prepare for a journey to Mecca
for the purpose of performing the circuit. This was a privilege
which could be claimed by anyone, and it was not permissible to
hinder its exercise. The Prophet announced that the only purpose
of his party, which numbered fifteen hundred men, was to perform
the circuit in peace and then to return to Medina. He had no
hostile intent against anybody. The Meccans decided not to
permit him and his party to enter Mecca for any purpose whatever, and sent out a strong force to the north to intercept him.
The Prophet, approaching Mecca from the west, refrained from
entering the limits of the Sanctuary,* and made camp a few miles
outside these limits. He announced that he would accept any
conditions the Meccans might choose to impose upon his party
during the period they would be in Mecca, so only that they
might perform their acts of worship in peace.

Soon an envoy arrived from the city and made it clear that the
chiefs would on no account permit the Muslims to enter Mecca,
at least not that year, for this would be interpreted as a triumph
for the Prophet and a humiliation for the Meccans. Continuing
his efforts to persuade the Meccans to let his party perform an act
of worship which was the undoubted right of every Arab, the
Prophet sent one of his principal companions, Uthman, into
Mecca to talk to the chiefs, but to no purpose. Eventually, the
Meccans did propose certain conditions, all of which the Prophet

* The Sanctuary, an area encompassing the Ka'aba and its precincts and
extending for twenty miles in each direction from the limits of Mecca, is a
region in which no fighting is permitted. Pillars mark the boundaries of the
Sanctuary.

accepted, and a treaty, known as the Treaty of Hudaibiyya (after the place where the Prophet was then encamped), was drawn up. The treaty specified that hostilities be suspended for ten years; that any tribe choosing to do so could enter into treaty relations with the Muslims or the Meccans; that both sides were under obligation to respect these treaties; that any Meccan young man who left the town without the permission of his father or guardian and joined the Prophet would be returned to Mecca, but that any Muslim who left the Prophet and went over to the Meccans would not be returned to the Muslims; that the Prophet and his party would return to Medina, but would be permitted to perform the circuit the following year and could stay in Mecca for that purpose for three days; that they would not enter Mecca with any arms other than sheathed swords; that the Meccans would vacate the town during that period in order to eliminate all risk of clash.

The Muslims felt that the terms of the treaty were not only onerous and one-sided, but humiliating. The Prophet, however, explained that unequal as it was, it did secure great benefits, the principal ones being that the Meccans had recognized the Muslims as a people with whom they could enter into treaty relations, and that they had agreed to a ten-year truce period. During that time Islam could be freely preached, and, he added, perhaps peaceful conditions would be established throughout Arabia before the truce period ended. He also stressed that the terms of the treaty were not contrary to his vision; in fact, they opened a way for its fulfillment, inasmuch as the performance of the circuit of the Ka'aba the following year was now assured. Concerning the one-sided arrangement with regard to the return of Meccan young men who might accept Islam, the Prophet pointed out that any person whose heart was illumined by faith would continue to spread the light wherever he was, while Muslims had no use for anybody who chose to repudiate his faith and desert them.

While the Prophet and his party were on their way back to Medina from Hudaibiyya, the Prophet received a revelation which described the peace treaty as a great victory (48:2).

Peace having been secured, with every chance of its being made permanent before the treaty lapsed, the Prophet was now able to turn, without distracting diversions, to the carrying forward of his principal mission. He addressed letters to the various rulers holding sway over territories which were part of, or contiguous to, the Arabian peninsula, inviting them to accept Islam. Among those to whom these letters were sent were the Chief of Bahrain, the Emperor of Iran, the Byzantine Emperor, his Viceroy in Egypt, and the Emperor of Ethiopia. The Chief of Bahrain and many of his people accepted Islam. The Iranian Emperor treated the Prophet's communication with haughty contempt, not only tearing it up, but sending directions to his Viceroy in Yemen to have the Prophet arrested. The Byzantine Emperor, to whom the letter was delivered, took some interest in its contents and even made inquiries concerning the Prophet. His Viceroy in Egypt treated the letter with great veneration and sent back presents to the Prophet. The Emperor of Ethiopia accepted the Prophet's invitation and declared himself a Muslim.

The Jews who had been expelled from Medina and were settled in Khaibar, a short distance to the north, found that their incitement of Arab tribes against the Prophet had, in view of the Treaty of Hudaibiyya, little chance of success; therefore, 'they turned their attention to the Christian and pagan tribes in the north, who were under the protection of the Byzantine Emperor, and they also started intriguing with the Jews settled in Iraq and with the Iranian Emperor. Thus, though the Prophet and the Muslims might have peace in south and central Arabia, they were to be exposed to fresh and even greater dangers from the north and northeast. If the whole of that region were not to flare up at once against the Muslims, the least that was necessary was to remove the Jews from Khaibar because the place served as a dangerous spying post as well as a center of disaffection and incitement close to Medina. The Prophet led a force against Khaibar and called upon the Jews to surrender, but, relying on the strength of their fortifications, they chose to fight. After a siege lasting some days they surrendered, but were allowed to depart unharmed on condition that they settle in some place far from Medina.

When the time came, the Prophet and two thousand followers performed the circuit of the Ka'aba—and did so with scrupulous observance of the conditions which had been laid down the previous year in the Treaty of Hudaibiyya. Shortly after, Khalid and 'Amr, two of the Meccan generals who had distinguished themselves in the battle of Uhud, accepted Islam and joined the Muslims.

On return from Mecca, the Prophet received intelligence that Christian tribes on the Syrian border, instigated by the Jews and

pagan Arabs, were making preparations for an attack upon
Medina. He dispatched a party of fifteen to make a reconnais-
sance. They found an army massing on the Syrian border, and
hoping that an exposition of the principles of Islam might serve
to reassure the Christian tribes of Syria and to preserve peace, they
attempted to establish contact with these hostile forces. They
were, however, attacked with arrows, and all were killed.

Upon receipt of this news, the Prophet planned an expedition
against Syria, but receiving intimation that the forces which had
been concentrating on the border had dispersed, he abandoned
the project. Instead, he addressed a letter to the Byzantine
Emperor through the chief of the Ghassan tribe, who exercised
authority in the name of Byzantium, in which he protested against
the military preparations which had been observed on the Syrian
border and the unjust killing of the party of fifteen whom he had
sent to report on the border situation. His envoy was arrested by
the Ghassan chief and was put to death. When this came to the
Prophet's knowledge, he dispatched a force of three thousand to
Syria under the command of Zaid, his freedman.

The Prophet, together with some of his companions, traveled
some distance out of Medina with these forces, to speed them on
their way, and when parting with them he reminded them that
they should consider themselves all the time in the presence of
God, and that the commanders should deal justly with those
over whom they had been placed in authority. They should fight
in the cause of God courageously, but humanely. They should not
molest priests and monks and those who occupied themselves
with the remembrance of God in their houses of worship, nor
should they kill women or children or old people or those who
were in any manner afflicted and were not able to fight. Nor
should they cut down any tree or pull down any building.

When these forces arrived at the Syrian border, they found
that the Emperor himself had taken the field with one hundred
thousand of his own soldiers, and a like number recruited from
the local Christian tribes. A discussion arose among the Muslims
whether they should go forward to encounter this huge force, or
should return to Medina and report the situation, or should send
to Medina for instructions. It was decided to march forward, and
the battle was fought at a place called Muta. The fighting was
fierce and desperate and first Zaid, and after him Jafar, a cousin
of the Prophet, and then Abdullah, each of whom had been

named commander by the Prophet in that order, were killed. Then Khalid took over the command and continued the fight till dark. The next day he changed the disposition of his small force; those on the right were posted on the left and those in the rear were brought to the front. This created the impression among the enemy that the Muslims had received reinforcements during the night. There was desperate fighting throughout the day, and at nightfall the Byzantine forces withdrew from the field. Khalid returned to Medina with the remnant of the Muslim force.

The following year the Meccans committed a flagrant breach of the Treaty of Hudaibiyya. Without warning or cause, they sent a force with the Banu Bakr tribe, with whom they were in alliance, to attack the Khuza'a, a tribe in alliance with the Muslims, and killed many of their people. The Khuza'a immediately dispatched a party of forty fast riders to Medina to give the Prophet intimation of this treacherous attack and to call upon him to redress the breach of the treaty. The Meccans, perturbed at this piece of news, sent Abu Sufyan to Medina to patch up the matter. Nobody there paid any attention to him and he returned to Mecca, where he reported that though he had not succeeded in securing a new agreement, neither had he observed any warlike preparations in Medina. Abu Sufyan and the Meccans were soon undeceived, however, and were taken completely by surprise when they found the Prophet only a day's march from Mecca at the head of a force of ten thousand, composed partly of Muslims from Medina, but mainly of Muslims from among the tribes in alliance with the Prophet.

The Meccans, feeling helpless, sent Abu Sufyan and two others to the Prophet's camp to see whether anything could be done to save the situation. They found the Prophet much distressed over the wanton breach of the treaty by the Meccans and the slaughter among the Khuza'a that they and their allies had perpetrated. Abu Sufyan, recalling all that the Meccans had done to, and attempted against, the Prophet and the Muslims, feared the worst. He passed a night in the Prophet's camp and was deeply impressed by the love and devotion which the Muslims entertained for the Prophet. Realizing that there was no way of escape for the Meccans, he asked the Prophet whether the Meccans could have peace if they did not draw the sword. The Prophet answered in the affirmative and announced a series of measures which would secure a peaceful entry of his followers into Mecca and obviate the possibility of a clash. These measures were widely proclaimed in Mecca and the Muslim forces marched in, the Prophet himself bringing up the rear. At one point the party led by Khalid was attacked by the Meccans and there was a clash resulting in the death of about a dozen men. News of this was brought quickly to the Prophet, and he immediately issued orders which stopped further bloodshed.

The Prophet proceeded to the Ka'aba, and himself smashed one by one the idols that had been installed therein. As each idol fell, he recited the verse: "Truth has come and falsehood has vanished away. Falsehood does indeed vanish fast" (17:82). Thus was the Ka'aba restored to its true purpose, the worship of the One God, as was intended by Abraham.

Having performed these immediate and necessary tasks, and having prayed inside and outside the Ka'aba in thankfulness to God for all His favors, the Prophet sent for the leaders of the Qureish and asked them how he should deal with them. They replied that they fully merited whatever punishment he might choose to inflict upon them, but that they knew he was a generous brother and would deal with them as such. The Prophet pronounced judgment in the words addressed by the Prophet Joseph to his brethren: "No retribution shall be exacted from you this day" (12:93).

All the scorn and ridicule poured on him by the Meccans; their implacable hatred and enmity; the long years of bitter, cruel, and sustained persecution; all the fighting, the hardship and suffering; the loss of dear and devoted companions—all, all was in the moment of triumph laid aside, banished from the mind and forgiven in the name of the Lord on High, the Gracious, the Merciful, the Creator and Master of all. God's glorious command was carried out to the uttermost: "Good and evil are not alike. Repel evil with that which is best and lo, he between whom and thyself was enmity will become as though he were a warm friend. But none attains to it save those who are steadfast, and none attains to it save those who possess abundant good" (41:35–36). The gates of love and mercy were opened wide. Bitter enemies of the morning became warm friends by nightfall. Some hearts were still sullen; the humiliation, though softened by magnanimity, was hard to endure, but even these could not long withstand the healing effect of the balm so generously and so beneficently applied by the Prophet. History furnishes no parallel instance of such complete forgiveness, such utter beneficence, on so large a scale.

A dozen individuals had been marked down for punitive action on account of the atrocities of which they, individually, had been guilty. One of them was Hindah, the wife of Abu Sufyan, who had constantly incited the Meccans against the Muslims. After the battle of Uhud she had cut out the heart of the Prophet's uncle, Hamza, killed in battle, and had chewed it up. Even on the day that Mecca opened its gates to the Muslims, she was so outraged when her husband conveyed to her news of the surrender that she took hold of his beard and gave him a violent shaking, calling upon the Meccans to come and kill him for his treachery in having agreed to the surrender instead of taking up arms against the Muslims. However, when she realized that the situation was hopeless, she joined a group of women who went to the Prophet to make their submission. During their talk with the Prophet, Hindah, veiled, intervened several times with pert remarks. The Prophet, thinking the voice was familiar, inquired: "Is that Hindah?" Hindah replied: "Yes, but Messenger of Allah, you cannot proceed against me now for I am a professing Muslim." The Prophet smiled and said: "Of course, you are free."

Another Meccan of the same type was Habbar, who had cut the girth of the camel which carried the Prophet's daughter Zainab as she was about to proceed to Medina during the Emigration. Habbar's action caused Zainab to fall from the camel. She suffered a miscarriage, which later resulted in her death. Habbar also appeared before the Prophet, and professing sorrow for his misconduct begged forgiveness, intimating that he had accepted Islam. In his case also the Prophet said: "You may go free. I can take no action against you now."

It will be recalled that Abu Jahl, the commander of the Meccan army killed during the battle of Badr, had been the Prophet's bitterest enemy in Mecca. His son, Ikramah, was one of the Meccan commanders in the battle of Uhud who had spotted the inadequately guarded rear pass and had led the attack which ended in near disaster for the Muslims.

When Mecca fell, Ikramah left the town and proceeded to the coast, intending to cross over to Ethiopia, being convinced that he could have no security in Mecca or anywhere near it. His wife approached the Prophet and asked whether Ikramah could return to Mecca while professing his idolatrous beliefs. The Prophet replied that faith was a matter of conscience and conscience was free. If Ikramah returned to Mecca he would not be molested, and could live there in security professing whatever he chose to believe in. On this assurance she followed Ikramah and persuaded him to return to Mecca. On arrival there, he repaired to the Prophet and received the assurance which the Prophet had already given to his wife. Thereupon he announced his acceptance of Islam, and the Prophet asked him if there were anything he wished for. Ikramah replied that he could wish for no greater bounty than God had already bestowed upon him in opening his heart to the acceptance of Islam, but he did desire that the Prophet should pray God to forgive him all the enmity that he had borne toward the Prophet and the Muslims.

The Prophet prayed accordingly and then bestowed his own cloak on Ikramah, saying: "He who comes to me believing in God can claim my house as his." Ikramah proved himself a sincere and zealous believer and set the seal on his faith by laying down his life in defense of it on one of the Syrian battlefields some years later.

The Prophet, having returned to Mecca, as had been foretold before the Emigration (28:86), felt that the people of Medina might wonder whether he intended to take up his residence there. He called their leaders and told them that he had no such intention. Mecca was very dear to him, but having cast in his lot with the people of Medina, who had stood by him when he was rejected by the Meccans and had to leave Mecca, he would not now leave them for Mecca. They were delighted to hear this and felt as if he had bestowed the world's abundance upon them.

Mecca had fallen, but this did not bring peace. The Prophet's march against Mecca had been so sudden that the first intimation of it that reached the tribes of central and southern Arabia was the fall of the town. They were greatly agitated by the news, and felt that the time had come for the last desperate effort to be put forth against Islam. Within a month of the fall of Mecca and while the Prophet was still in the town, he had to go forth to face an army of seventy thousand men at Hunain. On this occasion a force of two thousand Meccans, many of whom had not yet professed Islam, had also joined him, for though not Muslims they had accepted the Prophet's authority.

The battle, even before it was fairly joined, took an adverse course, and the Muslim forces were thrown into utter confusion. The Prophet was left with only twelve companions, but he spurred his mule forward, saying: "I am a true Prophet and no impostor. I am the grandson of Abdul Muttalib." At the same time he asked his uncle, Abbas, who was near him, to stand on an eminence and call out to the Emigrants and the Helpers that the Prophet of God summoned them. This helped rally the Muslim forces and the battle that ensued ended in complete victory (9:25–26). On this occasion Abu Sufyan, a recent and reluctant convert, gave proof of his rapid inner conviction by holding fast to the stirrup of the Prophet and exposing himself to extreme danger. The enemy abandoned great booty on the field of battle and many prisoners were taken, which brought in large sums in ransom. Instead of distributing all this among the Muslim forces, according to custom, the Prophet chose to distribute it among the people of Mecca and those living in the neighborhood of Mecca, Muslim and non-Muslim alike. This occasioned some disappointment among sections of the Muslim army, but most of them reconciled themselves to the Prophet's decision and accepted it cheerfully.

The result of the battle of Hunain seemed to assure peace in the peninsula proper, but when the Prophet returned to Medina he found that owing mainly to the activities of some of the disaffected elements, the leading figure among whom was Abu 'Amir of the Khazraj, there was serious apprehension of an attack from the north. Abu 'Amir and his associates had been active in creating tension between the Muslims and the Christian tribes of Syria. They went to and fro spreading rumors on each side that the other was preparing to attack. These rumors became so persistent that the Prophet considered it necessary to lead in person an army against Syria. In Medina itself the disaffected element tried to scare the Muslims by painting dreadful pictures of the sufferings and destruction that surely awaited any force that might dare to challenge the great might of Byzantium, while yet hoping that the Prophet would go north at the head of a group so small and weak that none of them would be suffered to return. Medina was at that time in the grip of a famine and the season was at its hottest, so that marching through the desert involved terrible suffering. Some of the desert Arabs sought to make excuses why they could not join the expedition. Others who were eager to join could not find mounts, nor even shoes to protect their feet against the burning sands of the desert (9:90–96). Nevertheless, a force was got ready, and marched to the border of Syria. Arriving there, the Prophet dispatched parties in different directions to report on the situation. These returned and reported that they had not observed any concentrations anywhere. Being assured that in fact no preparations were going forward in Syria for an attack against the Muslims, the Prophet decided to return to Medina, stopping only for a few days near the border to conclude peace treaties with some of the tribes on the border. There was no fighting at all. The expedition involved the Prophet's absence from Medina for about two and one-half months.

Delegations now poured in from all parts of Arabia offering their submission and announcing their acceptance of Islam. In a short time the whole of Arabia adhered to the Pax Islamica.

In the ninth year after the Emigration, the Prophet went on pilgrimage to Mecca. On the day of the pilgrimage he received the revelation: "This day have I perfected your religion for you and completed My favor unto you and have chosen for you Islam as your faith" (5:4).

The Prophet, as was his wont, announced the revelation and delivered an address—known as the Farewell Address—to the huge assemblage in the valley of Arafat outside Mecca. He started by saying that he did not know whether he would be able to meet them again on the occasion of the pilgrimage, and he asked them to lend an attentive ear to what he had to say. He went on to admonish them to order their lives in accordance with the commandments of God; to take particular care that no trespass was committed against any person in respect of his life, property, or honor; to treat women with due regard and consideration, fully observing their rights, which corresponded to the rights that the men had. He expressed solicitude for the welfare of prisoners of war, some of whom they still had among them, saying that they must be accorded the same treatment as members of the captors' own families; he stressed that all human beings were equal, whatever their individual status, and that no one could claim any privilege or superiority against any other.

He ended by asking them to bear witness to the Unity of God, and to affirm the principal articles of faith. He then inquired whether he had conveyed God's message to them, and had discharged his trust. There was a deafening response that he had.

He asked those present to convey what he had said to those who were not present on the occasion.

The pilgrimage over, the Prophet returned to Medina and occupied every available moment in expounding and teaching the principles of Islam and the philosophy that lay behind them and in urging the Muslims to order their lives accordingly.

One day he announced that he had received the revelation: "In the name of Allah, Ever Gracious, Most Merciful. The help of Allah having come, and the Victory, and thou having witnessed men entering the religion of Allah in troops, hymn the praises of thy Lord, and seek His protection against their weaknesses. Surely He is Oft-Returning with compassion" (110:2–4).

Abu Bakr concluded from this that as the Prophet's mission had been fulfilled, he would not be spared to them for long, and he was overcome by emotion. The Prophet, observing this, remarked: "If it were permissible to love a human being with the heart's full devotion, I would have so loved Abu Bakr, but such love is only for God," and he went on to add that all doors that opened into the mosque should be closed except Abu Bakr's.

Soon the Prophet fell ill. For some days he continued to go to the mosque and lead the Prayers, but then he became too weak to do this. He directed Abu Bakr to lead the Prayers. One day he told those present that if there were anyone whom he might have injured by mistake or unwittingly, that person should come forward now so that he might make suitable amends, as he did not wish to appear before his Maker with any obligation undischarged. One of them came forth. He reminded the Prophet of an inconvenience, even though slight, which he had once suffered at the Prophet's hands. It was merely that the Prophet's elbow had by chance once grazed his back. "Come then," the Prophet offered, "and stick your elbow into my back." "But, oh Messenger of Allah, my back was bare while yours is covered." The Prophet offered to bare his back, and did so. The man approached, and with great tenderness kissed the Prophet's back. It was his way of demonstrating his deep love for the Prophet.

The end approached. The Prophet expressed great anxiety lest after his death his followers might be tempted to have recourse to practices which might assign him a position above that of a human being, as had been done in the case of some other prophets by their followers. He impressed repeatedly upon those who visited him that he was but a human being to whom God had vouchsafed revelation for the guidance of mankind. He breathed his last with the words: "To the Companion on High, to the Companion on High."

The Prophet's death (A.D. 632) struck the Muslims as a fearful calamity, and many of his intimate companions were crushed with grief. Umar drew his sword and said he would cut off the head of any who dared to assert that the Prophet was dead; he could not die. Abu Bakr arrived. Entering the chamber where the Prophet's body lay, he kissed it on the forehead and said: "God will not inflict two deaths upon thee," meaning that the death of the body was inevitable, but that God would preserve forever the Prophet's teaching concerning the Existence and Unity of God. He then came out and asked Umar to desist while he addressed the people briefly. He recited from the Quran: "Muhammad is but a Messenger. All Messengers have passed away before him. If then he die or be slain, will you turn back on your heels? He who turns back on his heels shall not harm Allah at all. Allah will certainly reward the grateful" (3:145). And he added: "Hearken: he who worshiped Muhammad should know that Muhammad is dead, but he who worships God should remember that God is Ever-Living and does not die."

This helped those present to balance their emotions, and to realize that though the parting was heartrending, God's will was supreme and must be accepted in a spirit of steadfastness.

The poet Hassan gave expression to his poignant grief at the death of the Prophet in Arabic verse:

> Thou wert the pupil of my eye;
> My eye is now sightless.
> After thee I care not who dies;
> I was fearful only of losing thee.

E

6

The Excellent Exemplar

MUHAMMAD WAS A LAWBEARING PROPHET. THE Quran says that he was not a Messenger who brought new-fangled doctrines (46:10). There had been lawbearing prophets before him, for instance Moses, through whom God had proclaimed the advent of a lawbearing Prophet "like unto him" (Deut. 18:18). This means that Muhammad had been selected by God as a fit and appropriate channel for conveying the Divine law and guidance to mankind. His claim that he had been so selected implied that his personality had been molded to that end and that he illustrated conformity to that law and guidance in his own conduct. It is necessary, therefore, briefly to study his personality and character in order to see whether that implication was justified. What type of man was he? How did he deal with his fellow beings? How did he discharge his duty to God?

Though Muhammad lived in a region which had slight contacts with the rest of the world and at a time when the art of history was still in its infancy, his was a truly historical personality. He lived his life in the full light of day. Enough is known of his early life to enable us to form a fair idea of his qualities and character. After he received the Divine Call his every word, act, and gesture were observed, and a complete record of them has been preserved. It was necessary that that should be so, for otherwise not only would certainty and confidence be lacking, but his life could not furnish us with an example of what he taught.

Muhammad was a human being—no more, no less—and therefore he could serve as an example for mankind. He possessed and claimed no supernatural powers. He was subject to the same conditions and limitations as the rest of us. He suffered more than most and achieved outstanding success in his lifetime. His life had many facets and passed through many phases. Like other men he was a son, a husband, and a father. He had been a servant employed by a master, a citizen subject to the authority of his town. God appointed him a teacher and a guide. He immediately became an object of scorn and ridicule and soon of bitter persecution. He was a loving and anxious shepherd of his little flock. Through bitter persecution and hard fighting, he gave proof of the highest courage, endurance, and perseverance.

During the last ten years of his life he was called upon to discharge the duties of chief executive and chief magistrate of a heterogeneous community, divided into sections in conflict with each other. He became the head of a state fraught with internal frictions and beset with external dangers of every description. In addition to the heavy duties and responsibilities pertaining to his Prophetic office, he was called upon to display qualities of administration and statesmanship which taxed him to the utmost.

He was a man of peace. The due discharge of the trust and responsibility which God had been pleased to place on him demanded the establishment and preservation of peace. His enemies would let him have no peace. They forced him to take up arms in defense of the most fundamental human right: freedom of conscience. He hated war and conflict, but when war was forced upon him he strove to render it humane. He abolished all savage and barbarous practices. He commanded in battle, but scrupulously refrained from personally shedding blood. His strategy was faultless and was always designed to reduce loss of life and human suffering to the minimum. Binding obligations and demands of justice imposed upon him the duty of avenging wrong and punishing evil in a harsh world, but his judgments were always tempered with mercy.

The Prophet was fair of feature and form. He was a model of health, strength, and manliness; withal gentle of heart, sensitive, full of sympathy, tender toward suffering of every description. He had been early commanded to "lower the wing of tenderness" toward those with him (26:216). This became his second nature. His habits and ways were simple; he was modest and humble. In his personal life he was austere, yet he was, like Abraham, appreciative of the "bounties of his Lord" (16:122).

The testimony of Khadeeja with regard to his character and qualities has been noted. Someone inquired from Ayesha, daughter of Abu Bakr, whom he married two years after the Emigration, how the Prophet occupied himself during the time that he was at home. She said that he helped in the performance of household duties, patched up his clothes, mended his shoes, and was a kindly and affectionate companion. She was asked for her estimate of his character. She answered: "His character was the Quran."

During the period of persecution in Mecca he endured all without complaint and proved himself a good and law-abiding citizen. Yet he was never afraid and was not deterred from doing all that he considered was due from him. It has been mentioned that he had, in association with some others, undertaken the obligation to go to the assistance of any person who might have been wronged and to procure justice for him. He never failed or faltered in the discharge of that obligation, even after he himself became the object of persecution. On one occasion an outsider sought help from the Meccans in respect of the recovery of a sum of money owed to him by Abu Jahl. Those whom the man approached directed him cynically to the Prophet. The Prophet immediately accompanied him to Abu Jahl's house, and knocked at his door. Abu Jahl, amazed to see Muhammad there, admitted the debt. The Prophet then asked him to discharge his obligation, which he promptly did. When Abu Jahl later appeared among his fellows, they jeered at him and taunted him with having submitted meekly to Muhammad's demand. He said he had been so awed that he could not do otherwise.

Even during the Meccan period, the widow, the orphan, the needy, the wayfarer, the slave, and the distressed were the objects of the persecuted Prophet's special care and concern.

At Medina he continued his simple ways and austere habits. For days together his hearth remained unlit. He and his family subsisted on a meager diet of dates, or parched and ground barley. Sometimes water alone sufficed. He had but one change of clothes. His dwelling was of the simplest and barest. He slept on a leather sack filled with twigs and branches of trees. He never slept in a bed; never ate bread made out of ground flour; never ate his fill.

Indeed, his personal requirements were always kept at the barest minimum, and that minimum he accepted and appreciated as a generous Divine bounty. This was strikingly illustrated on the day Mecca surrendered and opened its gates to him. That was a day of great triumph. The Prophet busied himself with settling and supervising the orderly carrying through of the complicated and delicate operation, and when everything had been satisfactorily accomplished, he bethought himself of procuring some nourishment. He went to the house of his aunt, Umm-i-Hany, who was delighted to welcome him, but was distressed that she had nothing in the house which she could offer him except a piece of very stale bread, too hard to be swallowed. When she mentioned this to the Prophet, he smiled and said, "Surely, Umm-i-Hany, it can be softened by being soaked in water. And have you anything which could make it more palatable?" She replied, "There is a little of the dregs of vinegar left over from long ago." The Prophet said, "That would be excellent." He then proceeded to soak the piece of bread in water, and when it was softened, he ate it with the few drops of black vinegar, first pronouncing the name of God over the "meal" and rendering thanks to Him when he finished, as if it had been a banquet. He thanked his aunt and observed, "Umm-i-Hani, what a bounty bread and vinegar is."

At night, between the prescribed services, he spent long hours in Prayer. He stood so long in Prayer that sometimes his feet became swollen. This once moved Ayesha to venture a mild protest. The Prophet said: "Ayesha, God has been so profuse in bestowing His bounties upon me that it behooves me to be the most grateful of His servants."

The character of his domestic life may be gathered from one of his own well-known sayings: "The best among you is he who treats the members of his family best."

He constantly exhorted his people toward moderation in all respects. Noticing that some were inclined to carry austerity to the extreme, and to occupy themselves so much with prayer and fasting that they were apt to neglect their normal obligations, and to injure their health, he admonished them thus: "I fear God more than any of you fear Him, yet I fast and I eat; I pray and I discharge all my obligations toward my family and my people. It is not right to carry any matter to the extreme. God loves best those acts of worship and piety which, though moderate, are carried out without being felt a burden. Having performed what is prescribed, pray and fast and worship God while you may do so cheerfully; stop when your spirit or your body begins to feel the strain."

He did not disdain humor and with all his grave preoccupations did not altogether neglect the lighter side of life. On one occasion when he was sitting at home with Ayesha, an old woman came to visit her. Thinking that it was a good opportunity to ask a favor of the Prophet, the visitor begged him to pray that she might be admitted to heaven when her time came to depart this life. The Prophet said: "There will be no old women in heaven." Distressed, the old lady began to bewail her fate. The Prophet hastened to explain that what he had meant was that there would be no question of age, of old or young in heaven; all would be alike. He comforted her till she was restored to cheerfulness. On one occasion he challenged Ayesha to a race, which she won. A year or two later he challenged her again and this time he won. He laughed, saying, "Ayesha, we have come out even."

Ayesha once confessed to him that she had suspected him of an unfairness, but had soon found out that she was mistaken. He remarked, "Ayesha, there is a Satan inside every one of us, of whose promptings we should beware."

"Is there a Satan inside you also?" she rejoined.

"Yes," he replied, "but he has accepted submission."

One day he happened to pass near a date-palm garden where some people were grafting trees. He inquired what they were doing, and when they explained the process he asked them why they did not do it another way. The following year these people complained that they had adopted his suggestion, but that the trees had yielded less fruit. "But I had merely made an inquiry from you," he said. "You know more about these things than I do. You should have followed the method which experience had taught you was best."

He was often called upon to decide disputes and give judgment. He warned, however, that he had no means of discovering the truth except through what was stated before him. It was quite possible that one party to a dispute might succeed by plausible arguments in persuading him that right was on his side, when in fact the other party was in the right, and that he might give judgment in favor of the first. Even so, a person in whose favor judgment was given must remember that he was answerable to God. The mere fact that he had obtained a judgment from the prophet would not serve to absolve him if he were not in fact in the right.

The Prophet's clemency was well known. A poor man confessed to him publicly that he had been guilty of a certain offense. The Prophet imposed a mild penalty by way of a fine, which would be distributed in charity, but the man said he was unable to pay. In the meantime somebody brought a basket of dates to the Prophet to be distributed in charity. The Prophet bade the guilty man to take the dates and distribute them among the poor. Said the man: "Sir, I know of no one more deserving of charity than myself." The Prophet laughed and replied: "Well then, take them yourself and that will suffice as your penalty."

His treatment of Hindah, Habbar, and Ikramah after the fall of Mecca has been mentioned. An incident of a more personal nature is also worthy of recall. During the course of a journey his party rested among a grove of trees to avoid the noonday heat. The Prophet hung up his sword by the branch of a tree and lay down to rest under its shade. An enemy who had been on the lookout for an opportunity to kill him stole into the camp, and finding the Prophet sleeping unguarded, approached him, secured his sword, and sat down on his chest. The Prophet woke up in surprise as the man, brandishing the sword, said: "Who can save thee now?" The Prophet gently uttered the single word, "Allah," moved away from under the man, raised himself and took hold of his assailant, wresting the sword from him. The position was now reversed.

"Who can save thee now?" inquired the Prophet.

"No one!" exclaimed the man in terror.

"Why do you not say 'Allah'?" asked the Prophet as he released the man. When the man returned to his tribe he told them that he had encountered a man whose mercy and forgiveness were beyond belief. He then related what had occurred, and this led him and his tribe to accept Islam.

The Prophet had been sent as a manifestation of God's mercy to mankind (21:108). His mercy was all-embracing, without limit, and without discrimination. He was not niggardly about it, as lesser men might have been (17:101).

But that which inspired him first and last was his duty to God. His beneficence toward all human beings was only one aspect of the performance of the duty which he owed to his Maker. No consideration could stand in the way of the performance of that duty. When the Meccans gave his uncle, Abu Talib, the choice between adhering to Muhammad or retaining the chieftainship of the tribe, Abu Talib put the matter before the Prophet. The Prophet told him that he could withdraw his protection, but that as for himself, he must continue till the end to do what God commanded him. He would not desist even if the Meccans placed the sun on his right and the moon on his left. That stand he maintained till the last.

At Uhud, when the Meccan commander, Abu Sufyan, believed that the Prophet and his principal companions had been killed, he shouted: "Glory to Hubul," naming the principal idol worshiped by the Meccans. The Prophet, out of prudence and considerations of security, had told his companions who had gathered round him after he had been wounded and had been revived, not to answer Abu Sufyan's calls when one by one he had challenged Muhammad, Abu Bakr, and Umar, to answer him. Following his instructions they kept quiet and maintained silence even when Abu Sufyan proclaimed the glory of Hubul. But when the Prophet heard this last exclamation, he turned impatiently to his companions, prudence and all concern for security thrown to the winds, and exclaimed: "Why don't you say, 'Allah is the Most High, the Most Exalted'?" The shouts went up and convinced Abu Sufyan and the Meccans that the Prophet was alive. The Meccans thereupon held a council whether they should attack the small party round the Prophet and put an end to all of them. But they thought better of it, and calling it a day, withdrew from the field.

On the day of Hunain when the Prophet had at the very start of the battle been left alone with only a dozen supporters, even Abu Bakr could not restrain him from spurring forward his mule toward the enemy, proclaiming that he was a true Prophet and no impostor.

With him God always came first. So much was this so that even his enemies in Mecca were wont to say, "Muhammad is intoxicated with love of God."

Such is the testimony of man and events. What of the testimony of God, Who had commanded him to shoulder the responsibility of conveying His message to mankind and of leading them back to Him? The Prophet's enemies did not believe in his mission nor that what he proclaimed as revelation was received by him from God, but even for them God's testimony concerning him became conclusive in the sense that it was openly and widely proclaimed. They found it so true that on no occasion and in no particular did they ever call it in question. It was a standing challenge to his opponents. They never took it up.

The Prophet was commanded to proclaim: "If Allah had so willed I should not have recited the Quran to you, nor would He have made it known to you. I have indeed lived among you a whole lifetime before this. Will you not then understand?"

(10:17). Thus God put forward the purity and righteousness of the Prophet's life, which those who opposed him so bitterly had observed at close quarters, as proof that he was not capable of uttering a lie against God. Not without reason had his fellow townsmen bestowed upon him the title "*El-Ameen*," the Trusty, the Faithful.

Faced squarely with this challenge, not one of them ever attempted to assert that Muhammad had on any occasion been guilty of saying or doing that which was not utterly true, completely righteous.

Yet all the time he had to stress that he was but a man like the rest, lest, observing the security that he enjoyed in the midst of constant danger, the success that he extracted even from persecution and defeat, and the ultimate triumph of his cause to which the whole of Arabia was witness, some might be tempted to ascribe to him supernatural capacities and powers or superhuman status. "Say: 'I am but a man like yourselves. I have received revelation that your God is only One God. So let him who hopes to meet his Lord act righteously, and let him join no one in the worship of his Lord' " (18:111).

When challenged by his opponents to show them a sign, like causing a spring to gush forth from the earth, or causing the heavens to fall upon them in pieces, or ascending to heaven and bringing down with him a book which they could read, he was commanded to reply: "Holy is my Lord. I am but a man sent as a Messenger" (17:91-94).

It was necessary to stress this both in view of what had happened in the case of some previous prophets who were exalted as divinities by their followers and also for the simple reason that only a man can be an exemplar for men. An angel or a god cannot set an example which man can follow. The dimensions would be utterly disparate. It is a curious inversion that a prophet's opponents often seek to justify their rejection of him on the ground that he is but a man, a single individual from among themselves (54:25). Yet, as the Quran points out, it is only a man who can serve as God's Messenger to men. An angel would be sent as a prophet if the earth were peopled with angels (17:95-96).

The Prophet's disclaimer of any supernatural powers or capacities is repeatedly emphasized in the Quran. For instance, he is commanded to say that he does not possess knowledge of the unseen, save only that much which God reveals to him (2:256;

72:27–28). Had he possessed such knowledge, he would have
collected abundant good for himself, and no evil could have
touched him (7:189). It is true that the Prophet had full faith in
God's promises of help and the ultimate triumph of the cause, but
he set a clear example that faith in God and in His promises en-
tailed the putting forth of the utmost effort toward the achievement of the purpose and the goal which God himself had
appointed.

For instance, the Prophet had been assured of God's protection
against his enemies (5:68), of his victorious return to Mecca
(28:86), of the ultimate success and triumph of his cause (58:22–
23), but he did not for one moment slacken his vigilance or his
effort in respect of the complete discharge of his own duty and of
exhorting his followers to do the same (3:140, 201).

He was not only kindly and affectionate toward those who came
in contact with him, praying for them and exhorting them constantly to order their lives in accordance with Divine commandments and guidance, but also exerted himself to the utmost to
train them in every aspect and sphere of life, so as to prepare and
equip them for the discharge of the responsibilities that lay upon
them and for much heavier ones that were due to be placed upon
their shoulders (3:150). He was commanded to exhort his followers to pray for even those who persecuted them and paid no
heed to the warnings of God, and to overlook and forgive their
trespasses (45:15).

He was "a mercy for mankind." God called him so and he did
indeed prove himself such in every respect (21:108). It was
grievously painful for him that his people should be distressed,
and he was ardently desirous of promoting their welfare
—tender and compassionate at all times and anxious to apply
balm to their oft-harassed and wounded spirits (9:128).

When persecution became unbearable in Mecca, the Prophet
directed those of his followers who could do so to migrate across
the Red Sea to seek shelter and peace in the dominions of the
Emperor of Ethiopia. Later, when life was made almost impossible
for him and for the Muslims in Mecca, the migration to Medina
was decided upon but the Prophet himself stayed on in Mecca till
all those who could be the objects of the Meccans' resentment and
who were free to do so had departed from Mecca. Of the free,
male adults only Abu Bakr, Ali, and himself were left. Abu Bakr
accompanied him, and Ali, who had been entrusted with the re-

turn of money and articles which some Meccans had left with the Prophet for safe keeping, soon followed him.

On one occasion when there was an alarm in Medina at night, the people began to collect in the mosque, as they had been directed by the Prophet, awaiting his instructions. Presently they saw him riding into the town from the plain. He had already been out to investigate, and assured them that there was no danger, that they could go back to sleep. He was the most alert of them at all times concerning their security, as a good shepherd should be concerning his flock.

Passing along one afternoon he noticed a freedman sweating over his task. The Prophet approached him quietly from behind and covered his eyes with his hands as children sometimes do in sport. The man put up his hands to his eyes and from the softness of the hands covering them concluded that this intimate and affectionate gesture could come only from the Prophet. The Prophet began to laugh and removed his hands from the eyes of the man. This was his way of bringing comfort to one who might have considered himself lonely and friendless and might have been weary of his task.

On shaking hands with a laborer and perceiving that his hands were rough and calloused from hard toil, the Prophet held the man's hands within both of his and massaged them gently, repeating several times: "These hands are very dear to God."

That is why God affirmed that the Prophet possessed the highest moral excellences (68:5) and that God's Grace had been bestowed upon him in abundance (17:88).

The highest yearning of the human soul is to win the love of God through its own devotion to, and love of, Him. The Quran succinctly points the way for the satisfaction of that yearning. The Prophet was commanded to say: "If you love God, follow me: then will God love you and forgive you your faults. Surely, God is Most Forgiving, Merciful" (3:32).

When Ayesha said that the character of the Prophet was the Quran, she meant that the Prophet illustrated in his own person to the highest degree the excellences that the Quran teaches. It was because he had become a living example and illustration of the highest excellences that man is capable of achieving, that God's testimony affirmed: "Verily, you have in the Messenger of Allah an excellent exemplar, for him who fears Allah and the Last Day, and who remembers Allah much" (33:22).

Muhammad's soul being in travail over the moral and spiritual degradation of his people did strive to approach the Majesty of God, seeking and praying for a remedy. His striving found favor with God, Who, on Muhammad's approach, drew near to him, and the spiritual communion between the two wrought a unity of purpose. Muhammad's will and purpose were completely subordinated to those of God, and were, so to speak, fused with them. This spiritual fusion is metaphorically expressed in the Quran as "one chord serving two bows and even closer still." God then revealed to Muhammad that which was needed for the guidance of mankind (53:9–11).

The Prophet has explained this experience very simply. He has said that if a servant of God submits himself wholly to the will of God, and commits the whole direction of his life to it, he gradually achieves a condition in which God becomes the eyes with which he sees, the ears with which he hears, the hands with which he labors, and the feet with which he walks. This comes as close to expressing the mystic spiritual reality involved as it is possible to do within the limits of human speech.

The Quran expresses the same idea in several contexts. In the battle of Badr, what appeared to be an utter impossibility was converted into an achievement and the three hundred-odd ragged, half-starved, ill-armed Muslims gained complete victory over the thousand or so well-armed, seasoned Qureish warriors, proud of their might and arrogant in their pride. During the height of the battle, the Prophet took up a handful of pebbles and sand, throwing it in the direction of the Meccan army. A fierce gust of wind happened to rise suddenly, blowing from the Muslim side in the direction of the Meccans, and carried with it a whole storm of pebbles and sand, which so confused and bewildered the Meccans that they could not see aright, and were seriously handicapped. It contributed materially to their defeat. This incident is referred to in the Quran as: "You slew them not, but it was Allah Who slew them. Thou threwest not when thou didst throw, but it was Allah Who threw, that He might overthrow the disbelievers and that He might confer on the believers a great favor from Himself. Surely, Allah is All-Hearing, All-Knowing" (8:18).

Again, the Quran affirms that those who swear allegiance to the Prophet swear allegiance to God. "God's hand is upon their hands" (48:11). This verse has particular reference to an incident during the negotiations which resulted in the Treaty of Hudai-biyya, but it is of general application also. The expression "God's hand" is, of course, metaphorical. God has no physical attributes of any kind, but the meaning is obvious: those who swear allegiance to the Prophet enter into a covenant to subordinate their wills and purposes completely to the will and purpose of God. Thus, though they make a covenant by placing their hands upon the Prophet's hand, their true purpose is to make a covenant with God; and in that sense God's hand is upon their hands.

In short, the whole of the Prophet's life—every thought, every motion, every action, his very being—was devoted to God in the effort to seek closer communion with Him. This is clearly affirmed by Divine testimony: "Say: 'My prayer and my sacrifice and my life and my death are all for Allah, the Lord of the Worlds. He has no associate. So am I commanded, and I am the first of those who submit wholly to Him' " (6:163–164).

Such was the Prophet in the eyes of man and in the estimation of God.

God has proclaimed: "Allah sends down His blessings on the Prophet, and His angels constantly invoke His blessings on him; do you, O believers, also invoke Allah's blessings on him and offer him the salutation of peace" (33:57).

In obedience to this command, all through the centuries Muslims have constantly prayed for, and invoked Allah's blessings upon, the Prophet. It is estimated that there are today over four hundred million Muslims in different parts of the world—and the number is daily increasing—of whom at least half carry out this Divine command several times daily. An average Muslim invokes God's blessings on the Prophet forty times during the course of each day, and many of them do it a great many more times. In fact, every time the Prophet is referred to in conversation, by name or by reference to his Prophetic office, Allah's blessings are invoked upon him and Allah's peace is called down upon him. Thus, having regard to the distribution of Muslim peoples round the world, every moment of the night and day millions of hearts supplicate the Almighty for His blessings on His Prophet. One who devoted his life so utterly to the service of God and His creatures as did the Prophet is deserving of the deepest gratitude on the part of the whole of mankind. By constantly invoking the blessings of God upon him, those who do so seek to repay a fraction of the debt that humanity owes him.

7

Revelation

IN ITS BROADEST CONNOTATION, REVELATION signifies guidance vouchsafed directly by God to man. It may take various forms. The most obvious and most familiar form of revelation is revealed law; for instance, the Books of Moses and the Quran. The difference between the two, so far as the form of revelation is concerned, is that while the Books of Moses contain an account of the law and the guidance accompanying it as revealed by God to Moses, only small parts of them are a literal translation of verbal revelation. The rest is claimed to be revelation in the sense that the substance or purport was revealed by God to Moses, but the actual words are not the words of the revelation. The meaning of the revelation was communicated by Moses to his people in his own words, and what were believed to be these words were recorded at some later period. In contrast with this, the Quran is a record from beginning to end of the verbal revelation vouchsafed by God to Muhammad, the Prophet of Islam, comprising the law and the guidance and the philosophy behind them. What the Prophet himself said in exposition or illustration of the verbal revelation is not comprised in that revelation, but is separately preserved.

But revelation is not confined to the law and the guidance vouchsafed for the benefit of sections of mankind during various stages in their history and evolution, or, as in the case of the Quran, vouchsafed for the benefit of the whole of mankind. Revelation may also be vouchsafed by God from time to time, drawing attention to the manifold aspects of that which has already been revealed, but which may not yet have been fully appreciated in juxtaposition to the growing complexity of human life, or which may have been overlooked or neglected after having been put into effect over a period of time. In a dynamic universe, guidance, even revealed guidance cannot be permitted to become static.

Again, revelation may be an individual experience illustrating the possibility and constituting the enjoyment of direct communion with God. In such cases it is confined mostly to true dreams and clear visions, though verbal revelation is not entirely excluded. Revelation fulfills diverse needs and purposes.

For revelation to fulfill its main purpose, mankind must respond ever afresh to the revelation that already exists or that may be vouchsafed from time to time in further exposition of it. The co-relation is necessary between revelation and man's response to it. That man may be able to see, it is necessary that the eye respond adequately to light. A blind man or a man whose eyes are diseased is unable to see or to see clearly. Equally, a man with perfect eyesight is unable to see or to see clearly in the dark. Revelation is to reason and intellect what light is to the eye. If one is closed or the other is shut out, no vision is possible.

Thus revelation is a continuous experience, and must remain so. All God's attributes are eternal. God has through the ages spoken and revealed Himself in myriad ways to His servants and creatures, and will ever continue to do so. This attribute of His, like all His other attributes, will never fall into disuse. If this means of direct communion between man and his Maker were to be withdrawn, all spiritual life would wither. Spiritual life is constantly renewed and invigorated through the experience of revelation, direct or indirect, in various forms. If this vitalizing and refreshing process were to cease, mankind would be left without active spiritual experience, and faith would be reduced from a living reality to mere speculative reasoning. Reason by itself may or may not lead a person to affirm that there must be God; it is revelation alone that enables him to proclaim with complete certitude and in utter confidence that God *is*.

Indeed, revelation as an individual experience is both a need and a fulfillment of spiritual life. Only experience of direct communion with God through revelation establishes in men's minds and hearts the absolute certainty of faith in a living and beneficent Creator, and furnishes the motive power for the acceptance and realization of the highest spiritual values. If a religion sincerely accepted and faithfully acted upon does not lead its followers into the enjoyment of such a communion, it fails to serve the ultimate and highest purpose of religion. Concerning such a religion it must be concluded that it is no longer adequate to the spiritual needs of mankind. Islam claims to fulfill these needs in all ages.

That reason by itself could have led to the discovery of, and faith in, the existence of God is a complete inversion of the truth. God is the Creator of the universe and by virtue of His attribute of Providence has throughout made provision for man's spiritual as well as for his material needs.

Up to a certain stage in the course of creation, that is to say before man's capacities had been perfected to a degree which made him conscious of the need of communion with God, or enabled him to experience it, he needed only a general concept of good and evil, right and wrong, that which was beneficent and that which was harmful. The Quran says that it is of the essence of man's nature with which God has endowed him that it prompts him toward good, and seeks to restrain him from evil (30:31; 91:8–11). The Prophet has said that every child is born with that nature. Outside influences tend to confirm him in it or to divert him from it. Before man's capacities were perfected, the promptings of his inherent nature, if attended to and not interfered with by external influences, were sufficient to furnish him with the simple guidance he needed.

Man's insistent spiritual need is a living faith in, and realization of, God's existence. God has made provision for the fulfillment of that need through revelation. The Quran says that it is for God to provide guidance (92:13). As soon as the human mind became capable of perceiving the need of, and experiencing direct communion with, God, in other words, as soon as man's capacities were perfected and he began to deserve the name of man, spiritual guidance began to be vouchsafed to him through revelation, and the angels were commanded to aid and succor him in the carrying forward of his good and righteous purposes and designs (15:30; 38:73).

God proclaimed for all time that guidance would be provided for mankind at each stage, and that whoso shall follow God's guidance "on them shall come no fear, nor shall they grieve" (2:39).

The advent of messengers and prophets from among mankind was announced. They would be the bearers of Divine guidance and would seek to establish and strengthen faith in God through rehearsal of His Signs. These Signs should be pondered and reflected over. They are the means of sustaining and enriching spiritual life, which ultimately expresses itself and finds fulfillment in communion with God (7:36).

There has been a whole succession of prophets and messengers who have been sent at various times among different peoples so that no section of mankind has been left unprovided with Divine guidance corresponding to its needs. The Quran is explicit that every people has had its messenger, guide, or warner (10:48; 13:8; 35:25). God's Providence in the spiritual sphere is as comprehensive as it is in the material one.

Through the messengers and prophets, God has revealed His guidance for the benefit of the people. This guidance is often referred to in the Quran as "the Book," and to emphasize that the guidance was in each case adequate for, and appropriate to, the needs of the people, it is stated that it was sent down "in accordance with the requirements of truth and wisdom" (17:106). Attention is also drawn to a particular aspect of Divine guidance which is apt to be overlooked: that it provides a balance, or a standard of values, which should enable people to make beneficent adjustments in their lives and to determine the fact and measure of progress in all spheres (72:18). The rule of conduct should be to weigh and adjust all factors in justice and neither to transgress nor to fall short of the Divine measure (55:8–10). This would help establish human relations on a basis of justice and along beneficent lines (57:26).

As stated, however, revelation is not confined to its main purpose of conveying or interpreting Divine law and guidance to mankind. Through acceptance of the law and the guidance (i.e., faith) and conformity thereto (i.e., righteous action), a person begins to have experience of individual revelation; or, in other words, he begins to enjoy direct communion with God. This revelation becomes the means of fulfillment of the highest spiritual needs and yearnings of man. In default of direct communion with God through different forms of revelation—vivid dreams of a certain type, clear visions, verbal communications—there could be no certainty for man that he was progressing along the path that leads to God. There is little comfort in the assurance that if we would regulate our lives in accordance with the dictates and values inculcated by our respective faiths we would witness and experience the beneficent consequences thereof in the Hereafter. From the Hereafter, once we reach it, there is no return (21:96). That is a truth of tremendous significance and consequence. If in

F

the Hereafter it is realized that our assumption with regard to our
ultimate goal and the means of arriving at it, on the basis of which
we had ordered our life on earth, was not in fact well-founded,
there would then be no margin left for voluntary correction of
our error. Surely there must be some means of making sure as we
go along that we are on the right path and that we are making
progress along it. This assurance, this certainty, could only be
achieved through revelation.

We are assured that if we make God our shield in every respect
and act in conformity with the guidance vouchsafed to us, we
shall realize in this life the fruits thereof in the shape of progressive
elimination of our faults and shortcomings, and in the actual
enjoyment and experience of God's beneficence (8:30). Light will
be provided wherein we may walk (57:29).

There is the promise that those who have firm faith and put
their full trust in God, realizing that He alone is the true source
of all beneficence and that everything else is only a means of
approach to Him and is under His power and control, and then
remain steadfast and act righteously, will, in this very life, receive
God's assurance and comfort that they are under His protection
both in this life and in the Hereafter (41:31–32).

The certainty of being on the right path, which alone can enable a person to devote all his faculties and capacities all the time
to winning the pleasure of God through service to his fellow beings, in the face of every kind of opposition and persecution, can
be achieved only through such an assurance.

In today's circumstances, experience of that kind is even more
necessary than it has been in the past, in face of the temptation
to treat everything as resulting solely from man's own effort, skill,
and knowledge. Man's contributions are indeed essential for all
progress and achievement, but they are only part of the means
and not the source of the beneficence which alone makes human
effort worthwhile and human life a glorious bounty of God.

8

The Quran

THE QURAN, AS ALREADY STATED, IS THE RECORD of the verbal revelation vouchsafed by God to Muhammad, the Prophet of Islam, over a period of approximately twenty-two years (610–632). It is the very words that God put in the mouth of that Prophet (Deut. 18:18). It contains all truth (John 16:13) for the guidance of mankind. Its message is universal. It affirms the truth of all previous revelations and the righteousness of all Prophets (2:137; 5:45, 47).

The arrangement of verses in the Quran does not follow the chronological order. Whenever a verse or group of verses was revealed, the Prophet indicated its place in the order and sequence of the Quran. Obviously, the compilation of the whole in the form of a book could not be undertaken so long as the revelation to the Prophet continued; but it is a mistake to suppose that the present arrangement was determined by the second or third Khalifa some years after the death of the Prophet. That is not so. The Prophet himself instituted and authorized this arrangement. In fact, during the Prophet's lifetime the Quran was committed to memory and was recited in the order in which we find it. Each fresh revelation found its place in that order as indicated by the Prophet. His opponents sometimes made objection to the manner in which the Quran was being revealed, that is to say, in portions spread over a long period, and they asked: "Why is it not revealed all at once?" The revelation itself pointed out the reason and the wisdom underlying its manner and arrangement (25:33; 17:107).

One reason why the present arrangement does not adhere to the chronological order is that the revelation came as it was needed in the contemporaneous state of the people to whom it was immediately addressed—the purpose being, first, to create faith in the Existence and Unity of God; then, to lay the foundations of a beneficent society in accordance with the principles of Islam; then, to reconstruct society on those principles and to train it in their exercise so that the people could become the bearers of the Divine message and illustrate it in practice in daily living. This necessitated that revelation be vouchsafed stage by stage over a period of years, reinforcing the cardinal, central doctrine of the Existence and Unity of God throughout, but working out the pattern of a beneficent society gradually, adding new features after those revealed earlier had been firmly grasped and put into practice. Once this purpose was achieved, it was no longer necessary to have the revelation arranged in that order. It had then to serve the need of an established, though constantly growing, community. The order to be followed henceforth was that which was appropriate to those conditions.

In view of the lack of the mass-printing facilities to which mankind has since become accustomed, the method adopted for safeguarding the revelation was to commit it to memory rather than to preserve it in the form of a book, though the text of each revelation, comprising one or more verses, was also written down as it was received. The Prophet himself was not literate, but others who were competent in that respect were employed for the purpose (29:49).

Guidance having been furnished to mankind through a series of revelations vouchsafed to the various Prophets, what is the position of the Quran with respect to those revelations whose truth it affirms? Previous revelations were limited in their scope. Each was designed to meet the needs of the people to whom it was sent during the stage of development upon which that people was about to enter. Each contained fundamental truths, valid through the ages in respect of the whole of mankind, but it also contained guidance, directions, commandments, and prohibitions which were of a local or temporary character. Moreover, in course of time, portions of those revelations were lost or forgotten. That which was of universal and permanent application in previous revelations, in other Scriptures, has been reaffirmed in the Quran. Such portions as had been lost or were overlooked or forgotten, but were still needed, have been revived. That which was of purely local or temporary application and was no longer needed has been omitted. That which was not contained in previous revelations, the need for it not yet having arisen, but which would henceforth be needed by mankind, was added (2:107; 3:8).

This does not mean that the Quran makes obligatory upon the Muslims all the commandments and ordinances contained in to-day's version of the previous revelations and Scriptures. Indeed, it emphasizes repeatedly that these versions have suffered griev-ously at the hands of some of those who profess to be their sup-porters (2:80). What the Quran affirms is the actual revelation vouchsafed to the previous Prophets. Thus: "Surely, We sent down the Torah wherein is guidance and light. By it did the Prophets, who were obedient to Us, judge for the Jews, as did the godly people and those learned in the Law" (5:45). And again: "And We caused Jesus, son of Mary, to follow in their footsteps, fulfilling that which was revealed before him in the Torah; and We gave him the Gospel which contained guidance and light, fulfilling that which was revealed before that in the Torah as an admonition for the God-fearing" (5:47). The Gospel here means the revelation vouchsafed to Jesus, and not the books which are today commonly so described.

Not only are today's versions of previous revelations open to serious question on the score of authenticity of the text and accur-acy of translation and interpretation; many of the details concern-ing commandments and ordinances and even doctrine which were of a temporary or local character are now out of date or in-applicable. Today's doctrine is also in many cases based on sub-sequent interpretation and formulation which appear to have little connection with what was contained in the revelation and even contradict it. Attention is drawn to all this in the Quran, and yet the Quran emphasizes the unity of the fundamental teaching contained in all previous Scriptures and insisted upon by the Prophets, namely belief in the Existence and Unity of God and in the Hereafter, and conformity to God's will through righteous action.

As already stated, the Quran reaffirms all that was funda-mental in previous revelations and which is still needed by man-kind. That is part of the guidance which the Prophet, and through him the Muslims and, indeed, all mankind are exhorted to follow —the guidance revealed by God through the prophets (6:91).

Thus the Quran, while affirming the truth of all previous revelations, itself comprises all truth for the whole of mankind for all time. It has been described as "pure Scriptures, comprising lasting commandments" (98:3-4).

The Quran is thus a universal possession and inheritance; its

message is directed to the whole of mankind (7:159). It is sent
down as a guidance for mankind, with clear proofs of guidance
and with discrimination between truth and falsehood (2:186).

It expounds and explains all that is or may be needed by mankind for the complete fulfillment of life (16:90). It seeks to create
faith in God through rehearsal of God's Signs; it makes provision
for mankind's welfare, material, moral, and spiritual; it teaches
all that is needed for the beneficent regulation of human life
and expounds the philosophy underlying it, so that reason being
satisfied, wholehearted conformity to what is taught may be
assured (62:2–3). It expounds the significance of establishing and
maintaining communion with God. It draws attention to various
Divine attributes, their operation and the manner in which mankind may derive benefit from the knowledge thereof. In short, all
that is basic for the promotion of human welfare in all spheres,
whether pertaining to principles or conduct, is set forth and
expounded (16:90).

It is this comprehensiveness of the Quran, the need to make
provision for guidance in every respect for all peoples for all time,
that made it necessary that the guidance should be conveyed in
verbal revelation. The Quran is literally the Word of God and
possesses the quality of being alive, as the universe is alive. It is
not possible to set forth at any time the whole meaning and interpretation of the Quran or, indeed, of any portion of it with
finality. It yields new truths and fresh guidance in every age and
at every level. It is a standing and perpetual miracle (18:110).

The world is dynamic and so is the Quran. Indeed, so dynamic
is the Quran that it has always been found to keep ahead of the
world and never to lag behind it. However fast the pace at which
the pattern of human life may change and progress, the Quran
always yields, and will go on yielding, the needed guidance in
advance. This has now been demonstrated through more than
thirteen centuries, and that is a guarantee that it will continue
to be demonstrated through the ages.

The Quran has proclaimed that falsehood will never overtake
it. All research into the past and every discovery and invention
in the future will affirm its truth (41:43). The Quran speaks at
every level; it seeks to reach every type of understanding, through
parables, similitudes, arguments, reasoning, the observation and
study of the phenomena of nature, and the natural, moral, and
spiritual laws (18:55; 39:28; 59:22).

It reasons from the physical and tangible to the spiritual and intangible. For instance: "Among His Signs is this; that thou seest the earth lying withered, but when We send down water on it, it stirs and swells with verdure. Surely He Who quickens the earth can quicken the dead. Verily, He has power over all things" (41:40). Here, by quickening of the dead is meant the revival and rebirth of a people. As the dead earth is quickened by life-giving rain from heaven, a people that appears to be dead in all respects is revived and regenerated through spiritual water from the heavens, that is to say, through Divine revelation. This idea is expressed in the Quran in several places. Both resurrection and renaissance are explained with reference to the phenomenon of the dead earth being revived through life-giving rain (22:6–8).

The Quran repeatedly urges observation and reflection, the exercise of reason, and understanding (22:270). For instance: "In the creation of the heavens and the earth and in the alternation of the night and the day there are indeed Signs for men of understanding, who remember Allah while standing, sitting, and lying down, and ponder the creation of the heavens and the earth. This leads them to exclaim: 'Our Lord, Thou hast not created all this without purpose; Holy art Thou' " (3:191–192).

Whenever attention is drawn in the Quran to God's Signs, the object is to urge reflection upon the event or phenomenon cited, that we may proceed to draw lessons therefrom which would help us grasp the Truth; to understand the operation of Divine attributes and of Divine laws; to appreciate spiritual values and to adjust and order our lives accordingly, so that all our activities in every sphere should become wholly beneficent. It is in that sense that the guidance contained in the Quran is described as "a healing and a mercy for those who put their faith in it" (17:83). We are reminded: "O mankind, there has indeed come to you an exhortation from your Lord and a healing for whatever ills there are in the hearts, and a guidance and a mercy for those who believe" (10:58).

With all this, man is left to his own free choice and acceptance of the Truth. Faith is not commanded on the basis of authority, but is invited on the basis of understanding (12:109). "This is a Book that We have revealed to thee, full of blessings, that they may reflect over its verses, and that those gifted with understanding may take heed" (38:30). There is complete freedom to believe or to deny. "Say: 'It is the Truth from your Lord;

wherefore let him who will, believe, and let him who will, disbelieve' " (18:30). But of course, though the choice is free, the
consequences of the choice follow in accordance with Divine law.
No one is forced. Everyone must choose and seek the purpose of
his life on the basis of faith or turn his back upon the Truth and
destroy his soul, according to his choice.

It has sometimes been suggested that belief in Divine revelation
and acceptance of revealed truth tend toward intellectual rigidity
and narrowness. The exact reverse is the truth. Revelation stimulates the intellect and opens all manner of avenues for research
and expansion of knowledge. The constant and repeated exhortation to reflect upon and ponder every type of natural phenomenon
with which the Quran abounds is an express urge in that direction.
History furnishes incontrovertible proof of this. Within an
astonishingly brief period following the revelation of the Quran,
darkness and confusion were dispelled over vast areas of the earth,
order was established, all manner of beneficent institutions
sprang into life, a high moral order was set up, and the blessings
of knowledge, learning, and science began to be widely diffused.
Human intellect, which for some centuries had been almost
frozen into inactivity, experienced a sudden release and upsurge,
and the world became witness to an astounding revolution. This
was no freak occurrence, no sudden flare-up followed by an even
more sudden collapse. This was a phenomenon characterized by
strength, beneficence, and endurance. It fulfilled to a pre-eminent
degree the needs and yearnings of the human body, intellect, and
soul. It changed the course of human history. It flung wide open
the gates of knowledge and progress in all directions. Its impact
continues to be felt today through many and diverse channels.

The Quran has been described as a Light and as a clear Book,
whereby "does Allah guide those who seek His pleasure along the
paths of peace, and leads them out of every kind of darkness into
the light by His will, and guides them along the right path"
(5:16–17).

On the other hand, the Quran itself discourages the tendency to
seek regulation of everything by Divine command, pointing out
that such regulation would become restrictive and burdensome
(5:102).

One of many characteristics of the Quran which mark it as the
Word of God is that to arrive at the comprehension of its deeper
meaning and significance the seeker must, in addition to a certain

degree of knowledge of the language and the principles of interpretation, cultivate purity of thought and action. The greater
the purity of a person's life the deeper and wider will be his
comprehension of the meaning of the Quran (56:80). This has
always been strikingly demonstrated.

The Quran contains Divine assurance that the guidance em-
bodied therein will be guarded under Divine protection (15:10).
This comprises several aspects:

First, the text of the revelation should be preserved in its purity
and entirety for all time. Considering that the revelation contained in the Quran was vouchsafed to the Prophet over a period
of twenty-two years, first in Mecca and then in Medina, that this
period was marked by persecution, disturbance, and fighting, that
the Prophet himself was not literate, and that there was no sure
method for preserving a record of the revelation except through
human memory, it is a truly miraculous fact that the text of the
Quran has been preserved absolutely pure and entire, down to
the last vowel point. Even non-Muslim scholars, who do not
accept the Quran as Divine revelation, affirm that the Quran is
word for word that which Muhammad gave out to the world as
Divine revelation.

Second, the language in which the revelation was sent should
continue to be a living language. Classical Arabic is today understood and used as a means of communication over much vaster
areas of the earth and by many hundred times more people than
it was in the time of the Prophet.

These factors, so essential for the safeguarding of the guidance
contained in the revelation, could not have been assured by the
Prophet in advance. Yet they are not enough. For life is dynamic,
and the pattern of human life is subject to constant change. The
process of evolution is at work all the time. Besides, history testifies
that the passage of time brings about a decline in spiritual and
moral values in a civilization. It is inevitable, therefore, that over
the centuries there should be a falling-off in the true appreciation
of Divine guidance set forth in the Divine revelation as applicable
to current conditions and situations. The complete safeguarding
of the Divine revelation necessitates a constant process of spiritual
revival and rebirth. In the nature of things this must also come
about through revelation. It was announced by the Prophet that
to meet this need God would continue to raise from among the
Muslims, at the beginning of each century, someone who would

be inspired to revive the faith by drawing attention to the guidance contained in the Quran apposite to existing conditions. History has confirmed the truth of this assurance conveyed by the Prophet.

The last half-century has, however, witnessed the onset of a tremendous revolution in human values in all spheres of life. Standards that had been accepted and subscribed to through centuries are undergoing rapid revision and modification. The very dimensions of human life are being reshaped, so that scholars and thinkers are beginning to stress the need of a new revelation. Yet, the Quran is quite clear that the guidance contained therein will be found adequate during all stages at all times.

What provision, it may be asked, is there in the Quran to meet the contingency with which mankind is faced today, and which is likely to grow ever more insistent during all the tomorrows that lie ahead? To meet this contingency the Quran announced that the Prophet not only had been raised in the generation among whom he lived, but would also be raised among others "who have not yet joined them" (62:3–4). This means a spiritual second advent of the Prophet for the purpose of setting forth from the Quran guidance that may be needed in the New Age, and for illustrating the values demanded by the exigencies with which man may then be faced. This promise has been fulfilled in the advent of Ahmad, of Qadian (1836–1908), who warned that mankind stood at the threshold of an era which would bear the same relation to his age, that is, the beginning of the twentieth century, as the beginning of that century bore to the days of Adam, and who proceeded to set forth from the Quran, in the light of revelation vouchsafed to him, the guidance that mankind now desperately needs.

9
Concept of God

THE CENTRAL PIVOT AROUND WHICH THE WHOLE doctrine and teaching of Islam revolves is the Unity of the Godhead. From this concept proceeds the fundamental unity of the universe, of man, and of life. The object of Islam is to establish a balance and to bring about accord in the relationship of man to God and to the universe through beneficent adjustment.

The Quran is insistent upon the Unity of God and emphatically condemns any doctrine, idea, or concept which might directly or indirectly tend to associate any other thing or being with God as a partner or equal. "Say: 'He is Allah, the One; Allah, the Independent, and Besought of all. He begets not, nor is He begotten; and there is none like unto Him'" (112:2–5). It needs to be observed that the word "Allah" is the proper name of God and is not derived from "*ilah*" meaning "god." Of course, Allah is God, but the word does not signify merely that Allah is God to the exclusion of all other gods. Western scholars have often failed to keep this distinction in mind and have erroneously assumed that Allah merely signifies God rather than a god. In fact there is no etymological relationship between "*ilah*," god or a god, and "Allah," which is the substantive for God. To appreciate the juxtaposition employed by the Quran in this respect, it is necessary to keep the distinction in mind. God is "*ilah*," and there is no other "*ilah*" beside Him, and His name is Allah; as, for instance, "Verily, Allah is the only One God" (4:172). The Quran, like other Scriptures, teaches "your God is One God" (16:23), and it reveals that Allah is His substantive name.

It then proceeds to emphasize the Unity of God, to expound His attributes, and to explain and illustrate their operation.

The primary object of all revelation is to emphasize this concept of God, that is to say, that He is One, has no equal or partner, and that all adoration, glorification, worship, and obedience are due to Him alone. He is the object of the heart's deepest love and devotion. To seek nearness to Him, to do His will in all things, to win His pleasure, to become the manifestation of His attributes—that is to say, His image—is the purpose of man's creation (51:57). He is the Source of all beneficence, everything proceeds from Him, and is dependent upon Him. He is Independent and stands in no need of help or assistance from any other source, inasmuch as all sources and means proceed from Him, and none exists or subsists outside Him or outside His control and authority.

"He sends down the angels with revelation by His command on whomsoever of His servants He pleases, saying, 'Warn that there is no god but I, so take Me alone for your Protector'" (16:3).

This concept is reinforced by various arguments. For instance: "Allah has not taken unto Himself any son, nor is there any other god along with Him; in that case, each god would have taken away what he had created, and some of them would surely have dominated over others. Glorify, then, Allah above all that which they attribute to Him, Knower of the unseen and of the seen; exalted is He, therefore, above all that which they associate with Him" (23:92–93). Mythology furnishes ample illustration of the confusion and chaos that would prevail if there were a plurality of gods. There would be an end to all certainty and order and consequently to all beneficence. Man and the universe instead of being manifestations of Divine beneficence would present a spectacle of capricious and cruel sport, and instead of progressing constantly toward perfection, would be speedily destroyed. "If there had been in the heavens and the earth other gods beside Allah, then surely the twain would have come to ruin. Glorified then be Allah, the Lord of Power, above what they attribute" (21:23).

God has throughout affirmed and borne witness to His Existence, His Unity, His various attributes, and revealed these to mankind at each stage to the degree to which their awareness was needed by mankind for the complete fulfillment of life in all its dimensions. The discovery of all this was not left to man. If that had been so, countless generations would have perished before a concept of God, even remotely approaching the reality, could have been evolved. "Allah bears witness that there is no god but He—and so do the angels and those possessed of knowledge—Maintainer of Justice; there is no god but He, the Mighty, the Wise" (3:19).

The Quran not only excludes all idea of any equal or partner with Allah, it specifically excludes all idea of His having a son except in the purely metaphorical sense in which all mankind are His children, and in which the peacemakers are spoken of, in the Bible, as "the children of God" (Matt. 5:9). God is Ever-Living, All-Knowing, All-Hearing, the Creator of all, whose authority extends over everything. To attribute a son, in any but the purely metaphorical sense, to God, would amount to a denial of His Unity and in effect to a denial of His Godhead. "Verily, Allah is the only One God. Far is it from His attributes of Holiness and Perfection that He should have a son. To Him belongs whatever is in the heavens and whatever is in the earth. Sufficient is Allah as a Creator" (4:172).

God is not only the First Cause. He is the Creator, the Maker, the Fashioner, and He exercises control over the universe at all times. "Allah is the Creator of all things, and He is the Guardian over all things. To Him belong the keys of the heavens and the earth" (39:63–64). All His attributes are eternal. None of them ever falls into disuse. His attribute of Creation is equally in operation all the time. "Allah originates Creation; then He repeats it; then to Him shall you be brought back" (30:12). "To Him belongs whatsoever is in the heavens and the earth. All are obedient to Him. He it is Who originates the Creation, then repeats it, for it is most easy for Him. His is the most exalted state in the heavens and the earth. He is the Mighty, the Wise" (30:27–28).

He creates and perfects; He designs and guides (87:3–4). He has bestowed upon everything its appropriate form, which enables each thing to perform its function properly, and has then guided everything to its proper function (20:51). He bestows life and He causes death (53:45), and to Him do all things ultimately return (53:43).

"To Allah belongs the kingdom of the heavens and the earth, and He has mastery over everything" (3:190). Having created the universe and all that is in it, He did not sit back and, as it were, abdicate His control over it. Nothing can continue in existence except with His constant support. "In His hand is the dominion over all things and He grants protection to everything, but against Him there is no protection" (23:89).

Nature and all its phenomena, life and all its exigencies,

including its termination here below, have all been created in God's wisdom, obey His laws, and are under His control (21:34; 36:38–41; 67:2–5).

God regulates it all and clearly explains His Signs that men may have firm belief in communion with Him and in their accountability to Him (13:3).

The various attributes of God have been set out in the Quran in different contexts. He forgives faults and shortcomings. He accepts repentance, He judges and imposes penalties, He is the Lord of Bounty. Toward Him is the final return (40:4).

His principal attributes, to which all other Divine attributes are related, are mentioned at the very outset in the opening chapter of the Quran. He is the Creator and Sustainer of all the worlds and leads them stage by stage toward perfection. He is the Gracious One, Who has made provision for the fulfillment of the purpose of the creation of man and of the universe. He is the Merciful One, Who causes beneficent results to follow upon righteous action. He is the Master of the Day of Judgment (1:2–4).

The distinction between *Ar-Rahman* (the Gracious One) and *Ar-Rahim* (the Merciful One) is that the former connotes that aspect of God's Grace which precedes, and is independent of, human action, while the latter connotes the Divine Grace or Mercy that causes beneficent results to follow upon righteous action. In other words, the operation of the former is without reference to human action, and the operation of the latter is consequent upon human action.

It is also to be observed that the fourth attribute describes God as Master of the Day of Judgment, and not merely as Judge. It is true that the operation of all Divine attributes is in accord with the requirements of justice, but the concept of justice leaves ample scope for the operation of other attributes such as, for instance, Mercy, Bountifulness, Appreciation. It is a misconception that justice demands punishment or a certain degree or type of punishment of all defaults and offenses, and that it restricts reward and bounty to a scale proportionate to the action or quality that deserves appreciation. Justice demands that all shall have their just due, that is to say, that no penalty shall be severer than that which is appropriate to the default or offense, and that no reward, remuneration, or compensation shall fall short of that which is deserved or has been earned. The reduction of a penalty, or its total remission, is not inconsistent with justice, nor is the multiplication of reward in conflict with its spirit. God's Mercy and His Grace and Bounty are without limit. Indeed, God does not punish every default or offense; many He overlooks and forgives altogether (42:31). His Law is that He chastises where chastisement is needed for reformation, but that His Mercy encompasses all things (7:157).

The subject of Divine attributes is a very extensive one, and the Quran treats it with a wealth of variety and detail. Indeed, each attribute could in itself form the subject of a whole treatise. As illustration of the manner in which the Quran approaches and treats various aspects of Divine attributes, it may perhaps suffice to conclude with the following:

Allah—there is no god but He, the Ever-Living, the Self-Subsisting, the All-Sustaining. Slumber overtakes Him not, nor sleep. To Him belongs whatsoever is in the heavens and whatsoever is in the earth. Who is he that will intercede with Him except by His leave? He knows what has gone before them and what will come after them; but they encompass nothing of His knowledge save that which He pleases. His knowledge comprehends the heavens and the earth; and the care of them burdens Him not. He is the High, the Great (2:256).

Allah is the Light of the heavens and the earth. Similitude of His Light is as a lustrous niche, wherein is a lamp. The lamp is enclosed in a globe. The globe is, as it were, a glittering star. It is light from a blessed tree—an olive—neither of the East nor of the West, whose oil would well-nigh glow forth even though fire touched it not. Light upon light! Allah guides to His light whomsoever He will. Allah sets forth parables to men, and Allah knows all things well (24:36).

He is Allah, there is no god beside Him, the Knower of the unseen and the seen. He is the Gracious, the Merciful.

He is Allah, there is no god beside Him, the Sovereign, the Holy One, the Source of Peace, the Bestower of Security, the Protector, the Mighty, the Subduer, the Exalted. Holy is Allah far above that which they associate with Him.

He is Allah, the Creator, the Maker, the Fashioner; His are the most beautiful attributes. All that is in the heavens and the earth glorifies Him. He is the Mighty, the Wise (59 : 23–25).

There is nothing that participates in His Being or Attributes (42:12); so coin not similitudes for Him and liken Him not to anything (16:75).

10

Man and the Universe

THE UNIVERSE WAS CREATED; IT DID NOT JUST happen. So much is the attribute of Creation regarded as a concomitant of the Godhead that the Creator has become a synonym for God.

Not only did the universe not just happen of itself, but it was created with a purpose. It is inconsistent with the Godhead that He should bring into being anything merely by way of sport or pastime. "We created not the heaven and the earth and all that is between the two in play. If We had wished to find a pastime We would surely have found it in what is with Us, if at all We were to do such a thing" (21:17–18). Indeed, to imagine that God does anything without purpose, in effect amounts to a denial of God (38:28). All God's attributes operate in accordance with the requirements of wisdom (71:14). The creation of the heavens and the earth has also been in accordance with the requirements of wisdom (15:86; 39:6; 46:4).

The whole of God's creation is in harmony. There is no discord, disorder, or incongruity. Everything is adjusted and co-ordinated so as completely to fulfill the purpose for which it was created (67:2–5). Such disorder or maladjustment as may be observed results from misuse or contravention of the laws governing the universe.

The purpose of the creation of the universe is to aid man in achieving the object for which he has been created. This is part of the measure of God's unlimited bounty to man. The universe and the laws that govern it constantly work out under Divine direction the consequences, beneficent or otherwise, of man's use of God's bounties (14:8; 16:15; 23:79; 56:69–71).

The creation of man has passed through many stages (71:15,

18). Over aeons, having originated from water and clay, man began to be created from the sperm, was endowed with sense and understanding, and began to be guided through revelation (32:5–10; 23:13–15; 35:12).

The Quran stresses the unity of mankind, emphasizing that man has been created of one kind (4:2; 16:73).

Like the universe, man has not been created without purpose and has not to pass his life aimlessly (75:37). His life has a purpose, and he is responsible and accountable in respect of it. In the phraseology of the Quran, the principle of accountability is expressed in terms of man having to be "brought back" to God (23:116). The purpose of man's creation is that he should receive the impress of God's attributes and should become a manifestation of them within the limits of his capacities. In other words, he should *become* God's image (51:57). The Prophet has explained this by saying: "Equip yourselves with the attributes of God."

To aid man in the achievement of this purpose, he has been endowed with appropriate faculties and capacities. He has been created "in the best of molds" (95:5).

In addition to man's inherent capacities, which are best fitted for the achievement of the purpose of his life, God has bestowed upon man dominion over the forces of nature in the sense that the whole of nature is governed by laws; the operation of these laws has as its object the beneficent service of man. These laws are ascertainable, and through their knowledge man can progressively increase his mastery over the forces of nature and extract greater and greater beneficence from them.

The Quran describes man as God's "vicegerent upon earth" (2:31). It affirms that man has been created by stages, and that he began to be guided through revelation when his faculties had been perfected. He then found that the universe was subjected to him for the enrichment and consummation of his life. So much so that the angels were commanded to assist in the fulfillment of his righteous designs (15:30; 38:73).

> Allah it is Who has subjected the sea to you that ships may sail thereon by His command, and that you may seek of His Bounty and that you may draw benefit therefrom. He has subjected to you whatsoever is in the heavens and whatsoever is in the earth; all of it is from Him. In that surely are Signs for a people who reflect (45:13–14).

G

Again:

> Allah is He Who created the heavens and the earth and caused
> water to come down from the clouds and brought forth therewith
> fruit for your sustenance; and He has subjected to you the ships
> that they may sail through the sea by His command, and the rivers
> too has He subjected to you. He has also subjected to you the sun
> and the moon, both pursuing their courses constantly. He has sub-
> jected to you the night as well as the day. He gave you all that you
> wanted of Him. If you try to count the favors of Allah, you will not
> be able to number them. Verily, man is apt to misuse and abuse the
> bounties of God (14:33–35).

God's favor in bestowing upon man all that was needed for the
fulfillment of the purpose of life and in subjecting to his service
the whole of the universe and all its phenomena is repeatedly
stressed, and man is exhorted to reflect upon, and to draw lessons
from, all these phenomena.

> He it is Who sends down water for you from the clouds; from it
> you have your drink; and there grows by it vegetation on which
> you pasture your beasts.
> Therewith He also grows for you corn, and the olive, and the
> date palm, and the grape, and all kinds of fruit. Surely in that is a
> Sign for a people who reflect.
> He has constrained into service for you the night and the day, and
> the sun and the moon; and the stars too have been constrained into
> your service by His command. Surely, in that are Signs for a people
> who make use of their reason.
> He has constrained into service the things He has created for you
> in the earth, of diverse hues. Surely, in that is a Sign for a people
> who take heed.
> He it is Who has subjected to you the sea, that you may take there-
> from fresh flesh to eat, and the ornaments that you wear. And thou
> seest the ships ploughing it, that you may journey thereby, and
> that you may seek of His bounty, and that you may be grateful
> (16:11–15).

As already stated, reference to God's Signs emphasizes the need
for study and research so that the proper use of each thing may be
discovered by acquiring knowledge of its properties and the laws
governing them.

These gifts and bounties are for the benefit of man as such; that
is to say, of the whole of mankind without discrimination. They
are not intended for, or confined to, any particular section.

Considerations of space forbid even a brief reference to the multitude of directions in which man is capable of expanding his beneficent uses of everything that God has provided in the universe for his benefit. The assurance that the whole universe is subjected to man's service and the certainty that everything in it is governed by laws, the knowledge of which can be progressively acquired by man, throws wide open to man all avenues of knowledge, which he is not only encouraged, but is repeatedly urged and exhorted, to explore unceasingly. The only limitation is imposed by another of God's laws: that so long as man continues to make beneficent use of God's bounties, God will continue to multiply them unto man without limit, but, on the other hand, if he misuses or abuses them, he will be called to account in respect of them, and these very bounties may become the instruments of his ruin and destruction (14:8).

Further, as has been seen, God has always provided guidance through revelation so that mankind may be enabled to regulate their lives beneficently in all spheres.

Thus, equipped with his own inherent faculties and capacities appropriate to, and adequate for, the purpose of achieving his object in life; with Divine guidance available at all stages, adequate to his needs; and with the whole of the universe subjected to his service, man has through Divine beneficence been placed in the most favorable position for the complete fulfillment of his life and for the achievement of its goal and purpose. It is a glorious prospect.

A host of questions may be raised with regard to the nature of good and evil; man's propensity toward, and the likelihood of his falling into, evil; the chances and means of his retrieving himself and working his way back to beneficence; and with regard to the problems, real or fancied, encountered in connection therewith. The Quran deals with all these questions, and it does so with indubitable relevance for modern man.

Prayer

PRAYER AND THE REMEMBRANCE OF GOD, THAT IS,
contemplation of His attributes, are the principal means of
establishing communion with God. In its highest expression,
prayer itself constitutes an experience of communion with the
Divine. The Islamic concept of prayer is a direct pouring forth of
soul by the suppliant before the Divine Majesty. There is no need
for, nor does Islam tolerate the notion of, any intermediary between God and man. It is true that Prayer in congregation is led
by one of the congregation, but the leader, called the Imam, does
not in any sense act as an intermediary.

The reaching out of the soul toward its Creator—particularly
when it is in travail and seeks to pour forth its anguish to the
Almighty, Who possesses the knowledge and the power to come
to its aid, to bestow solace and comfort, to grant relief, to raise it
up from its lowly estate—is a natural urge that will not be denied.
That urge is in itself an affirmation and proof of both the Existence
of God and of the need and possibility of establishing communion
with Him. "Who hears the prayer of the anguished person when
he calls upon Him, and relieves his distress? . . . Is there a god
besides Allah? Little is it that you reflect" (27:63).

That sincere prayer is heard and answered is proof which excludes all question and all doubt of the Existence of God. The
Quran is explicit on the subject of the acceptance of prayer,
putting it as simply as: "Your Lord says, 'Pray unto Me. I will
answer your prayer'" (40:61). Indeed, prayer and the answer
to prayer constitute the one means of attaining to certainty concerning the Existence of God and the possibility of establishing
communion with Him. "When My servants ask thee concerning
Me, say that I am near; that I answer the prayer of the supplicant
when he prays to Me. So they should hearken to Me and have

firm faith in Me, that they may be rightly guided" (2:187).

We need, however, to remember that God is Master; we are His creatures and servants. He gives us the assurance that prayer is a means of approach to Him and that He answers prayer. This does not mean that the relationship of Master and servant is in any way affected through our prayers being answered. He is still the Master. He is also All-Knowing and All-Aware. No sincere prayer is in vain; though we, with our limited knowledge and our circumscribed vision, can never be certain what may be to our benefit and what may in the end do us harm. At times the literal acceptance of prayer may even not be the manifestation of God's Mercy and Grace, but the reverse. But all sincere prayer brings us nearer to God, which is the ultimate object, and there is an answer, though the answer may not, in God's Wisdom and Mercy, be manifested as we, in our haste and ignorance or in the stress of grief or emotion, may desire.

God alone is worthy that prayer be addressed to Him. There is no other being beside God to whom prayer may be addressed or who can answer prayer. Indeed, that is the principal reason for the rejection of all claims to divinity, complete or partial, that may be advanced on behalf of any other being. "Unto Him is the true prayer. Those on whom they call beside Him answer them not at all, except as he is answered who stretches forth his two hands toward water that it may reach his mouth, but it reaches it not. The Prayer of those who do not believe is but a thing wasted" (13:15).

The Quran offers the acceptance of prayer as a decisive proof of Divine power. Prayer may be addressed only to God Who alone has power to answer. All others are powerless to answer it. "Surely those whom you call on beside Allah are mere servants like you. Then call on them and let them answer, if you are justified in your claim" (7:195).

Then who can be more astray than those who instead of praying to God, the All-Knowing, the All-Hearing, the All-Aware, the Almighty, pray unto such as cannot answer them till the Day of Judgment. Indeed, they are not even conscious that any prayers are being addressed to them (46:6).

God accepts prayer as a manifestation of His Existence and His attributes. He has an individual relationship with each of His servants, and the acceptance of prayer is largely affected by the degree and the quality of each person's relationship to God, which means the degree to which the person responds to the guidance provided by God (42:27).

The concept of prayer in Islam finds expression in many ways. The most important is the one known as *Salat*, sometimes described as one of the pillars of the faith, which is obligatory. It comprises five daily services, which consist of congregational Prayer, all of them except one being preceded or followed by individual worship in the same form as the congregational Prayer. The times of the five services are dawn, noon, afternoon, after sunset, and nightfall (11:115; 17:79). The only service during which a sermon is delivered is the Friday noon service. The length of time for each of these services varies from fifteen minutes to a half hour. The Friday noon service takes longer, depending upon the time occupied by the Imam's address; on the average it occupies about one hour. When the worshiper is traveling or is under pressure of valid necessity, the noon and afternoon services may be combined, and the sunset and the late evening services may be combined.

The service is normally held in a place dedicated to the worship of God, called a *musjid*, or mosque, but it may be held anywhere, the only requirement being that the place chosen be clean. The Prophet has said: "The whole earth has been purified for me for the worship of God." When a mosque is not easily available, services are often held in private rooms, in an open park, in the desert, on board a vessel on the ocean, and even in a train. Two persons form a congregation; three, in the case of the Friday service. All worshipers participating in a service face toward the Ka'aba in Mecca, which ensures unity of direction throughout the world, and spiritual concentration.

The Call to Prayer, *azan*, is made by word of mouth and is in itself an epitome of the teachings of Islam. The person making the Call chants in a resonant, melodious voice, designed to carry as far as possible, the words of the Call, in Arabic, which may be rendered into English as follows:

Allah is Great [four times]; I bear witness that there is no being worthy of worship save Allah [twice]; I bear witness that Muhammad is the Messenger of Allah [twice]; come to Prayer [twice]; come to Salvation [twice]; Allah is Great [twice]; there is no being worthy of worship save Allah [once].

Whatever pursuit or occupation a person may be engaged in

when he hears "Allah is Great," which also means Allah is above all, the Call comes to him as a reminder that he must immediately transfer his attention from the business in hand to the worship of God, which is the ultimate goal and object and, indeed, the fulfillment and consummation of one's being.

There is a short interval between the Call to Prayer and the service, which gives the worshipers time to prepare for the service and to proceed to the mosque. The preparation for the service consists of cleaning the mouth and the nostrils and of washing the face, the arms up to the elbows, and the feet if they are uncovered, which secures both physical cleanliness and an attitude of attention and concentration toward the act of worship.

The service is led by one of the congregation, preferably the one who possesses the best understanding of the Quran. There is no priesthood or anything corresponding to ordination or taking Holy Orders in Islam. Every Muslim is, or should be, competent to lead a congregation in the service.

It may be thought that five services daily is a little too much and may become burdensome. In fact that is not so. It is a matter of comparative values. All five services taken together do not take up more than about two hours—no more time than a person in the West is apt to spend watching television. In the eyes of a Muslim, a diversion such as television, or the formalities attendant upon a ceremonial dinner, together with the preparations concerning dress, etc., that go with it, or a rubber of bridge has little value, whereas participation in congregational worship is nutriment for the soul. It can be, and in most cases is, a cathartic experience.

The frequency of the services has also a very special value. The beginning and the end of each day are devoted to communion with God during the morning and evening services. The greater part of the day must perforce be occupied with mundane pursuits, though, from the Islamic point of view, there is no sharp division between the material and the spiritual, the secular and the religious. Nevertheless, it is recognized that the dominant character of some pursuits and occupations has one or the other of these qualities. In the middle of these pursuits and occupations a person is reminded, two or three times in the course of the day, of his duty to God and his duty to his fellow beings, and he is summoned to participate with others in the common act of homage to, and communion with, the Maker of all. The preparation

for the service by way of ablutions has its own cleansing and refreshing effect, which attunes a person in advance to participation in the solemn worship of the Divine. Each Call to Prayer
arrests the further progress of the thoughts and pursuits in which
the worshiper is engaged immediately before the service. Participation in the service lifts his whole being to a higher plane, from
which he returns to his normal pursuits and duties refreshed and
invigorated. Each service provides a sanctuary for the soul,
wherein it may stand in the presence of its Maker, in communion
with Him. Thus the spiritual frame and structure of a worshiper's
being is strengthened and reinforced several times a day.

The Prophet said: "When you are engaged in the *Salat* you
should realize that you are in the very Presence of God; at the
very least you should be conscious that God is looking at you."
Throughout the *Salat* the worshiper's mind, indeed his whole
being, must be centered on God. If his thoughts wander, he
should rally them and shepherd them back into the Divine
Presence.

The principal part of the service is the recitation of the opening
chapter of the Quran, called the *Fatiha*. The *Fatiha* is recited
aloud by the Imam during the sunset, late evening, and morning
services, in which he is followed by the congregation, who recite
it silently after him. It is recited silently by each worshiper in the
other two services. This is followed by a brief recitation from
some other part of the Quran in the same manner. These recitations are made in the standing posture. The congregation then
bows and proceeds to make two prostrations. While bowing and
prostrating, the worshipers glorify God and silently praise Him.
These three postures constitute a *rak'a*. The different services
comprise two, three, or four *rak'as*. After every second *rak'a* and
after the final *rak'a*, the congregation prays while seated. In this
posture, among other prayers, Allah's blessings are invoked on the
Prophet (33:57). Prayers may be selected from the Quran or out
of those taught by the Prophet, or may be framed by each worshiper individually in his own words. They may be in Arabic as,
for instance, those from the Quran and those taught by the
Prophet, or they may be in the worshiper's own language or in
any other language that he may prefer.

Except the recitations that are made by the Imam, nothing else
is recited aloud during the service. At each change of posture, the
Imam indicates the change by proclaiming: "Allah is Great" or

"Allah hearkens to him who utters His praise". At the conclusion of the service, the Imam turns his face to the right, saying: "Peace be on you and the blessings of Allah," and then to the left, repeating: "Peace be on you and the blessings of Allah." This concludes the service. It is usual for members of the congregation not to disperse immediately, but to remain in their places for a minute or two, occupied in praise and glorification of God, usually in the words, "Holy is Allah, and worthy of all praise; Holy is Allah, of Vast Bounty."

The *Fatiha* is, as it were, the heart and soul of the service. It is one of the shorter chapters of the Quran, comprising only seven verses, but its significance is very wide. It may be rendered as follows:

> In the name of Allah, Who sustains us and has made all manner of provision for us in advance, and Who rewards righteous action with beneficent results. All worthiness of praise belongs to Allah, the Sustainer of all the worlds, Who leads them stage by stage toward perfection; the Gracious, the Merciful, Master of the Day of Judgment. Thee alone do we worship, and from Thee alone do we implore help. Guide us along the right path—the path of those on whom Thou hast bestowed Thy blessings, those who have not incurred Thy displeasure, and those who have not gone astray.

Thus the worshiper, at the very outset, finds himself in the presence of his Maker, and seeks to impress his mind and soul with a certain concept of the Majesty of God by reminding himself of His four principal attributes. He then gives expression to his conviction, resulting from the contemplation of these attributes, that He Who possesses these attributes in perfection is alone worthy of worship and is the Only Being from Whom help may be sought in all contingencies for all righteous purposes. Even for the purpose of being enabled to offer proper worship to Him, the worshiper seeks His help. He then makes his supplication that in all his affairs he may be rightly guided and may be enabled to adopt and pursue beneficent means for success: such means as would enable him to be included among those upon whom the Grace of God descends, to keep him from incurring God's displeasure, and to safeguard him from going astray.

In the *Salat* the worshiper repeatedly returns to contemplation of the Majesty of God, imploring Him to guide and direct his life and effort along beneficent channels. This repeated effort made in the right spirit, in humility and sincerity, must leave its impress on the mind and soul of the worshiper and cleanse him thoroughly of all dross. The Quran says that the *Salat* purifies a worshiper and washes him clean of all evil and misbehavior (29:46). The Prophet has said: "If a person has a stream of pure water running at his doorstep and washes himself thoroughly in it five times a day, no impurity would even approach him. Remember, the *Salat* is such a stream."

The Quran has laid it down as an obligatory duty that the *Salat* must be duly observed (2:4). This injunction is repeated many times. The *Salat* is also described as the principal means of seeking God's help. The Quran urges the seeking of Divine help through steadfastness and *Salat* (2:154). It is pointed out that it is not easy except for the humble in spirit, who know for certain that they will meet their Lord and that to Him will they return (2:46–47). Those who seek success wholly through their own effort, skill, and knowledge, and take little account of the certainty that each human being must face his Maker and render an account to Him of the great and priceless gift of life, are apt to consider the *Salat* a wearisome formality, and even a waste of time. Their idea of success is often limited to financial competence, office, dignity, or power, and does not extend to moral and spiritual fulfillment, to the constant reaching out of the soul toward perfection. As already stated, it is a matter of comparative values.

In addition to participating in the five obligatory services, Muslims are exhorted to get up during the latter part of the night for individual Prayer, in the same form as the *Salat*, as a supererogatory service (17:80). This generally comprises eight *rak'as*, offered in four units of two *rak'as* each. In addition, the Prophet often offered Prayer in two units during the early part of the forenoon. In this, also, he is followed by many Muslims.

Thus having regard to the times of the various services, obligatory and supererogatory, at all hours of the day and night, millions of human beings, of all races, colors, and conditions, humble in spirit, "whom neither merchandise nor traffic diverts from the remembrance of Allah and the observance of Prayer" (24:37–39) are engaged in glorifying Allah and celebrating His praise. As hour succeeds hour, in country after country, region after region, and continent after continent, millions pass on to others this holy pursuit. Seven times in the course of each twenty-four hours every part of the terrestrial globe is made witness of this purifying and ennobling exaltation of Allah's Holy Name by His humble creatures in adoration and gratitude, and of the invocation of His blessings upon His Messenger.

Besides the *Salat* there is constant occasion for, and urge toward, prayer. No time is prescribed; no formalities have to be observed; there is no set form of words. The heart and the soul make submission to their Maker and seek communion with Him as they may be moved. The difference between the *Salat* and prayer in its ordinary concept may be symbolically expressed as the difference between a public audience to which one is bidden and which one must attend on peril of being accounted a defaulter if one does not, and one's seeking an audience every time one's eagerness urges one to it.

Following the example set by the Prophet, the habit of prayer should be very constant. The Prophet was eager to maintain communion with God through prayer every moment of his life. The process of prayer and remembrance of God was practically continuous with him, and has been so with countless Muslims. The prayer most frequently resorted to is the first verse of the opening chapter of the Quran, which is repeated at the beginning of each chapter: "In the name of Allah, Who sustains us and provides for us and blesses all righteous action with beneficent reward." Occasions for this prayer are numberless during the course of a day. It is said as grace before meals; it is said when a glass of water or a cup of tea or any other refreshment is taken; it is said when any task is commenced, whether light or heavy. The idea is that everything, including our faculties and capacities, belongs to God and is a bounty from Him, which we use only with His permission. The concluding grace at meals, taught by the Prophet, is: "All praise is due to Allah Who has given us to eat and drink and has made us obedient to His will."

The prayers most often used are taken from the Quran for the obvious reason that a prayer taught by God Himself fulfills completely its own purpose and is also more in accord with the yearnings of the soul. Some of these are here set out:

"Our Lord, grant us Thy joyful bounties in this world as well as Thy joyful bounties in the life to come, and protect us from the torment of the fire" (2:202).

"My Lord grant me that I may be duly grateful to Thee for Thy favors which Thou hast bestowed upon me and upon my parents, and that I may act righteously so as to please Thee, and make my progeny righteous also. I do turn to Thee; and, truly, I am of those who submit themselves to Thee" (46:16).

On boarding a vessel: "In the name of Allah be its course and its mooring. My Lord is assuredly Most Forgiving, Merciful" (11:42). This is the prayer that Noah made when he embarked with his companions in the ark.

On riding an animal or a vehicle: "Holy is He Who has subjected this to us; we had not the strength to subdue it ourselves. To our Lord surely shall we return" (43:14–15).

On entering a building for any legitimate purpose whatever, slight or serious: "O my Lord, make my entry an entry of truth and then make my coming forth a coming forth with truth, and grant me from Thyself a helping power" (17:81).

The following would suggest its own relevance: "Our Lord, grant us of our spouses and our children the delight of our eyes, and make us a model for the righteous" (25:75).

This is a part of the prayer of Moses, usually offered silently by a person who is about to address an assembly or take part in a discussion: "My Lord, expand me my breast, and ease for me my task, and remove the impediment from my tongue, that they may understand my speech" (20:26–29).

The following is the prayer of Joseph: "O my Lord, Thou hast bestowed upon me a portion of authority and hast taught me the art of interpretation. O Maker of the heavens and the earth, Thou art my Protector in this world and the Hereafter, let not death come to me but in a state of submission to Thy will, and join me to the righteous" (12:102).

The prayers taught by the Prophet are also very helpful and strikingly illustrate the Prophet's own attitude of mind and the values that determined his conduct. On going out of his house he always prayed: "I go forth in the name of Allah, putting my full trust in Allah. There is no power to do good nor strength to resist evil save through Allah. O Lord, I seek Thy protection that I go not astray, nor cause any to go astray; that I stumble not, nor cause any to stumble; that I transgress not against any, nor any transgress against me; that I behave not ill toward any, nor any behave ill toward me."

On approaching a town, he prayed: "O Allah, Lord of the heavens and of all that they cover; Lord of the earths and of all that they are weighted with; Lord of the winds and of all that they waft; Restrainer of the forces of evil and of all that they cause to go astray, I beg of Thee the best of this town and the best of its people and the best of all that is in it and seek refuge with Thee from the evil of this town and the evil of its people and the evil of all that is in it. O Lord, provide us with that which is agreeable in this town, and protect us against all that is harmful in it; put affection for us in the hearts of its people, and put in our hearts affection for such of its people as are righteous."

On going to bed: "In Thy name, O Lord, I pass into a state resembling death, and come out of it. O Allah, I commit my soul to Thee and set my face toward Thee and commit my affairs into Thy care and rest my back against Thee in love and fear of Thee. O Allah, there is no refuge from Thee save in Thee. O Allah, I believe in the Book that Thou hast sent down and in the Prophet that Thou hast raised."

On waking up: "All praise is due to Allah, Who has caused us to come out of a state resembling death after He had made us enter it, and unto Him is the final resurrection."

On taking medicine: "In the name of Allah; He is the Healer."

When husband and wife come together: "O Allah, safeguard us against all evil and keep all evil away from the issue with which Thou mightst bless us." As soon as a child is born, the Call to Prayer is recited into its right ear and then into its left ear. Thus the child is exposed to the moral and spiritual call from the very moment of its inception.

Before taking a final decision on any grave or serious matter it is customary to pray—if possible, for seven days in succession, and over a more extended period if time permits—immediately before going to bed, in the following words taught by the Prophet: "O Allah, I seek good from Thee out of Thy Knowledge and seek power from Thee out of Thy Power and beg of Thee out of Thy boundless Grace, for Thou hast Power and I have no power, Thou hast Knowledge and I have no knowledge, and Thy Knowledge encompasses all that is unseen. O Allah, if it be within Thy Knowledge that this particular matter is good for me in the matter of my faith and in the matter of my worldly affairs and in respect of my ultimate end, then make it possible for me and make it easy for me and bless it for me, but if it be within Thy Knowledge that it is harmful for me, then cause it to move away from me and cause me to move away from it and enable me to attain good wherever it may be and then make my heart pleased with it."

Another form of prayer is the remembrance of God, that is to say, reflecting upon His attributes and the manner of their manifestation. The Quran describes this as a Sign of wisdom and a characteristic of "men of understanding, who remember Allah while standing, sitting, or lying down, and ponder over the creation of the heavens and the earth" (3:191–192).

The Arabs in the pre-Islamic period took great pride in the exploits of their ancestors and celebrated these with great éclat in their poetry. The Quran reminded them of this and exhorted them to celebrate Allah's praise with even greater emphasis and intensity (2:201). The Prophet Zachariah urged his people to celebrate the Glory and Holiness of God morning and evening (19:12). The Quran at various places exhorts the Muslims to glorify the name of their Lord, the Most High (87:2). There are several expressions used for that purpose, the commonest being: "Holy and Perfect is Allah"; "All praise is due to Allah"; "Allah is Great and above all"; "Holy is my Lord of Vast Bounty"; "Holy is my Lord, the Most High."

Some of the expressions in which remembrance of God is expressed are woven into the fabric of Muslim vocabulary in all parts of the world. The termination and consummation of all effort finds expression in: "All worthiness of praise belong to Allah, the Creator and Sustainer of all the worlds, Who leads them stage by stage toward perfection" (1:2). The Quran states that in Paradise also the righteous will give expression to their gratitude to Allah in the same terms (10:11). Whenever any event is mentioned or observed which excites wonder, it is greeted with "Holy and Perfect is Allah." On observing or hearing anything disagreeable or on any occasion when one is conscious of one's weakness and lack of strength in respect of achieving what is desirable or of resisting what may be undesirable, the expression employed is: "There is no strength and there is no power save through Allah, the Most High, of Vast Bounty." A misfortune or calamity, whether individual or national, evokes an expression of sympathy and a seeking after steadfastness and solace in: "Surely to Allah we belong and to Him shall we return" (2:157).

On an urging or incitement toward anything undesirable or harmful, protection is sought in the words: "I seek the protection and forgiveness of Allah." Before beginning the reading or recitation of the Quran, the protection of Allah is sought against all thoughts and promptings of evil (16:99).

The Quran constantly exhorts toward remembrance of God through observation (43:52; 51:22), reflection (2:220, 267; 7:185; 34:47), meditation (4:83; 47:25), the exercise of reason and understanding (6:152; 16:13; 23:81; 28:61), the seeking of knowledge (20:115; 30:7–8), the pondering over intellectual problems (17:45, 57; 9:122), the proper use of the emotions (2:155; 26:114; 39:56; 49:3), the fostering of spiritual vision (7:199; 11:21; 28:73), the drawing of lessons from past events (2:222; 6:153; 14:26; 45:24), and the expression of gratitude to God for all His favors and bounties, both by reminding oneself of them and through their proper use (14:8; 16:15; 23:79; 56:71).

The glorification of God and the celebration of His Praise are not confined to any set phrase or formula. The yearning of the soul to approach ever nearer to its Maker and to celebrate His Praise and Holiness, to express its homage to Him, and to proclaim its gratitude for His numberless favors and bounties, may find expression in a thousand different ways.

In short, Islam requires that whatever task or activity a person may be engaged in, his soul be anchored in God, and he constantly seek nearness to Him. A Muslim mystic has described this condition as "one's faculties being occupied with the business in hand, and one's soul being engaged with God."

12

Fasting

THE QURAN LAYS DOWN: "FASTING IS PRESCRIBED for you as it was prescribed for those before you, so that you may attain to righteousness" (2:184).

Fasting is prescribed during the lunar month of *Ramadhan*. The revelation of the Quran began in that month (2:186).

A person who is observing the fast is required, throughout the month, to abstain from food and drink and from sexual intercourse between the first flush of dawn and sunset. The fast is obligatory upon every adult, with certain exemptions. A sick person, one who is traveling, a woman with child or giving suck to a child, an old person, one who finds the severity of the fast hard to bear on account of age or other infirmity, are exempt. When the reason for the exemption is only temporary, as for instance illness from which the sufferer recovers, the number of days of the fast which are missed should be made up at any time during the succeeding eleven months. Should the cause of the exemption continue over a lengthy period of time or become permanent, as in case of old age or a chronic infirmity, the exemption is absolute; but the person concerned, if he can afford it, should arrange to provide food for a poorer person throughout the month of *Ramadhan* (2:185).

The month of fasting, being a lunar month, comes ten days earlier every year, thus rotating through the year, so that in every part of the world it falls in all seasons in turn. In the tropics, when the month falls in the summer season the fast entails considerable hardship because normal occupations have to be carried on, and in the intense heat and dryness a severe degree of thirst may have to be endured for several hours each day. However, the fast is not a penance. It is a physical, moral, and spiritual discipline. A similar discipline has been prescribed in other faiths,

though in some it has now only a symbolical significance. The
object of the fast is, as already observed, the attainment of
righteousness. Through the experience of the fast, the worshiper
should be led to exalt Allah for His having provided the guidance
relating to the fast and to the beneficent use of His favors and
bounties (2:186).

The fast places everybody, rich and poor alike, on the same
level. The well-to-do experience the pangs of hunger and thirst
identically with their less-favored brothers and sisters, so that, for
the former, hunger and privation cease to be mere expressions
and become an experience shared in common.

Besides the observance of the regulations regarding such matters
as food and drink, the month of fasting provides an opportunity
for concentration on, and intensity of, communion with God.
The supererogatory service in the latter part of the night becomes
obligatory during *Ramadhan*, though some people find it more
convenient to perform it immediately before the late evening
service. Also more time is devoted to the study of, and reflection
over, the Quran than at other times. Every opportunity is sought
to intensify the exercise of the moral and spiritual values, and
though normal occupations and duties are carried on as usual,
everything is subordinated to the main purpose.

In this context it would be useful to complete the perspective
by considering briefly the ordinances of Islam regulating food and
drink.

In the matter of food and drink the prohibitions are: blood, the
flesh of an animal that has died of itself, the flesh of swine, and the
flesh of an animal on which the name of any other than Allah has
been invoked, meaning thereby sacrifices made to idols or other
gods, and offerings to saints or any being other than Allah
(2:174; 5:4). The first three categories are prohibited because
they are harmful to the body, and that which is harmful to the
body is necessarily harmful to the spirit. The last prohibition
relates to something which is directly harmful morally and spiritually, inasmuch as it amounts to association of others with God.

A relaxation is made in the case of a person who is driven by
necessity and to whom no other means of sustenance and nourishment is for the time available. He may partake of a prohibited
article of food, using only that much which he considers necessary
for his immediate need. In such an instance, priority is given to
the need of maintaining and sustaining life, as against any possible

harm that might result from the use of a minimum quantity of
the forbidden article (2:174).

All intoxicants are also prohibited. It is recognized that some
people may derive some pleasure or advantage from the use of
liquor or other prohibited article, but such use is prohibited because the harm that it might do is greater than any pleasure or
advantage that might be derived from it (2:220). The prohibition,
however, is clear and total (5:91). The Quran points out that
indulgence in liquor tends to create dissension and enmity and
that people who indulge in it are liable to neglect Prayer and the
remembrance of Allah (5:92).

It must also be remembered that in the matter of any pleasure
or advantage to be derived from liquor, and the harm that may
result from its use, it is not only a particular individual or a class
that has to be considered; the whole community must be taken
into account. It may well be that the harm resulting to an individual or a number of individuals may not be clearly manifested, but there is no denying that society as a whole suffers a
great deal of harm from the use of liquor and other intoxicants.
The purpose of the Quran is not only to furnish guidance for the
individual, but to furnish guidance to the individual as a member
of society and to society and, indeed, to mankind as a whole.

These are the prohibitions, but not all that is permissible may
be used as food and drink in all circumstances. Of all that is permissible, only that may be used as food and drink which is clean
and wholesome (2:169). Even that which is permissible and is
clean and wholesome may be partaken of only in moderation
(7:32).

Within these limitations there is neither harm nor sin in eating
and drinking of the good things provided by God out of His
Beneficence, so long as the objective is that life may be sustained
and health promoted for the purpose of carrying out God's will
through firm faith in the guidance that He has provided, and
righteous action in accordance therewith, which ensures conformity to all His commandments (5:94).

Here, then, is a gradation which is elastic and takes account of
the immediate as well as the ultimate purpose of food and drink.
That which is on the whole harmful is prohibited altogether,
except in case of extreme necessity, when the preservation of life
must take precedence over any possible harm that might be done
to the individual concerned. Even then the exemption or relaxa-

tion is only in respect of the minimum quantity that would meet the immediate need. Thus restricted, the harm itself, if any at all in such a case, would be reduced to the minimum, and once the need has been met, the prohibition would continue to operate. Out of that which is permissible, only clean and wholesome articles may be used as food and drink. This has a relative aspect, also. That which is wholesome has a wider range for a healthy adult and a very restricted one for a child or an invalid. Even clean and wholesome food and drink must be used in moderation, and that again is a relative matter, having regard to the needs of each class and individual. Finally, not only the immediate purpose of food and drink, but also the ultimate purpose, namely, the promotion of the moral and spiritual values, must be kept in view.

That which is prohibited as being harmful, whether in the matter of food and drink or in any other connection, is abstained from at all times. In the month of *Ramadhan*, during the period of fasting there is abstention even from that which is lawful and permissible: food and drink, which sustain life, and marital intercourse, which promotes the continuance of the species. It is a symbolical pledge or covenant that a worshiper enters into, signifying that if in the course of his duty of submission to the will of God he should be called upon to put his life in jeopardy or to sacrifice the interests of his progeny, he would not hesitate to do so. Such a discipline carried on through a whole month every year should ensure that after each *Ramadhan*, the participant would, in the remaining eleven months of the year, progressively achieve greater and greater adherence to moral and spiritual values.

During the last ten days of *Ramadhan* some people stay continuously in a mosque and devote the whole of the time, not occupied by the obligatory and supererogatory services, to the study of the Quran and to the remembrance of God—reflection over His attributes and the manner of their manifestation. This period of complete devotion of a worshiper's time to the exercise of the purely spiritual values, is the culmination of the moral and spiritual discipline instituted by Islam. To carry this discipline farther would be a sort of monasticism or asceticism, which is not permissible in Islam (57:28).

On the other hand, it must not be forgotten that the whole purpose of fasting, whether obligatory, as during the month of *Ramadhan*, or supererogatory, as at other times, is to promote righteousness, which is a progressive cultivation of spiritual values.

The Prophet was very emphatic in drawing attention to that aspect of fasting. He said: "He who abstains from food and drink during the period of fasting, but does not strive to safeguard himself against moral lapses starves to no purpose." As against this, he pointed out that it had been revealed to him that, whereas there are high spiritual rewards for all other worship and righteous action, the ultimate reward of a person who observes the fast solely for the sake of God, is God Himself.

At the end of the month of fasting there is the Festival of the breaking of the fast. This is one of those occasions when even a supererogatory fast may not be observed. But again, in conformity with the spirit of Islam, the only matter prescribed for the Festival is an extra service during the forenoon, comprising two *rak'as*, which is followed by an address by the Imam. This service is held in the open where all the people of a village, several villages, or of a town, may gather together for the service, or in the biggest mosque or mosques of a large town. The purpose is to glorify God, to celebrate His praise, and to render thanks to Him for the guidance provided by Him, particularly with regard to all that relates to the observance of the fast, and for having enabled those upon whom the fast was obligatory to observe it duly.

13
Pilgrimage

ABRAHAM, PATRIARCH AND FRIEND OF GOD (4:126)
saw in a vision that he was offering his only son Ishmael as a
sacrifice to the Lord.* He said to the boy: "Son of mine, I have
seen in a dream that I am slaughtering thee. So consider what
thou thinkest of it." The boy replied: "Father, do as thou art
commanded; thou wilt find me, if Allah please, of those who are
steadfast."

Abraham made the necessary preparations. When all was ready
and he was about to proceed to the fulfillment of what he thought
he had been commanded to do, he received the revelation that he
had indeed fulfilled his dream (37:103–107). The true meaning
of the dream was not that he should sacrifice his son in the manner
in which he had seen himself doing in the dream, but that both
he and his son should be ready to make a great sacrifice to win the
pleasure of God (37:108). This great sacrifice was that the boy
and his mother should be settled in a distant, barren valley, so
that the boy should be made an instrument for the purpose of
establishing the true worship of God in and around the Sacred
House (14:38).

The first House consecrated to the worship of God was at Mecca
(3:97). It became a resort of pilgrimage and a sanctuary (2:126).
Abraham and Ishmael raised the foundations of the House
(2:128), and Abraham prayed that Mecca should be a town of
peace, that its dwellers be provided with fruits, and that God might
be pleased to raise up among them a Messenger from among themselves, who should recite to them His Signs and teach them the

* The Bible makes mention in this context of "thine only son, Isaac" (Gen.
22:2). Later in the same chapter, vss. 12 and 16, the "only son" is mentioned
without any name. But the truth is that Isaac was never the "only son" of
Abraham. His only son, up to the birth of Isaac, was Ishmael (Gen. 16:15).

Book, and wisdom, and should purify them and foster their welfare (2:127, 130). This prayer found its answer and its fulfillment in the advent of the Prophet of Islam (62:3).

Abraham was commanded: "Proclaim unto mankind the Pilgrimage. They will come to thee on foot, and on every lean camel, coming by every distant track" (22:28). The object of the pilgrimage was that the participants should derive social benefits therefrom, join in the worship of God, offer sacrifices, fulfill their vows, and perform the circuits of the House while glorifying and praising God (22:29–30).

The pilgrimage thus begun through Abraham became a well-recognized religious institution. In course of time, the original object was obscured, though the outward ceremonial remained. The pure worship of God degenerated into the worship of idols, whom the Arabs regarded as minor deities who could serve as intermediaries or intercessors between them and God (39:4). By the time of the Prophet as many as three hundred and sixty idols had been installed inside the Sacred House itself. These were demolished and the Ka'aba was restored to its original purpose— the worship of the One True God—on the day when Mecca opened its gates to the Prophet. The pilgrimage has since then continued as one of the obligations incumbent upon every Muslim adult who can afford the journey (3:98).

Like the month of fasting, the time appointed for the pilgrimage, ten weeks after the Festival of the breaking of the fast, is fixed according to the lunar calendar, and rotates through the year. The pilgrimage thus falls in all seasons of the year. The ceremonies and acts of worship connected with it are performed both around the Ka'aba inside Mecca and in a neighboring valley. The principal ceremonies in connection with the Ka'aba are the circuit of the House, at various times during the days of the pilgrimage, and running between Safa and Marwah, two hillocks situated close to the Ka'aba, in the middle of the town (2:159). This running between the two hillocks is in memory of the agony of Hagar, mother of Ishmael, running in search of water for her son and herself after Abraham had left them there. God revealed to Hagar the existence of a spring close to the place where Ishmael, who had grown very weak from thirst, was lying. This spring is still running, and every pilgrim drinks from it during the pilgrimage season.

While particular days are prescribed for the performance of

the pilgrimage, the *umra*, sometimes called the lesser pilgrimage, may be made at any time of the year. This consists of performing the circuit of the House and running between Safa and Marwah.

The circuit of the House is not a mere physical ritual. A pilgrim while performing the circuit is occupied in glorification of God and celebrating His praise and offering various prayers. The same is true of the running between Safa and Marwah.

The Quran points out that honoring that which has been declared sacred by Allah and revering the Signs of Allah promote righteousness of the heart (22:31, 33). This is related more to emotion than to reason, but reason itself recognizes the inspiring role of emotion. Indeed, it is emotions that fertilize the roots of action, particularly when the action requires sacrifice of things and objects held dear, for the sake of achieving a higher purpose. The love of wife or husband or children, the love of relations and friends and fellow beings, the love of place or country, the love of truth and righteousness, and finally the love of God—all are based on emotion and are the most powerful incentives for action and conduct.

The pilgrimage is a highly emotional experience. When a person makes up his mind to go on pilgrimage, and leaves his home for that purpose, his heart and mind are captured by a deep emotion. He is leaving all to whom he is deeply attached, and in the vast majority of cases is venturing forth into strange lands hitherto known to him only through report and rumor, for a spot which has, since early in the course of human history, been the scene of the manifestation of God's beneficence and God's love for His righteous servants. By responding to the call of God, laying aside all other preoccupations, deferring all other claims upon him, renouncing such comfort and loving association as constitute his joy and happiness, journeying to the barren valley where, under God's direction, Abraham left his wife and son so that a center might be established for God's true worship, and by taking part in that worship, the pilgrim hopes that he may himself be inspired with that spirit which inspired Abraham and Ishmael, and, later, the Prophet as well as numerous other righteous servants of God; and he hopes that he may ultimately be counted among those who are blessed with the love of God. The journey—in many cases long and arduous, and full of hazards—across deserts and oceans is undertaken and completed in this frame of mind. It is easy to appreciate the whirl of exalted emotion which uplifts the pilgrim's spirit, rising higher and higher as the goal approaches.

At a certain point the pilgrim discards his usual clothing and puts on the *ihram*, which, in the case of males, consists of two pieces of white, unsewn cloth draped and fastened round the body in such manner that the head, the hands, the right shoulder and arm, and the feet and ankles are left uncovered. From all parts of the globe, men and women converge on Mecca, coming by sea, by land, and now also by air, clad in the pilgrim's garb, which effaces all marks and insignia of wealth, rank, office, family, and places everyone on the same level. The simple garb signifies that the pilgrim has responded to the call of Allah as he will answer the last call when his time to depart this life arrives. All vanity is purged, and king and subject, master and servant, the white and the black, the yellow and the brown, hasten from all directions to the Sacred House, repeating:

> Here am I, O Allah, here am I;
> Here am I, there is no associate with Thee;
> All praise is Thine and all Bounty;
> There is no associate with Thee.

This response to the call of Allah is interspersed with:

> Allah is Great, Allah is Great, there is no being worthy of worship save Allah;
> Allah is Great, Allah is Great, all praise belongs to Allah.

The first concern of each pilgrim on his arrival in Mecca is to proceed to the enclosure of the Ka'aba and to perform the circuit of the Sacred House. The Ka'aba is, par excellence, the House of God. Of course, all places of worship are Houses of God, and as the Prophet declared, the whole earth is a mosque, but the Ka'aba has been declared by God Himself to be the Sacred House, being the first House consecrated to the worship of the One True God (3:97). When the expression "House of Allah" is used, it is understood throughout the Muslim world to mean the Ka'aba. The tumult of the heart when the pilgrim approaches the Sacred House and has his first sight of it is indescribable.

The Ka'aba itself—not to be confused with the precincts of the Ka'aba which extend over the central sector of Mecca—is a very simple stone structure, laying no claim to grandeur of size or beauty of architecture. It impresses by its very simplicity. Most of the time it is covered with a mantle of heavy black silk, which is renewed each year.

From whichever direction the pilgrim enters the enclosure and approaches the Ka'aba, he begins his circuit from the south-eastern corner, in which the Black Stone is placed. A circuit of the Ka'aba involves going around it seven times. Each round begins and ends opposite the Black Stone. At the end of each round, the pilgrim, if he can approach near enough and if he so wishes, may kiss the Black Stone, which again is an emotional expression calling to mind that the Prophet kissed it when he performed the circuit. The Prophet kissed it, not because any particular sanctity attaches to the stone, but as an expression of his emotion that the Ka'aba, originally constructed by Abraham and Ishmael, had been finally restored to the worship of the One True God, and would henceforth remain dedicated to that worship. Fearing that the Prophet's kissing the Black Stone might be interpreted as ascribing some special virtue to the stone, Umar, the second Khalifa, when performing the circuit, observed: "I know that this is only a piece of stone no different from other similar stones, and were it not for the memory that the Prophet expressed his gratitude to God for His favors and bounties by kissing it, I would pay no attention to it."

Similar emotions swell the pilgrim's heart when he runs between Safa and Marwah, thus calling to mind the distress of a mother, who, although resigned to her own and her son's fate, in the parched valley, because such was the will and pleasure of God, was, nevertheless, anguished by her son's extreme thirst. Hagar ran from one hillock to the other straining her eyes to catch some sign of habitation, a passing caravan, or even a solitary traveler—any source, or even a mere indication, from which water could be obtained.

All pilgrims drink from the Zam Zam, the spring disclosed to Hagar in her distress over Ishmael. This is no part of the cere-monial or ritual of the pilgrimage, but again the urge to drink from the same source which God in His Grace and Mercy dis-closed to the distraught mother and which has since continued to run as fresh and as plentiful as ever, can be well understood. The Zam Zam is within the precincts of the Ka'aba, between the Ka'aba itself and the two hillocks of Safa and Marwah, but closer to the Ka'aba.

Other places within the precincts and in the neighborhood of the Ka'aba that have particular associations are named accordingly. There is the Place of Ishmael, immediately outside the northern wall of the Ka'aba, and the Place of Abraham, a few paces from the eastern wall, between the Ka'aba and the Zam Zam; but, characteristically, there is no place named after the Prophet himself. The places associated with him in any way are known, but they are not named after him, nor are they marked in any special way. He was anxious to attribute everything to God and to preserve the memories of certain spots and of their association with certain events because they were God's Signs. He himself was only a servant of God who had been chosen by God's favor and bounty to be the recipient of revelation, which contained guidance for the whole of mankind. In his eyes God was all; he himself was nothing. The Ka'aba and its precincts stand as signs and witnesses of many things, but also proclaim forever the single-mindedness and self-effacing love and devotion of Muhammad, the Prophet, for Allah, his Lord.

The Ka'aba is situated in the center of Mecca, and though its enclosure is big enough to permit large groups of men to perform the circuit and to take part in the Prayer services, the services connected with the pilgrimage are held in a valley a few miles outside Mecca at Mina and Muzdalafa, and on the Plain of Arafat. It is at the latter place—where the Prophet delivered his Farewell Address—that all pilgrims gather on the actual day of the pilgrimage (the "day" to be distinguished from the "ceremonies," which include the entire period from the time the pilgrim leaves home until his return). At the end of the pilgrimage every pilgrim who can afford it sacrifices an animal or joins in making a sacrifice. Symbolically, the act pledges the pilgrim's life to the service of God and His creatures, and places that life at God's disposal as completely as the life of an animal owned by a person is at its master's disposal. As the Quran says, the flesh of the animals sacrificed does not reach Allah, nor does their blood; it is the pilgrim's spirit of righteousness that reaches Him. "Thus has He subjected these animals to you, that you may glorify Allah for His guiding you" (22:38).

As has been mentioned, one of the objects of the pilgrimage is that those taking part in it "may witness its benefits for them" (22:29). It is much to be regretted that the social, economic, and political aspects of this object of the pilgrimage have been greatly neglected by the Muslims.

The pilgrimage is obligatory only upon those who can afford the journey (3:98). This means not merely that the pilgrim should be in a position to defray the expenses of the journey to and from Mecca, and of his stay there for the period necessary for the performance of the pilgrimage, but that he should be able to afford the time needed for the journey, and also be able to make provision during his absence for those dependent upon him and for the proper conduct of his worldly affairs. In other words, the pilgrimage is obligatory only upon people who are in comparatively easy circumstances, those who constitute the more responsible sections of the Muslim community in different parts of the world.

All Islamic services, the five daily ones for congregational Prayer, the Friday noon service, in which an address is delivered, the two Festival services, one at the end of the month of fasting, and the other on the occasion of the pilgrimage, and the pilgrimage itself, are so organized as to ensure the co-operation of all sections of Muslim society for the promotion of human welfare in all its aspects.

The five daily services provide occasions for people who frequent a particular mosque, and for any others who may chance to be present at any of the services, to exchange greetings and to discuss before or after the service any matters, local or of a wider import, which might affect or interest them. The Friday noon service brings together in rural areas people from several neighboring villages and hamlets, and in the towns all the inhabitants of the town, or, in the case of large cities, of a section. The Imam's address should deal with questions in any sphere of life that are of common interest to those participating in the service. In the early days of Islam the Friday service was led in the capital by the Khalifa, the head of state, and in the provincial towns and rural areas, by the Governor, head of the district, or by some other prominent citizen deemed capable of leading the members of the congregation and stimulating their action and co-operation in the desired direction. This continues to be the practice in some parts of the Islamic world today, but in many backward or outlying areas the Imam's address tends to be a routine and formal affair, not calculated to forward the purpose it is meant to serve. There are signs, however, of a desire to restore to the institution its true spirit and to utilize it fully for promoting the moral, spiritual, social, and economic welfare of Muslim society.

On the occasion of the two annual Festivals, the people of a whole town and its neighboring areas come together to participate in the service. The Imam's address on this occasion should serve the same purpose as the Friday-service address, but in respect of a much larger number of people drawn from a wider area.

The pilgrimage draws Muslims together at Mecca from the ends of the earth. It should be a truly representative gathering of the whole Islamic world. In effect, it should be the World Assembly of Islam gathered together in spiritual association for the glorification of God and the promotion of human welfare. The week preceding it and the week following it, and indeed, a longer period if it be necessary, should be utilized for consultation, discussion, and examination of schemes and projects having as their object the strengthening of human fellowship, brotherhood, and co-operation and the promotion of human welfare in the whole world. As this very important aspect of the pilgrimage has now been neglected over centuries, ways of effecting these objectives must be well thought out. The first steps would, no doubt, be modest, but if the effort be inspired by the true Islamic spirit, the pilgrimage can, within a matter of years, become one of the most beneficent instruments for the promotion of knowledge, of co-operation, and of constructive achievement in all fields. Ultimately it may even serve to secure the formulation of agreed policies and the putting into effect of beneficent projects in every part of the world. This is an objective well worth striving for. The spirit and the occasion are already there; men of vision and understanding are needed to harness them for the service of man, which is the true service of God.

Before or after the pilgrimage, it is customary for large numbers of pilgrims to visit Medina, to supplement their knowledge of, and association with, the historic places connected with the life of the Prophet and with the beginnings of Islam, to revive the memories of the glories and inspiring events of that period, and, more particularly, to express their love for the Prophet by praying for him at his tomb. Until recently the journey from Mecca to Medina was an arduous one, occupying from eight to twelve days in either direction. It was made by camel, which is, under the best of circumstances, not the most comfortable or convenient mode of transport. A few years ago a macadamized road was completed through the desert between Jeddah (port and airport for Mecca) and Medina, and the journey can now be made by car in about six hours or by bus in the course of a day. More recently, local air services have also become available. The distance between Jeddah and Medina is, roughly, two hundred miles.

Hudaibiyya, where the famous truce was concluded between the Prophet and the Meccans, lies along the road almost half way between Jeddah and Mecca, a short distance before the boundary of the Sanctuary is reached. The pilgrim proceeding from Jeddah to Mecca may make a brief stop at Hudaibiyya or at any other place on the way. The road from Jeddah to Mecca is in excellent condition. The distance, some forty miles, can be covered by car in about an hour and a half, and by bus in approximately two hours. The journey from Mecca to Medina has to be made by way of Jeddah, which is the real starting point for the journey.

Two thirds of the way from Jeddah to Medina, a short distance to the left of the road, is the field of Badr, where the first battle with the Meccans was fought. This part of the road runs almost straight and level through the desert, parallel to the Red Sea. Beyond Badr and up to Medina the road winds in and out of, and around, bare hillocks. There are many places of historical interest in and around Medina. There is the mosque at Quba, the hamlet where the Prophet stayed for a few days on his first arrival from Mecca. There is the mosque in which the Prophet was leading the service when the revelation came which changed the *qibla*—direction toward which worshipers face during the service —from Jerusalem to Mecca (2:145). There is the graveyard where most of the early Muslims are buried, including Uthman, the third Khalifa; Haleema, the foster mother of the Prophet; Ibrahim, the Prophet's little son; several members of the Prophet's family and many of his companions. There is the battlefield of Uhud, a few miles east of Medina, where the second battle with the Meccans took place, the one in which the Prophet himself was wounded, and was at one time thought to have been killed, and in which his uncle, Hamza, was killed. Hamza and those Muslims who were killed during the battle are buried at Uhud. Those who were wounded were taken to Medina, and the ones who later died from their wounds are buried in the graveyard at Medina.

But of course the focal point of interest is the Prophet's mosque, in the center of Medina. The Prophet was buried in the chamber in which he died, and the mosque was later extended to include the burial site. Abu Bakr and Umar, the first two Khalifas, are also buried here, alongside of the Prophet, permission having been given by the Prophet's wife Ayesha, to whom the chamber belonged. The graves are enclosed within four walls and the only view of them may be obtained through a grille in the southern wall. This is a precaution both for safeguarding the graves and also against visitors indulging in any act or practice which might savor of ascribing a superhuman position to the Prophet or to his two companions buried next to him. The Prophet abhorred any act that bore even a semblance of deification, and he gave repeated expression to this feeling during his last hours.

A visit to Medina is, like the pilgrimage itself, a deeply emotional experience. No ceremonial is involved. The visitor seeks as many opportunities as may be available to join in the services in the Prophet's mosque, and also for supererogatory Prayers therein. During each visit to the mosque he prays for the Prophet, adding any other prayers and supplications that he may wish, standing as close to the grille or one of the walls enclosing the graves as he can approach, having regard to the number of other people seeking to do the same.

At Medina the soul of the visitor is deeply conscious of the manifestation of the love of Allah for Muhammad, His servant and His Messenger. There he witnesses throughout the hours of the day and the night the visible response of hundreds of thousands, to God's command: "Allah and His Angels send blessings on the Prophet. O ye who believe, do you also invoke His blessings on him and salute him with the salutation of peace" (33:57).

The visitor treads the streets and paths of Medina with his heart and soul surcharged with love, devotion, and gratitude to that pre-eminent Servant of Allah, who dedicated every moment of his life to the service of Allah and His creatures (6:163-4). The intervening centuries seem to vanish and the visitor experiences the feeling that only yesterday did that gracious Servant and Messenger of Allah tread those same paths in humility and devotion. He, too, is inspired with the feeling expressed by a Pakistani poet:

> Every path I view with eyes of love;
> Perchance along this one he might have trod.

14
Moral and Spiritual Values

ISLAM BASES ITSELF ON ACCEPTANCE OF LIFE, NOT on rejection or withdrawal. Monasticism and asceticism are not permissible in Islam (57:28). Righteous living, making proper and balanced use of one's faculties and of the bounties provided by God, is the rule of life (23:52). "Say, 'Who has prohibited the use of the good and pure things which God has provided for His creatures?'" (7:33).

Within this general concept the Quran lays down detailed instructions for the fostering of moral and spiritual values. The object is the beneficent and co-ordinated development of all faculties. Whatsoever God has bestowed upon man by way of inner faculties, and external possessions must all be put to appropriate use (2:4).

That use must be adjusted and regulated, otherwise it would cease to be a moral activity. Islam teaches that natural instincts and tendencies are converted into moral qualities through their proper regulation and adjustment by the exercise of reason and judgment. The Prophet has said that the value of human conduct is determined by the motive and intent that inspire it. An act done under the uncontrolled and unregulated operation of a natural instinct is not a moral act. It may do good or it may do harm, but it does not possess a moral quality.

The Quran classifies moral qualities from different points of view. For instance, there are those that relate to the mind and those that relate to the body. What becomes or can become known to others and what is contemplated by the mind and cannot become known to others except when disclosed by the person concerned may both possess a moral quality. The Quran directs: "Approach not evils and indecencies whether manifest or hidden" (6:152). Man is accountable in respect of both kinds of conduct:

that which manifests itself in action and that which is con
templated and meditated, but does not find overt expression
(2:285).

For example, a person who is openly arrogant acts immorally
but equally immoral is the person who, though outwardly meek
and humble, nurses pride in the secret depths of his heart. "They
were presumptuous in their hearts and were also very over
bearing" (25:22).

Again, moral conduct may be good or it may be bad. Among
other characteristics of something which is good is that it is posi
tive; it overcomes and prevails against that which is bad and
therefore, negative (11:115). A person who consistently foster
good morals subdues even the tendency toward bad morals.

Other classifications of morals include those that affect the in
dividual alone and those that are likely to affect others also. The
Quran places every person under the obligation to safeguard and
promote the welfare of his own soul as well as the welfare of hi
fellow beings (5:106; 3:111, 115). The Prophet has said: "Thine
own soul has also claims on thee, which must be fulfilled."

The Quran, however, makes a distinction between thought
and designs that are deliberately entertained and those that cros
the mind involuntarily, to be suppressed or discarded as soon a
they are perceived. The former possess a moral quality and in
volve responsibility and accountability (2:226). If a person re
sists or suppresses an involuntary thought which is an incitemen
to evil, his reaction is moral and constitutes a good action. The
same is the case if he seizes upon a passing thought which con
tains a suggestion for the doing of good and proceeds to translate
it into deed, but not so if he acts under a momentary surge o
emotion without deliberation or judgment coming into play. Or
the other hand, if he does not take advantage of the suggestion and
ignores it, he misses an opportunity of doing good, and that has a
negative moral character.

A few illustrations might help one appreciate the manner in
which the Quran teaches that natural instincts can be converted
into moral qualities. Take the natural instinct of revenge or retri
bution that manifests itself in many forms and incites a person to a
variety of acts. The regulation of this instinct, by placing it under
the control of reason and judgment, converts it into a moral
quality; whereas, if it be allowed to operate unrestrained and
uncontrolled by reason, it cannot acquire a moral character.

Regulation of a natural instinct may itself have several gradations. With regard to the instinct just mentioned, the first gradation is: A person who has suffered wrong may seek the imposition of a penalty upon the wrongdoer. This is often necessary to safeguard law and order, not only through its deterrent effect on potential lawbreakers, but also by removing the temptation to unrestrained violence on the part of the injured person. However, the penalty must not be out of proportion to the wrong suffered (2:195). The next gradation is: He who forgives a trespass committed against him, intending thereby to effect a reformation in the offender, achieves a higher standard of moral action than the one who insists upon the imposition of a proportionate penalty in all cases (42:40–44). A still higher gradation is: The person wronged should not only suppress his desire to take revenge, and, in cases where reformation may be reasonably expected, forgive the wrongdoer, but he should go further and exercise benevolence toward the latter (3:135).

Where the person who has committed the wrong is powerful and is in a position of authority, and the person wronged or aggrieved is unable to obtain redress or recompense, he might be tempted to descend to faultfinding and even to abuse. The Quran forbids indulgence in either. Abuse is prohibited because it is both false and immodest, and faultfinding is prohibited because it is likely to injure rather than to reform the conduct of the wrongdoer; for when a person's faults and shortcomings are publicly proclaimed, he begins to indulge in them openly (49:12).

An injured person unable to obtain redress for the wrong suffered by him might entertain spite and enmity in his heart toward the person who has wronged him, but this is also incompatible with right thinking and righteous conduct (15:48). Thus, the proper regulation of the natural instinct of revenge or retribution narrows down its operation within very strict limits. A penalty proportionate to the wrong committed is permissible, but it is better to forgive where forgiveness may be reasonably expected to help the offender improve himself—and it is even better to add benevolence to forgiveness. To endure wrong patiently and to forgive is described as a "matter of high resolve" (3:187; 31:18; 42:44).

Another natural instinct is love. Its proper regulation converts it into a high moral quality. Unregulated, it might do great harm. The Quran declares that the strongest and highest love of those who believe is for Allah, meaning that the love of God must come

I

before everything else (2:166). A detailed and specific gradation is prescribed. The love of Allah and the duty to Him and the love of His Messenger and the duty of striving in Allah's cause must come before the love of parents, children, brothers, wives, husbands, kinsfolk, country, home, possessions, business (9:24). The very notion of values involves the idea of gradation. Little difficulty arises where duty is clear and there is no conflicting inclination. Difficulty is encountered when duty points in one direction and inclination pulls in another, particularly when inclination also puts on the garb of a duty owed to one's parents, or children, or kinsfolk, or nation, or business, or profession. In such a case, even if there be a duty involved, the duty lower in the scale of values must give way to one that is higher; otherwise, conduct ceases to have a moral quality and is merely an expression of natural instincts and inclinations.

Another consideration affecting the regulation of the natural instinct of love is that preference must be given to a duty owed in respect of benefits received in the past as against an inclination to yield to the natural instinct of love or to do that which might hold out the hope of benefits to be received in the future. In this context, love of parents and the duty owed to them stands higher than the love of children and the duty owed to them. In the case of the latter, the natural instinct does not need to be stimulated, but has to be regulated to check indulgence. The Quran has put the duty owed to parents in close juxtaposition to the duty owed to God. "Thy Lord hath commanded that ye worship none but Him and that ye conduct yourselves towards your parents with beneficence. If one of them or both of them attain old age with thee, never say unto them any word expressive of annoyance, nor reproach them, but address them with kindly speech; and lower to them the wing of humility out of tenderness, and pray, 'My Lord have mercy on them, even as they nourished me tenderly in my childhood' " (17:24–25).

Again: "We have enjoined on man concerning his parents—his mother bears him in weakness upon weakness, and his weaning takes two years—'Be grateful to Me and to thy parents. Unto Me is the final return' " (31:15).

Yet again: "We have enjoined on man to conduct himself beneficently toward his parents. His mother bears him with pain and brings him forth in pain, and the bearing of him and the weaning of him take thirty months" (46:16).

The Prophet has said: "Paradise lies at the feet of your mothers." On one occasion a person asked him: "Which of my kinsfolk has the strongest claim upon me?"

"Thy mother," he replied.

"And after her?"

The Prophet smiled, and said: "Thy mother." Asked a third time, he still said: "Thy mother." When asked a fourth time, he replied: "After her, thy father."

On another occasion he said: "Most unfortunate is the person who is granted an opportunity of serving his parents, and fails to win Paradise through kindness and tenderness toward them."

Here is a very clear gradation in the matter of the duty derived from love and affection: "Worship Allah and associate naught with Him, and conduct yourselves with beneficence toward parents, and toward kindred, and orphans, and the needy, and toward the neighbor that is of the kindred, and the neighbor that is a stranger, and the companions by your side, and the wayfarer, and those who work for you. Surely, Allah loves not the proud and boastful, who are niggardly and enjoin people to be niggardly" (4:37-38).

Love of children is not stressed, for it is a natural instinct, but its regulation has been emphasized, for a lot of harm may be, and indeed is, done by a wrong concept of what may be owed to children. The Quran stresses the need of proper upbringing and points out that love of children involves the duty of safeguarding their future, both here and in the Hereafter (66:7).

The natural instinct opposed to love is hate, repugnance, or enmity. If not regulated, it may occasion great damage. Under proper regulation, it promotes dignity, self-respect, and righteousness. It is wrong to consider hate or repugnance in itself as an undesirable moral quality. In the first place it is not a moral quality at all; it is a natural instinct. In itself it is, so to speak, morally as neutral as love. Its proper regulation converts it into a moral quality. One must hate evil; one must resent certain types of wrongdoing. For instance, the Quran says: "Allah has endeared faith to you, and has made it attractive to you, and He has put repugnance in your hearts toward disbelief, disobedience and transgression. Such, indeed, are those who follow the right course, through the grace and favor of Allah. Allah is All-Knowing, Wise" (49:8-9).

A certain amount of misconception has been created in this connection by confusing wrong and evil with the wrongdoer and the perpetrator of evil. The two must be kept distinct. How a wrongdoer should be dealt with has already been noticed in dealing with the natural instinct of revenge. The just punishment of wrong or forgiveness or the exercise of benevolence, in appropriate cases, toward the wrongdoer does not mean that the wrong itself is approved of. Care must, however, be taken that repugnance toward evil or wrong should not cause one to be diverted from the path of duty. For instance, the hostility of a people should not incite one to injustice, however strong might be the resentment felt toward the hostile people. "Let not the hostility of a people incite you to injustice. Act justly always; that is nearer to righteousness" (5:9). While it is forbidden to let the heart incline toward transgressors (11:114) or to make friends with those who are guilty of transgression, one must deal kindly and equitably even with those opposed to the faith, for Allah "loves those who are equitable" (60:9).

Another natural instinct is the desire to outstrip one's fellow beings in the race for progress and in the acquisition of desirable objects. Islam seeks to regulate the operation of this natural instinct by directing it toward the purpose of achieving moral and spiritual progress. The Quran says that everyone has an urge toward the achievement of some purpose, but that the proper goal toward which to direct this urge is the progressive achievement of righteousness (2:149). If this instinct is not properly regulated it might generate envy, faultfinding, and lack of appreciation of the good qualities of others. It might make a man proud and boastful. All these are harmful qualities against which we have been warned and from which we must seek to safeguard ourselves. One of the prayers taught in the Quran is to seek refuge with God against envy and the mischief of an envious person (113:6). Against faultfinding, the Prophet has said: "If a person falsely imputes to another a moral or spiritual fault, let him beware lest the same fault manifest itself in him which he has falsely imputed to another." The Quran forbids holding other people in scorn or despising them. "Let not one people despise another, haply that people may turn out to be better than themselves, and let not women despise other women, haply these may turn out to be better than themselves" (49:12). Pride and boastfulness and other consequences of the unregulated operation of the instinct of ambition are condemned. "God loves not him who is proud and boastful" (4:37).

The urge toward the propagation of the race is another natural instinct. It is wrong to think that the exercise of this natural instinct is incompatible with the cultivation of the highest spiritual values. This is contrary to the entire concept of moral and spiritual values as inculcated by Islam. Natural instincts are a bounty of God as much as are mental and physical capacities. It is not their essential nature, but their proper or improper exercise, that is good or evil. Indeed, the neglect of any capacity is itself evil inasmuch as it amounts to misuse of it. That is why Islam does not permit celibacy or monasticism as a way of life. It recognizes that people who instituted these systems did it with a good motive, but inasmuch as the systems offended against the principle of the beneficent use of all faculties and capacities, they lent themselves to abuse and did harm (57:28).

Islam teaches that married life is the higher state because it is a means of complete and co-ordinated development of personality, and urges the adoption of that state as an aid toward such development (4:4). The Prophet has said: "The married state is our way. He who deliberately turns away from our way is not of us." He who, having arrived at marriageable age is unable to find a suitable mate, is exhorted to observe complete continence till the opportunity of making a suitable match presents itself (24:34). Extramarital relations are forbidden altogether (17:33).

The exercise of the right of ownership over property, goods, money, and the like is another natural instinct. Its unregulated exercise may, on the one hand, lead to extravagance, and, on the other hand, to miserliness and hoarding. The first regulation of this instinct imposed by Islam is that what is spent upon others must be pure and of good quality and should have been lawfully earned or obtained. It is only such spending that possesses a moral quality and can be productive of moral benefits, both for him who spends and for him who receives. "Spend of the good things that you have earned, and of what We produce for you from the earth, and seek not what is bad to spend out of it, when you would not yourselves receive it except with closed eyes. Know that Allah is All-Sufficient, Praiseworthy" (2:268).

The next consideration inculcated by Islam is that though individual legal ownership is recognized, and the owner's rights of possession, enjoyment, and transfer of property are safeguarded, all ownership is made subject to a moral trust in favor of those who may be in need. "And in their wealth was a share for one who asked for help and for one who could not ask" [that is, one who might be in need, but preferred not to ask others out of a feeling of modesty or self-respect; one who was unable to express his needs at all because he suffered from certain disabilities; and animals] (51:20). Giving to others should not be with the object of obtaining a better return from them (74:7), nor should it be on an extravagant scale, which might encourage idleness or leave the donor unprovided for (17:27). Beneficent spending is that which is neither extravagant nor parsimonious, but keeps to the middle path (25:68). Niggardliness is condemned (4:38), and hoarding is accounted a major sin, entailing severe punishment (9:34–35).

These instances should suffice to illustrate how Islam, by seeking to regulate the operation of natural instincts, elevates them into moral qualities. It does not, however, arbitrarily condemn certain qualities as evil and approve of certain others as good. It explains why certain qualities are good and others are evil. Because the object of man's existence is that he should become a manifestation of God's attributes, that which reflects a Divine attribute is good, and should be sought and fostered, and that which runs counter to a Divine attribute is evil, and should be avoided. No person can even make a start in pursuit of the ultimate object without a firm determination to keep strictly to the paths of purity and righteousness, and to eschew all that may be in conflict with them. The universe and the laws that govern it are designed to aid and assist in the process (18:8). Certain moral qualities have been described as good because they assist in this process. Those that obstruct this process are described as evil. It is, as already stated, a characteristic of good qualities that they are positive and prevail over bad qualities, which are negative (11:115).

With reference to each moral quality, the Quran explains why it is regarded as good or bad. For instance, the exhortation to repel evil with that which is good is justified on the ground that this is the surest means of striking at the root of hatred and enmity —by converting an enemy into a firm friend (41:35). Transgression and oppression are condemned because they tend to create disorder and to destroy peace (7:56–57). Scornful behavior toward other people is forbidden because it tends to set up a vicious circle. If it is persisted in, the weak and the poor, when they attain power and wealth in turn, will seek to humiliate those who used to despise them and to treat them with contempt (49:12).

Extravagance is bad because it leads a person into evil company and to the misuse of God's bounties (17:28). Niggardliness and hoarding, which is the consequence of niggardliness, are condemned because they put wealth out of circulation and deprive its owners as well as others of the beneficent use of it, thus affecting the general welfare prejudicially (47:39). As regards envy, the Prophet has said: "Safeguard yourselves against envy, for envy eats up the sources of happiness as fire eats up fuel." As to adultery and fornication, the Quran says: "It is an impurity and an evil way" (17:33). In other words, it is a vice which produces a feeling of secret guilt in the mind and sullies it, and it is a wrong way of achieving the object underlying the sexual instinct, namely, the propagation and preservation of the species. It prevents birth or renders the paternity of the child doubtful, thus imperiling its proper care and upbringing.

Benevolence and beneficence are incumbent upon man, since all that he possesses—his faculties, his capacities, his wealth, and his substance—he has received from God. He must share all this with his fellow beings and be beneficent and benevolent in his turn as God has been bountiful to Him (28:78).

Islam has set up a gradation in moral qualities which enables a person to take stock of his moral development and progress for the purpose of discovering in what respect special care and effort are needed. A gradation is as indispensable for the moral development of man as a graduated course of studies is indispensable for the instruction of the human mind. Religion must furnish guidance for people of varying capacities who are at different levels of moral and intellectual development. It is necessary, therefore, that it should set forth gradations of moral values which should enable people to determine where they stand and what needs to be done in each case for further development. In this connection, the Quran states: "God enjoins equity, beneficence, and treatment like that accorded to kindred; and forbids evils that are not manifest, and those that are manifest and cause annoyance and those that cause injury to others. He admonishes you, so that you may be rightly guided" (16:91). Thus virtue and vice are each divided into three grades. All grades of vice must be eschewed and all grades of virtue must be achieved.

The lowest grade of vice is conduct that causes injury to others; for instance, all trespass against the person, property, interests, or honor of a fellow being. Most of these are crimes; the rest are civil wrongs and are punishable or remediable as such; all of them are moral offenses. Legal effort at the regulation of human relations exhausts itself at that level. It is only moral effort that can carry the matter further. The next step in moral development is to avoid all conduct which, though not amounting to trespass and causing injury, would occasion annoyance to others and would offend their feelings. Examples of this are bad manners and various other kinds of social misbehavior. These two classes of evil are manifested in external action, but the source of all evil is the mind, where evil designs are initially harbored and later issue into action. The third prohibition relates to all such thoughts and designs. It is only when these are controlled and barred that a person safeguards himself completely against evil.

Similarly, three grades of virtue or righteous action are prescribed. The first (lowest) is described as equity, or equitable dealing. This means to do good equal to the good one receives from others; furthermore, it means that when one suffers a wrong, one should not impose, or insist upon the imposition of, a penalty in excess of the wrong suffered. This lowest standard of virtue finds expression in what is generally known as the Golden Rule. Although the Golden Rule by implication may enjoin turning the other cheek or walking the second mile, it does so by implication only. In Islam, the three grades of virtue are specified, and this step is merely the first one toward the goal. The next stage is that of conscious beneficence, the doing of greater good in return for good and the doing of good without expectation of any return; and forgiveness of wrong if in the circumstances it may reasonably be expected that forgiveness would help the wrongdoer reform himself. The last stage is instinctive beneficence, a beneficence that flows out from one as love and affection flow out toward one's kindred. Cultivated to that degree, beneficence would resemble a natural instinct; but having been acquired deliberately, it would be the highest moral quality. It would manifest itself toward a wrongdoer not only in forgiveness but in benevolence.

Islam attaches great importance to gradation in the process of the attainment of moral and spiritual excellence. The very first Divine attribute in the Quran is *Rabb*, meaning that aspect of the Providence of God which leads stage by stage toward perfection

(1:2). It is also stated that one of the functions of a prophet is to train people who could in turn assist their fellows in achieving moral and spiritual perfection, stage by stage (3:80). It must be remembered, however, that progress toward perfection must be constant and continuous. It does not end with this life, but continues in the Hereafter. Even in Paradise the prayer of the righteous will be: "Our Lord, perfect unto us our light and remove from us our shortcomings" (66:9).

The Quran furnishes guidance as to how bad moral qualities may be discarded and good ones fostered. The very first necessity, of course, is to recognize and accept Divine guidance, which is always available (7:36).

An essential element in the effort toward achievement of moral and spiritual excellence is the certainty that however low a person may have fallen, it is always possible for him to rise. Islam teaches that man has been endowed with a pure nature. The Quran says that God has created mankind in accord with the nature designed by Him (30:31). The Prophet said: "Every child is born in accord with a pure nature endowed upon him by God." It is true that each person is subject to influences of heredity, upbringing, and environment, but these can, where necessary, be corrected or eliminated. Evil comes from outside and can be kept out, or having entered, can be discarded. There is no room for despair. The Quran says: "O My servants, who have committed excesses against their own souls, despair not of the mercy of Allah: surely, Allah forgives all sins. Verily, He is Most Forgiving, Merciful" (39:54). The Prophet warned emphatically against despair. He said: "He who says the people are ruined is the one who causes them to be ruined," meaning that a feeling of despair is the surest means of bringing about failure and ultimate ruin.

The company of the righteous is another very important factor in the process of moral development (9:119). It is not necessary today to expatiate on the psychological aspect of this valuable direction—keeping company with the righteous. The influence of food and drink on moral and spiritual development has not yet been fully recognized, but it is clear, at least, that food and drink are directly related to physical health and growth, and these in their turn are surely related to moral and spiritual development. The Quran says that righteous conduct is promoted by observing purity in the matter of food and drink (23:52).

Social customs may sometimes constitute a hindrance in the way of moral development. In the scale of values, moral progress must be placed higher than conformity to social customs and habits, which have no inherent value beyond the fact that they have been observed over a long period of time. Such customs become burdensome impositions and should be discarded (7:158). All avenues from which evil might enter should be watched and guarded. Unregulated and unrestricted social intercourse between the sexes has led to the lowering of moral standards in many cases, and proper regulations are needed (24:32–33). The general rule of conduct in all matters where specific directions are not available is to follow the middle path, and to avoid excess of all kinds (2:144).

The greatest comfort, however, is to be found in the assurance that man has been created for the purpose of becoming a manifestation of Divine attributes (51:57). This means that he is capable of achieving that purpose. If in the pursuit of that purpose he should fall by the way, there is the further Divine assurance that God accepts repentance from His servants, and forgives their defaults (42:26).

Not every default entails a penalty. Many that we are not even conscious of are overlooked (42:31). Punishment follows upon deliberate wrongdoing, but Divine Mercy encompasses everything (7:157).

It is sometimes thought that the idea of wrong being wiped out by repentance fosters rather than checks wrongdoing. This is a complete misconception. Repentance does not mean that a person who deliberately commits wrong has only to say he repents and he can thereby escape the consequences of his evil conduct. The word for repentance used in the Quran is *taubah*, which means "turning away," turning completely away from evil and turning back to God along the path of righteousness. This involves a moral revolution which should engender intense repugnance toward evil and a constant yearning after righteousness, manifesting itself in conduct. All conduct, which includes thought, leaves an impress on the soul. True repentance means that the stain left by wrongdoing should be completely washed out through righteous conduct. Acceptance of repentance and forgiveness of wrongdoing imply that a stage has been reached where not only the evil committed is forgiven in the sense that the penalty involved is remitted, but that its consequences affecting the wrongdoer are also wiped out. A human being can forgive only in the limited sense of remitting the penalty, but Divine forgiveness has the quality of wiping out the consequences also. The Prophet has said: "He who truly repents is like one who has committed no default."

There is also the assurance that good is positive and overcomes and destroys evil. "Surely, good overcomes and destroys evil. This is a reminder for those who would remember. Be thou then steadfast; for, surely, Allah suffers not the reward of the righteous to perish" (11:115). The Quran lays down that the recompense of evil is a penalty in proportion thereto, but that the recompense of good is without limit: "Whoso does evil will be requited only with the like of it; but whoso does good, whether male or female, and is a believer—these will enter the Garden; they will be provided therein without measure" (40:41).

God does not wrong any of His creatures; on the contrary, He multiplies the consequences of all righteous conduct, and adds from Himself a vast reward (4:41).

Spiritual values are not separable from moral values, but they come into play more prominently with regard to the experience of communion with God. The exercise of moral values is in itself a valuable contribution in that regard. A true concept of the attributes of God, Prayer, remembrance of God, fasting, and all the other forms of worship are powerful aids toward spiritual development. The avenues of spiritual progress and development are open to all and are not barred against any. The essential condition is that a person should sincerely accept and firmly believe in Divine guidance and act in conformity with it. The concept of righteous action in Islam is action in conformity with the will of God, which is expressed in the guidance furnished by God to mankind through the prophets. Steadfastness in this course most surely leads to the enjoyment of communion with God (103:4).

The Quran says: "From among men are those who sell themselves in return for the pleasure of Allah: these are the true servants of Allah on whom the mercy and blessings of Allah descend" (2:208). All their thoughts, designs, and actions, their prayers, their worship, their sacrifices, in short, their life and their death, are solely for God (6:163). They arrive at a stage where, as the Prophet has said, God becomes their hands with which they work, and their feet with which they walk, and their eyes with which they see, and their ears with which they hear.

The same concept has been expressed in the Quran. It says that those who put their faith in Allah as the only source of true beneficence, and then remain steadfast, enter into communion with God and become the recipients of revelation (41:31–32). These are the friends of God, with regard to whom it is said: "Behold, the friends of Allah shall certainly have no fear, nor shall they grieve —those who believed and kept to righteousness—for them are glad tidings in the present life and also in the Hereafter" (10:63–65). They enter upon the enjoyment of God's perfect favors in this very life. The Quran says that for him who fears his Lord and stands in awe of His Majesty and Glory there shall be two Gardens, one in this world, and one in the life to come (55:47). The culmination is reached when the Divine call comes: "O soul at peace, return to thy Lord; thou, well pleased with Him; and He, well pleased with thee. So enter thou among My chosen servants, and enter thou My Garden" (89:28–31).

15
Social Values

IN THE WIDER SENSE EVERY ASPECT OF HUMAN relationships is governed by social values. It would, however, be convenient to discuss social values in the narrower sense, namely, those relating to personal relationships and those pertaining to an individual as a member of society, separately from those that may more appropriately be described as economic values and values pertaining to public affairs.

All values affecting man are based upon the concept that each human being is capable of achieving the highest stage of moral and spiritual development and that his personality must be respected. The Quran takes note of diversities of race, color, language, wealth, etc., which serve their own useful purposes in the social scheme, and describes them as Signs of God for those who hear and possess knowledge (30:23). But none of these confers any privilege or imposes any disability. The Quran says that God has divided mankind into tribes and nations for greater facility of intercourse. Neither membership in a tribe nor citizenship in a state confers any privilege, nor are they sources of honor. The true source of honor in the sight of God is a righteous life (49:14). In his Farewell Address, the Prophet said: "You are all brothers and are all equal. None of you can claim any privilege or any superiority over any other. An Arab is not to be preferred to a non-Arab, nor is a non-Arab to be preferred to an Arab."

Islam has established a universal brotherhood. It is stressed that a true brotherhood can be established only by virtue of mankind's relationship with one another through God. Other factors —common interests, common pursuits, common occupations— may help to foster friendship and brotherhood—to a degree, but the very same factors may also engender jealousy and hostility. It is only the consciousness that mankind are all equally creatures and servants of God and that they must all constantly seek the pleasure of God, that can bring about the realization of true brotherhood, which can stand the test of all the contingencies to which life is subject. "Hold fast, all together, by the rope of Allah, and be not divided; and remember the favor of Allah, which He bestowed upon you when you were enemies and He united your hearts in love, so that by His grace you became as brothers; and you were on the brink of a pit of fire, and He saved you from it. Thus does Allah explain to you His commandments, that you may be rightly guided" (3:104).

The family is the basic unit of human society. The foundation of a family is laid through marriage. One of the principal considerations to be kept in mind in the choice of a spouse is set out in one of the three or four verses that the Prophet always recited on the occasion of the celebration of a marriage. "O ye who believe, fear Allah, and let every soul look to what it sends forth for the morrow" (59:19). This means that the choice should be determined not only with reference to obvious and immediate considerations, but also with reference to the more lasting consequences of the contemplated union, both in this life and in the next. The Prophet has said: "Some people marry for the sake of beauty, others for family connections, others for wealth, but your choice should be determined by moral and spiritual considerations, as these are the sources of lasting happiness." Degrees of kinship within which marriage is prohibited are laid down (4:23–25).

It is one of the bounties of God that He has created male and female of the same species and has put love and tenderness between them, so that they constitute a source of peace and rest for each other. "In that surely are Signs for a people who reflect" (30:22). The relationship between husband and wife is described as that of a garment and its wearer. The Quran says that a wife is raiment for the husband, and the husband is raiment for the wife (2:188). A garment provides protection, comfort, and ornament. It is also the closest thing to a person outside his or her own self. A husband and wife bound together by the "love and tenderness" that God has put between them are surely garments for each other. The Quran says that the best garment is the garment of righteousness (7:27), so that a husband and wife should be such a garment for each other.

Women have rights *vis-à-vis* men corresponding to those that men have *vis-à-vis* women on a basis of fairness and equity

(2:229). Men are exhorted to consort with their wives in kindness and are reminded: "If you dislike them, it may be that you dislike something wherein Allah has placed much good" (4:20).

The Prophet, as noted earlier, said: "The best among you is he who treats the members of his family best." He was himself always most careful and considerate in respect of all that concerned women. On one occasion he was on a journey when women were also of the party. At one stage the camel drivers, fearing they were late, began to drive the camels fast. The Prophet admonished them: "Mind the crystal," meaning that they should have due regard to the comfort of the women. His reference to the women as "crystal" implied that woman is delicate and sensitive, and is easily hurt. On another occasion he explained that woman is by her nature like a rib. "You can straighten it out with persistent gentleness, but if you try to straighten it out suddenly, you are likely to break it."

Islam does not regard marriage as an indissoluble sacrament. It is a civil contract, importing mutual duties and obligations. An essential feature of the contract is a settlement by the husband on the wife, called dower (4:5), so that the wife should own some property of her own over which she has complete control. Divorce is permitted in Islam, but the Prophet has said that of all things permitted, the most obnoxious in the sight of God is divorce. The process of divorce is spread over a period, during which every effort must be made at smoothing out differences and at reconciliation. If differences become acute, the counsel and help of mediators, one from the wife's people and one from the husband's, should be sought (4:36). If divorce is finally decided upon, the husband cannot take away from the wife anything he has given her (4:21–22), and must make suitable provision for her over a period of six months, which is normally required for the process to be completed. If husband and wife are reconciled to each other during this period, the divorce proceedings are dropped (2:229–230).

Islam permits a plurality of wives, not exceeding four, but only on condition of strict equality of treatment among them. "If you fear you will not be able to deal justly with them, then marry only one" (4:4). The permission may be availed of in a national or domestic emergency, or where circumstances make it desirable that the ordinary rule of monogamy be departed from, but in every case, whatever the degree of affection that the husband may have for one wife as compared with the other, his treatment of each must be absolutely equal. He must make identical provision for each and spend the same period of time with each. There are detailed regulations and instructions which show that he who avails himself of the permission must submit himself to a severe discipline. The contingency that necessitates recourse to a plurality of wives may be worth the discipline, but there is certainly no allowance for self-indulgence. The Prophet has said: "A man who marries more women than one and then does not deal justly with them will be resurrected with half his faculties paralyzed." Preservation of the higher values and promotion of righteousness must be the constant objectives. Permission to marry more than one woman at a time is a necessary emergency provision for the preservation and fostering of high social values and for safeguarding society against promiscuity. In the Islamic social system no stigma attaches to the institution. Each wife occupies an equal position of dignity and honor and there is no discrimination among the children. The permission has undoubtedly been abused, but Islamic society is seeking to eradicate such abuse through legal regulation of the institution.

Great stress is laid on the proper upbringing and training of children. As has already been observed, attention must be paid to the child's proper training long before its birth. The prayer taught by the Prophet, "O Lord, safeguard us against evil and safeguard the issue that Thou mightst bestow upon us against evil," when husband and wife come together, is a striking reminder of the duty that the parents owe to their children in this respect. The prayers taught in the Quran in this context have the same object. Abraham's prayer, "My Lord, bestow upon me righteous offspring" (37:101), and Zachariah's prayer, "My Lord, bestow upon me from Thyself pure offspring" (3:39), illustrate this. So also the prayers, "Our Lord, grant us of our wives and children the delight of our eyes, and make us a model for the righteous" (25:75) and, "My Lord, make my offspring righteous" (46:16). The Prophet has said, "Honor your children," which again draws attention to their being brought up in ways of righteousness so as to make them worthy of honor. One aspect of the commandment of the Quran, "Do not destroy your offspring" (17:32), is that the development of their faculties and capacities should not be neglected inasmuch as that would amount to destroying them.

Infanticide, which was a common practice during certain periods of human history, is prohibited (17:32). The practice, prevailing in certain Arab families who prided themselves on their noble status, of infanticide of female children is severely condemned (81:9–10). As women and female children were generally held in low esteem among the Arabs, the Prophet was very emphatic on proper upbringing of girls, and due consideration being shown to women. He has said: "A person who is blessed with a daughter or daughters and makes no discrimination between them and his sons and brings them up with kindness and affection, will be as close to me in Paradise as my forefinger and middle finger are to each other."

While stressing kindness and affection toward children and uniformly treating all children tenderly, he did not approve of undue indulgence. He had laid it down as a rule for himself and his family and all his descendants that they should never accept charity. On one occasion when a quantity of dates was brought to the Prophet to be distributed in charity, a small grandson of his took one of the dates and put it into his mouth. The Prophet, putting his finger into the child's mouth and gently extracting the date, observed with a smile: "My dear, Muhammad's descendants are not permitted to partake of charity." On another occasion he said to his daughter: "Fatima, continue to be diligent in righteous action, for on the Day of Judgment you will not be asked whose daughter you are, you will only be asked how you employed yourself."

The Quran lays great stress on kindness toward neighbors (4:37). The Prophet emphasized on many occasions the duty owed to a neighbor, saying: "So repeatedly and so much has God impressed upon me the duty owed to a neighbor that I began to think that a neighbor might perhaps be named an heir." On one occasion while urging his companions to keep constantly in mind the need of kindliness toward their neighbors, he said:

This is not at all difficult; all that is necessary is that one should be willing at all times to share with one's neighbor; even if you have only broth for a meal, it is easy to add an extra cup of water and share the broth with your neighbor."

In the same way, the needy and the wayfarer must be looked after (4:37). The insistence upon kindness and help to the wayfarer is particularly striking. Only a person who has had occasion to travel in foreign lands where even the language is unfamiliar can properly appreciate this direction. The traveler need not be poor and wanting in means. The mere fact that he is in a strange

K

land, among strange people, and, perhaps unable to express
his needs in their language, should make him an object of kindly
and helpful attention. On some occasions it may be a great relief
merely to be given directions with regard to the road, the situation
of a hostelry, or a needed address. All this is part of "kindness to
the wayfarer," which is repeatedly enjoined in the Quran.

Those burdened with debt and those held in captivity because
they are unable to pay their ransoms or to purchase their freedom
are proper objects of "spending in the cause of Allah" (9:60).

Orphans have been made the objects of particular care. Their
proper upbringing, and the due administration of their property
must be ensured. Detailed directions are laid down with regard to
the guardianship of minors and the administration of their property. It is the duty of the guardian to check on the upbringing of
the orphan from time to time. When the orphan comes of age and
if he is of sound judgment, his property should be handed over to
him in the presence of witnesses. A guardian or administrator of
an orphan's property is entitled to a suitable allowance if he cannot afford to give the time necessary without compensation, but
if he is himself in easy circumstances he is not entitled to any compensation (4:7). If the orphan on attaining majority should prove
to be of defective judgment a suitable allowance should be made
for his upkeep, and he should be given such advice as he may
need, but his property should be duly administered and his
interests safeguarded (4:6).

The property of the orphan should not be dealt with to his
prejudice by exchange or by being held in common with the
property of the guardian (4:3). The Quran reinforces the guardian's obligation toward the minor in very emphatic language.
"Let those who deal with minors have the same circumspection in
their minds as they would wish for in respect of their own little
ones if they were to leave them behind. Let them, therefore, fear
Allah and always speak the straightforward word. Those who
consume the property of orphans unjustly only swallow fire into
their bellies" (4:10–11).

Younger people are admonished to show due respect and consideration for older people, and older people are exhorted to treat
younger people with kindness and affection. The Prophet has
said: "He who does not behave kindly toward younger people and
does not show due respect to older ones is not of us."

Islam aims at merging all sections of society into a single

community so that all persons may feel themselves to be members of the same family. A whole set of directions exhorts those who are better off to adopt simple ways of life and not to set up artificial barriers in the way of free social intercourse. For instance, the well-to-do are urged toward moderation in food and drink (7:32), and to shun all vanity (23:4). They should be neither stingy, holding back their wealth and substance from being shared by others, nor extravagant, indulging themselves and the members of their families without regard for others who also have a right to share in their wealth (25:58; 51:20). Simple ways of life, dispensing with artificial ceremonial, render social intercourse easy and agreeable. Islam lays great stress on cleanliness of body, clothing, dwellings, public places, and the like (74:5-6). Frequent ablutions and baths are prescribed.

It is recognized that there must be diversity of all kinds in a healthy society, and that it is not only futile but harmful to covet that in which others excel. Each must exercise his or her own capacities and talents and strive to promote both individual and common good. All asking of favors should be from God alone (4:33). Begging is prohibited except in case of extreme need.

Various aspects of good manners are insisted upon. "The true servants of the Gracious One are those who walk in the earth with dignity, and when they are addressed rudely they say: 'Peace'" (25:64). "Turn not thy face away from people in pride, nor walk in the earth haughtily; surely, Allah loves not any arrogant boaster. Moderate thy pace when walking and soften thy voice when thou speakest" (31:19-20).

The Muslim greeting, which is common throughout the Islamic world, is: "Peace be on you and the mercy of God and His blessings." The Quran directs that one should greet one's fellow beings with a better greeting than one receives oneself, or at least return the same (4:87). One is urged to adopt a straightforward manner of speech and not to equivocate (33:71).

When calling upon people or entering one's own house one must go in by the front door, as a matter of courtesy in order not to take a person by surprise (2:190); furthermore, when calling upon people, one must ask permission before one enters; and when one enters, one should greet the inmates with the salutation of peace (24:28). "If you find no one therein, do not enter until you have obtained permission from the owner. If it be said to you, 'Go back,' then go back; that is purer for you. Allah knows well what you do. There is no harm for you to enter freely uninhabited houses wherein are your goods. Allah knows what you disclose and what you conceal" (24:29-30).

Before starting on a journey, due provision must be made therefor, to obviate embarrassment (2:198).

Only three types of public associations are approved of. First, those formed for the purpose of promoting the general welfare, in other words, charitable associations and the like. Second, those the object of which is to promote the spread and propagation of knowledge and investigation and research into the sciences, arts, philosophy, etc. Third, those established for the purpose of peaceful settlement of disputes and for removing causes of friction, whether in domestic, national, political, or international spheres, and thereby promoting peace among mankind (4:115). When people are gathered together for a common purpose, they should behave in an orderly manner, and should not leave or disperse without permission (24:63). When required to make room in a gathering, this should be done cheerfully, and all directions should be carried out with eagerness (58:12).

All people should behave with dignity, and particular attention must be paid to maintenance of order in public places and thoroughfares and in keeping them clean. Persons using public places must take care that no undue inconvenience is occasioned to others using the same, nor should any person be exposed to risk or injury. The Prophet has said that a person passing through a street carrying anything pointed or with a sharp edge should cover it up, so that nobody is exposed to the risk of injury through his carelessness. He has also directed that people should not move from places where an infectious epidemic has broken out to other inhabited places, as this would result in spreading the infection.

The obligation is laid upon everyone to urge others toward goodness and to seek to restrain them from evil, but with kindness and affection (31:18). Spying, backbiting, and undue suspicion must be avoided (49:13). Someone asked the Prophet whether it was backbiting to mention a defect or shortcoming from which another did in fact suffer. The Prophet replied that that was exactly what backbiting meant, for if the defect or shortcoming did not in fact exist, the person attributing it to another would be guilty both of slander and of backbiting. If a person has been guilty of slandering another, this must not be communicated to the person slandered because it would create mischief. The Prophet has said that a person who slanders another shoots an arrow at him, which falls by the way, but a person who hears a slander and carries the tale of it to the person slandered is like one who directs the arrow to its mark.

It is the duty of every Muslim constantly to seek increase of knowledge (20:115). The Prophet has said that the seeking of knowledge is a duty cast upon every Muslim man and woman, and he went so far as to add "even if it should involve a journey to far-off Cathay." He has further said: "A word of wisdom is the lost property of a Muslim. He should seize it wherever he finds it."

With regard to servants, the Prophet has said: "They are your brothers, and you should treat them as such. Provide them with the kind of food that you eat and the kind of clothes that you wear, and if you set them a hard task, join them in it to help them complete it." He has directed that when food is prepared, the person who helped prepare it should be invited to partake of it.

The wages of a laborer must be paid to him "before the sweat dries upon his body."

The Prophet was very insistent upon kindness toward animals. On one occasion he noticed a dove flying around agitatedly, and discovered that somebody had caught its young. He was very annoyed and asked the person to restore the young to the mother immediately. When he saw a donkey that had been branded on the face, he said that this was a cruel practice. If branding be necessary, the Prophet pointed out, it must be done on the leg, where the muscles are not so sensitive. No animal, he added, should be beaten on the face, as the face is a most sensitive part of the body.

Perhaps the most comprehensive directive within the domain of social values is: "Help one another in righteousness and virtue; but help not one another in sin and transgression" (5:3). When the Prophet said on one occasion, "Go to the help of your brother whether oppressor or oppressed," he was asked, "We understand what is meant by going to the help of a brother who is oppressed, but how shall we help a brother who is an oppressor?" The Prophet replied, "By restraining him from oppressing others."

The Prophet has defined a Muslim as "one from whose hands and tongue his fellows apprehend no harm." He furnished a strong motive for mutual co-operation and help when he said, "If a person occupies himself in helping his brother, God occupies Himself in helping him."

16

Economic Values

THE BASIC ECONOMIC CONCEPT IN ISLAM IS THAT absolute ownership of everything belongs to God alone (3:190). Man is God's vicegerent on earth. God has subjected to man's service "whatsoever is in the heavens and whatsoever is in the earth; . . . In this surely are Signs for a people who reflect" (45:14). This has reference to man as such, to the whole of mankind and not to a particular individual or group. "Allah is He Who has appointed you [mankind] His vicegerents on earth. Know then, that he who fails to recognize this dignity and to act in accordance therewith shall be answerable for his neglect and will himself suffer loss and also incur the displeasure of his Lord" (35:40).

Legal ownership by the individual, that is to say, the right of possession, enjoyment, and transfer of property, is recognized and safeguarded in Islam, but all ownership is, as we have seen, subject to the moral obligation that in all wealth all sections of society, and even animals, have a right to share (51:20). Part of this obligation is given legal form and is made effective through legal sanctions, but the greater part is secured by voluntary effort put forth through a desire to achieve the highest moral and spiritual benefits for all concerned. In fact, this supplementing of legal obligations which secure the irreducible minimum with moral obligations to be discharged through voluntary effort runs through every part of the Islamic system. Its operation can be observed in every sphere. For instance, there are the obligatory Prayer services, and supererogatory Prayers, and prayer and remembrance of God at all other times. There is the obligatory fast during the month of *Ramadhan* and supererogatory fasts at other times. There is the obligation upon those who can afford it to perform the pilgrimage once, but *umra* may be performed at any time, and the pilgrimage itself may be repeated as often as a person desires. The same principle holds in the economic sphere.

The object of the Islamic economic system is to secure the widest and most beneficent distribution of wealth through institutions set up by it and through moral exhortation. Wealth must remain in constant circulation among all sections of the community and should not become the monopoly of the rich (59:8).

Islam recognizes the diversity of capacities and talents, which is in itself beneficent, and consequently the diversity in earnings and material rewards (4:33). It does not approve of a dead-level equality in the distribution of wealth, as that would defeat the very purpose of the diversity, and would amount to denying "the favor of Allah" (16:72). It is obvious that if the incentive of proportionate reward for labor, effort, skill, and talent were to be removed, not only would initiative and enterprise be adversely affected, but intellectual progress would also be arrested. That is why the theoretical doctrine of equal reward irrespective of the diversity of skill, capacities, and talents that have gone into the production of wealth has never been maintained for long, even where it has been proclaimed as state policy, and has had to be modified through recourse to various devices designed to secure diversity in reward. On the other hand, Islam does not leave the principle of competition and of proportionate rewards to work itself out mechanically; that too would lead to hardship and injustice, and would retard the moral and spiritual development of individuals as well as of society as a whole.

The principal economic obligation is the payment of the capital levy called the *Zakat* (22:79; 23:5). The word *Zakat* means "that which purifies" and "that which fosters." All original sources of wealth—the sun, the moon, the stars, the earth, the clouds that bring rain, the winds that drive the clouds and carry the pollen, all phenomena of nature—are the gift of God to the whole of mankind. Wealth is produced by the application of man's skill and labor to the resources which God has provided for man's subsistence and comfort and over part of which man enjoys proprietary rights, to the extent recognized by Islam. In the wealth that is produced, therefore, three parties are entitled to share: the workman, whether skilled or unskilled; the person who supplies the capital; and the community as representing mankind. The community's share in produced wealth is called the *Zakat*. After this has been set aside for the benefit of the community, the rest is "purified" and may be divided between the remaining parties that are entitled to share in it.

The *Zakat* is assessed on both capital and income. Its incidence varies with reference to different kinds of property, but on the average it works out at two and one-half per cent of the capital value. The proceeds of the *Zakat* are devoted toward relieving poverty and distress, winning over the cheerful co-operation of those who have not yet completely adjusted their lives to the Islamic system, providing ransom for prisoners of war, helping those in debt, providing comfort and convenience for travelers, supplying capital where talent is available but funds are lacking, providing stipends for scholars and research workers, meeting the expenses involved in collecting and administering the *Zakat*, and generally toward all things beneficial for the community as a whole, such as public health, public works, medical services, and educational institutions (9:60). It thus "fosters" the welfare of the community (9:103).

Besides the *Zakat*, which has been described by the Prophet, as "a levy imposed upon the well-to-do which is returned to the poorer sections of the people," implying that it is their just due and must be paid back to them, there are other institutions within the economic sphere operating constantly to further the objective of the whole system. One of these is the Islamic system of inheritance and succession. Under this system a person may not dispose of more than one third of his property by testamentary directions. While he is in the enjoyment of normal health he may dispose of his property freely, subject, of course, to the moral obligations, some of which have been noted; but neither by will nor by gift, once he enters upon a stage of illness which terminates in death, may he dispose of more than the permitted one third. By such disposition he may provide legacies for friends, for servants, and for charity.

The rest of the inheritance must be divided among prescribed heirs in specified shares. No part of the one third permitted to be disposed of by will may be used to augment the share of one or more heirs to the prejudice of the remaining heirs. Each heir can take only his or her prescribed share and no more; nor can any heir be deprived of the whole or any part of his or her share. There is a wide circle of heirs. If a person should die leaving a father, mother, wife or husband, sons and daughters, each is an heir and is entitled to a determined share of the inheritance. In some cases the share of a female heir in the same degree of relationship to the deceased as a male heir is equal to that of the male heir, but

normally it is one half of that of a male heir in the same degree
(4:8, 12–13).

The difference between the normal share of female heirs and
male heirs of the same relationship to the deceased is not in fact
discriminatory to the prejudice of the female heirs. Under the
Islamic system, the obligation of maintaining the family always
rests upon the husband, even when, as is often the case, the wife's
personal income may be larger than the husband's. To enable the
male to discharge his obligations toward the family, his share in
the inheritance is twice that of a female in the same degree of relationship as himself. Far from operating to the prejudice of the
female heir, this actually places her in a favorable position as compared with the male heir because she does not have financial
obligations to the family. The Islamic system of inheritance oper-
ates to distribute wealth so that a large number of people may
have a competence or, at least, a little, rather than that one or a
few should have a large share and the rest nothing.

Another major provision is the prohibition against the making
of loans on interest. The word used in this connection in the
Quran is *riba*, the connotation of which is not identical with that
of the word "interest," as commonly understood, but for our present purpose "interest" may be used as a rough equivalent. *Riba*
is prohibited because it tends to draw wealth into the hands of a
small circle and to restrict the exercise of beneficence toward
one's fellow beings. In the case of loans which bear interest, the
lender in effect takes advantage of, and makes a profit from, the
need or distress of another. Islam urges the making of loans, but
says they should be beneficent loans, meaning, without interest.
If the debtor finds himself in straitened circumstances when the
time for repayment of a loan arrives, he should be granted respite
till he finds himself in easier circumstance, but "if you remit it
altogether as charity, that shall be the better for you, if only you
knew" (2:281).

It is a mistake to imagine that transactions involving interest
bring about an increase in the national wealth. The Quran says
that in the sight of Allah it is not a beneficent increase. "But
whatever you give in *Zakat*, seeking the favor of Allah—it is these
who will increase their wealth manifold" (20:40).

Trade, commercial partnerships, co-operatives, joint stock
companies, are all legitimate activities and operations (2:276).
Islam does, however, lay down regulations with regard to

commercial activities designed to secure that they be carried on honestly and beneficently. All contracts, whether involving large amounts or small, must be reduced to writing, setting out all the terms thereof, as "this is more equitable in the sight of Allah, and makes testimony surer and is more likely to keep out doubts, and avoid disputes" (2:283). The writing should set out the terms agreed upon fairly, and as a further precaution it is laid down that the terms of the contract shall be dictated by the person who undertakes the liability. If the person on whose behalf the liability is undertaken is a minor, or of unsound judgment, then his guardian or the person representing his interest should dictate the terms of the contract (2:283).

Monopolies and the cornering of commodities are prohibited; so also the holding back of produce from the market in expectation of a rise in prices. All this is opposed to beneficence, and those who indulge in such practices seek to take advantage of the need or distress of their fellow beings. The seller is under obligation to disclose any defect in the article offered for sale. Goods and commodities for sale should go into the open market, and the seller or his agent must be aware of the state of the market before proposals are made for purchase of the goods or commodities in bulk. He should not be taken unawares lest advantage be taken of his ignorance of the state of the market and the prevailing prices. All this is very clearly laid down by the Prophet.

There are stern injunctions in the Quran with regard to the giving of full weight and measure (26:182–185). "Woe unto those who give short measure; those who, when they take by measure from other people, take it full, but when they give by measure to others or weigh out to them, they give them less. Do not such people know that they will be raised again unto a terrible day, the day when mankind will stand before the Lord of the worlds?" (83:2–7).

Defective or worthless goods or articles should not be given in exchange for good ones (4:3). In short, any kind of transaction which does not comply with the highest standards of honesty and integrity must be eschewed, "for God loves not the dishonest"(8:59).

Gambling is prohibited, inasmuch as it promotes dissension and hatred, and tends to deter those who indulge in it from the remembrance of God and from Prayer, thus occasioning a great deal more harm than any possible benefit that may be derived from it (2:220; 5:92).

All unlawful means of acquiring property are prohibited, as these in the end destroy a people (4:30). Acquisition of property or goods through falsehood falls in the same category. It is equally unlawful to seek to establish a title to property by obtaining judgment through corrupt means like bribery or false evidence (2:189). The Prophet has said that a party to a dispute which obtains a judgment in its favor, knowing that it is not in the right, only collects a quantity of fire for itself and not something from which it can draw any benefit.

On the other hand, goods and property lawfully acquired are a bounty of God which is provided by Him as a means of support. They should be properly looked after and should not be wasted through neglect. A person of defective judgment should not be permitted to squander away his substance. It should be managed and administered for him, and provision should be made for his maintenance out of the income (4:6). The duty of making such provision would normally appertain to the community or to the state.

Niggardliness is condemned as a negative and destructive quality. While, on the one hand, ostentation and vanity are disapproved of, on the other, it is not considered right that a person who is well-off should pretend to be poor, fearing lest he be called upon to help others. By doing this he makes himself poor in effect, and deprives himself of the benefits that may be derived from God's bounty (4:38). The wealth of misers, instead of bringing them any advantage, becomes a handicap and arrests their moral and spiritual development (3:181). The other extreme, extravagance, is equally condemned. Even when giving to, or sharing with, others a person should not go so far as to render himself in turn an object of charity (17:30). Hoarding is absolutely prohibited because it puts wealth out of circulation and deprives the owner as well as the rest of the community of its beneficent use (9:34). The truth is that God alone is All-Sufficient, and all prosperity proceeds from Him. It is men who are in need, and prosperity is achieved not through miserliness or holding back, but through beneficent spending, which is spending "in the cause of Allah," namely, in the service of His creatures (47:39).

As already stated, a legal owner of property is not the only person entitled to its use. Those in need who ask, and even those who do not ask or are unable to express their need, have a right in the property of those who are better off, inasmuch as all wealth is a

bounty of God and is acquired through the use of resources which
God has provided for the benefit of the whole of mankind (51:20).
That is why the Quran directs that kindred, the needy, the wayfarer, must be paid their due (30:39). To this end there is emphatic and repeated exhortation in the Quran. Such giving
should be in proportion to the need of the person to be helped and
in accord with the means of the giver, and should not proceed
from any expectation of receiving a return (17:27; 74:7).

It is indeed the highest bounty of God that He should have endowed man with appropriate faculties and capacities and then
subjected the universe to man's beneficent service to enable him
to achieve the fullest development of his faculties in every sphere
of life. Yet some people, instead of putting their faculties to
beneficent use in the service of their fellow beings and in spending
that which they possess for the same purpose, have a tendency to
hold back, not realizing that even from the purely selfish point of
view the greatest benefit is to be derived from beneficent spending
and not from parsimonious holding back. This is the fundamental
principle which is the basis of all prosperity, individual, national,
and universal. The Quran emphasizes this repeatedly. For instance: "Behold, you are those who are favored by being called
upon to spend in the way of Allah; but of you there are some who
hold back, yet whoso holds back does so only to the prejudice of
his own soul. It is Allah who is All-Sufficient, and it is you who are
needy" (47:39). Holding back renders a person progressively
poorer in the true sense inasmuch as he stultifies his faculties, and
by putting that which he possesses out of service and out of circulation, renders it completely barren and unfruitful.

The subject of charitable and beneficent spending has so many
aspects that they can be better appreciated in the juxtaposition in
which the Quran puts them. The following excerpts contain a
whole philosophy of spending, giving, and sharing, on which no
detailed commentary is necessary:

> The similitude of those who spend their wealth for the cause of
> Allah is like the similitude of a grain of corn which grows seven ears,
> in each ear a hundred grains. Allah multiplies even more for whom-
> soever He pleases. Allah is Bountiful, All-Knowing.
> They who spend their wealth for the cause of Allah, then follow
> not up what they have spent with reproach or injury, for them is
> their reward with their Lord, and they shall have no fear, nor shall
> they grieve.

A kind word and forgiveness are better than charity followed by injury. Allah is All-Sufficient, Forbearing.

O ye who believe, render not vain your charity by taunt and injury, like him who spends his wealth to be seen of man, and he believes not in Allah and the Last Day. His likeness is that of a smooth rock covered with earth, on which heavy rain falls, leaving it bare and hard. They shall not secure the benefit of aught of what they earn. . . .

The likeness of those who spend their wealth to seek the pleasure of Allah and to strengthen their souls is that of a garden on elevated ground. Heavy rain falls on it so that it brings forth its fruit twofold, and if heavy rain does not fall on it, then light rain suffices. Allah sees what you do.

Does any one of you desire that there should be for him a garden of palm trees and vines with streams flowing beneath it, and with all kinds of fruit for him therein—while old age has stricken him and he has helpless offspring—and that a fiery whirlwind should smite it and it be all consumed? Thus does Allah make His Signs clear to you that you may ponder.

O ye who believe, spend of the pure things that you have earned, and of what We bring forth for you from the earth; and seek not what is bad to spend out of it when you would not receive it yourselves except with closed eyes. Know that Allah is All-Sufficient, Praiseworthy.

Satan threatens you with poverty and enjoins upon you what is foul, whereas Allah promises you forgiveness from Himself, and Bounty. Allah is Bountiful, All-Knowing.

.   .   .   .   .

If you give alms openly, it is well; but if you keep them secret and give them to the poor, it is better for you. He will remove from you many of your evils. Allah is aware of what you do. . . .

Whatever of wealth you spend, it is to the benefit of your own selves, while you spend not but to seek the favor of Allah. Whatever of wealth you spend, it shall be paid back to you in full and you shall not be wronged.

Charity is for the needy, who are restricted in the cause of Allah and are unable to move about in the land. The ignorant person thinks them to be free from want because of their abstaining from asking. You shall know them by their appearance; they do not ask of men with importunity. Whatever of wealth you spend, surely Allah has perfect knowledge thereof.

Those who spend their wealth by night and day, secretly and openly, have their reward with their Lord, on them shall come no fear, nor shall they grieve (2 : 262–269; 272–275).

17

Public Affairs

THE PRINCIPLES GOVERNING THE ADMINISTRA-
tion of public affairs are a part of social values. The first matter
that calls for notice in this context is the concept of the state. Here
again the basic concept is that sovereignty over the universe belongs to God, but that mankind, God's vicegerents, are invested
with authority in certain spheres, as a trust, for which they are
answerable and accountable to God. The Prophet has said:
"Everyone of you is a shepherd, and everyone of you is accountable for that which is committed to his care."

Inasmuch as God's sovereignty extends over the whole universe,
the ultimate ideal of a state in Islam is a universal federation, or
confederation, of autonomous states, associated together for upholding freedom of conscience and for the maintenance of peace
and co-operation in promoting human welfare throughout the
world. In pursuit of this idea, the Islamic state, established by the
Prophet, which spread rapidly westward through Egypt and
North Africa to Spain, and eastward through Iraq, Iran, and
Central Asia to the confines of China, instituted a single citizenship entailing over-all allegiance to a single head of state, the
Khalifa (meaning vicegerent or successor) who was the guardian
of the Pax Islamica and was responsible for the welfare of all
sections of the vast population united and inspired by common
ideals. With the decline of moral and spiritual values, the ideal
was neglected. The central authority weakened progressively
until allegiance to the Khalifa was reduced to a mere formality
and local rulers became virtually independent.

Islam takes note of the diversity that exists among nations and
peoples, and promulgates directives for beneficent administration
of public affairs. These directives, as relevant to the present-day
world situation as to the times in which they were first revealed,

can lead mankind forward to the achievement of the ideal for which it has striven and toward which it still works.

A study of the Quran reveals that it contemplates two types of states, having the same ideals and objectives, but differing with regard to the scope of the authority of the state and the manner of its establishment. In this respect, also, the ideal is a state in which the head of state exercises authority in both the secular and the spiritual spheres. The Quran says: "Allah has promised to those among you who believe and act righteously that He will surely make them Successors in the earth, as He made Successors from among those who were before them; and that He will surely establish for them their religion, which He has chosen for them; and that He will surely give them security and peace in exchange for their present fear. They will worship Me, and they will not associate anything with Me. Then whoso is ungrateful after that, they will be the rebellious" (24:56).

The office of Khalifa is elective. He may be elected directly or, as happened in the case of Umar, the second Khalifa, he may be nominated by his predecessor, the nomination being subject to approval by the people after the death of the nominating Khalifa.

The Khalifa holds office for life and must devote his whole time, all his faculties, and his full capacity to the service of the people. He is bound by the ordinances of Divine law and by the principles on which they are based. He must carry them out both in the letter and in the spirit, and see that they are put into effect within the state in the most beneficent manner possible.

The Khalifa must decide questions of policy and all major questions of administration after consultation with the chosen representatives of the people, both for the purpose of informing himself in arriving at a decision with regard to the matter in hand, and also in order to train the representatives in the conduct of public affairs (3:160). Indeed, the administration of public affairs through appropriate consultation of competent persons is set down as a characteristic which Muslims should develop (42:39). On the part of the people, co-operation with, and obedience to, those set in authority and entrusted with the conduct of public affairs is placed in juxtaposition to the duty of obedience owed to God and to His Messenger (4:60).

The institution of the Khilafat therefore partakes of what is commonly called secular as well as of what is known as religious character. The Khalifa is the chosen representative of the people, and he has also promise of Divine support so long as the institution maintains the character with which the Quran invests it, and does not merely bear the title, as has unfortunately so often happened in the history of the Muslim peoples (24:56).

The other type of state is that in which also the head of state is a representative of the people, with duties and responsibilities corresponding to that of the Khalifa; but with regard to his tenure of office, the scope of his authority, and the limitations upon it, he is bound by the provisions of the Constitution in conformity with which he is elected to office and which he must uphold. In his case, too, the insistence is upon his role as representative of the people. This is mandatory, for the Quran says: "Verily, Allah commands you to entrust authority into the hands of those who are best fitted to discharge it" (4:59). It is clear that sovereignty in this context is vested in the people. They are commanded to entrust it to those who are best fitted to discharge the responsibilities attaching to it. The exercise of the franchise for the purpose of electing representatives for the discharge of the various responsibilities of state is thus elevated to a sacred trust. The verse continues: "And when you are called upon to judge between, or exercise authority over, the people, you must do so equitably and with justice." These two obligations, the one laid upon the people to choose their representatives wisely, and the other laid upon those who are chosen to exercise their authority equitably and with justice, are the very essence of good administration. The verse concludes: "Surely excellent is that with which Allah admonishes you. Allah is All-Hearing, All-Seeing." This implies that the Muslims might from time to time be tempted to depart from these two fundamental principles, and to try other experiments, but they are warned that what Allah has admonished them with is alone the most excellent and the most beneficent method by which these responsibilities may be discharged. Allah will watch the discharge of these responsibilities, and should the spirit which Allah desires to inspire all those concerned with their discharge begin to languish or disappear, those responsible for the default would be accountable to Him.

The head of a Muslim state is protected against judicial action in respect of the discharge of his public duties, but in respect of obligations undertaken by him in his private capacity as a citizen, he has no privilege and is subject to the same judicial process applicable to any other citizen. Umar, when he was Khalifa, was summoned to court to answer a civil charge preferred against him. When he appeared, the judge stood up as a mark of respect. Umar observed that he had come into court not in his capacity as the Khalifa, but as a private citizen and that it was utterly wrong and inconsistent with the judge's position for the latter to extend any courtesy to him which was not extended to all other citizens when appearing in court. He held that the judge, by his action, had failed in his duty of impartiality toward the parties and was no longer fit to exercise judicial functions.

Islam pioneered the first effective concept of the welfare state. The dignity of labor was unquestioned—indeed, we have seen that the Prophet emphasized this when he said to a laborer, "These hands are very dear to God"—but Islam also laid down that it was a duty of the state to ensure the provision of the average necessities of life for all citizens. This is regarded as the minimum requirement of a beneficent social organization (20:119–120). In fact, the first regular census in Islam, taken during the time of Umar, was carried out for the purpose of ensuring that everybody was supplied with the basic necessities, namely, food, drink, and shelter.

Once when Umar was on one of the many walking trips he made about the countryside during his tenure as Khalifa, he heard a whimper. Following the sound, he came upon a woman tending a pot on the fire. Beside her, three children were crying. In answer to Umar's question, the woman explained that her children had gone without food for two days because she was without means. As a last resort, she had put the kettle, filled only with water, on the fire in the desperate hope that the children would be lulled to sleep with thoughts of a meal soon to appear.

Umar returned to Medina, where he collected in a large bag some flour, butter, meat, and dates. A servant, whom he summoned for assistance in lifting the bag on to his back, protested, offering to carry the bundle himself.

"No doubt you will carry this bundle for me just now, but who will carry my burden on the Day of Judgment?" asked the Khalifa. He then carried the provisions to the woman.

"God bless you for your kindness!" she exclaimed. "You are far more fit to be Khalifa than Umar. He knows nothing of how the people fare."

"Well, Mother, perhaps Umar is not so bad," said the Khalifa gently, smiling.

L

The duties of the Islamic state are no different from those of any other enlightened state or ruler, but they must be conceived and discharged in the spirit which Islam seeks to infuse into all institutions. They are concisely expressed in the saying of the Prophet: "Every one of you is a shepherd, and is responsible and accountable for that which is committed to his care. The Sovereign is responsible and answerable for his people, every man is responsible and answerable for the members of his family, every woman is responsible and answerable for her home and children, and every servant is responsible and answerable for the property of his master that is in his charge."

Islam regards the state as a shepherd put in charge of a flock, and as a shepherd is bound to protect and look after the flock and provide for all its needs—keeping the sheep from straying, guarding them from the prowling wolf, feeding and housing them, protecting them against pestilence and disease—so it is the duty of the Islamic state to safeguard its people against dissension, disorder, disturbance, and oppression, to secure them against attacks from outside, and to make provision for all their intellectual and material needs.

A principal duty of the Islamic state is to safeguard the security of the state and to maintain the defense arrangements in a proper condition (3:201).

The duty of the Islamic state to make provision for the intellectual development of the people was early emphasized by the Prophet. He was himself so anxious concerning it that after the battle of Badr he announced that any Meccan prisoner of war who was literate could earn his freedom by instructing ten Muslim children in the elements of reading and writing. This duty was so well discharged by his immediate successors that within a brief period the camel drivers of the desert, despised by Iran and Byzantium, became the teachers of the world and the torchbearers of enlightenment.

Provision was made for the administration of justice at a very high level as soon as the Prophet arrived in Medina, at which time the Charter of the Republic of Medina was drawn up. Umar was appointed one of the judges, and the Prophet himself often performed that function. The Quran lays down as a condition of belief in Islam that a Muslim must accept the obligation of judicial determination of disputes, find no demur in his heart against the final judgment that may be handed down, and carry it out fully (4:66). In addition to the safeguards inherent in the orderly process of the administration of justice, a very emphatic admonition already mentioned was added by the Prophet. He said that a party which obtains a judgment in its favor should not consider itself as having a valid right to the subject matter of the judgment if in fact it is not entitled to such right. The mere fact of a judgment in its favor will not shield it against the consequences of the wrong that it would be guilty of in appropriating that to which in fact it is not entitled. The Prophet added that if such a party wrongly appropriates anything under color of the judgment, it only "takes home a quantity of fire."

Judges are admonished to carry out their duties with strict impartiality and justice. No party should attempt to corrupt the course of justice through bribery (2:189) or by presenting false evidence (25:73). A more emphatic and comprehensive injunction is: "O ye who believe, be strict in observing justice, and bear witness for the sake of Allah, even though it be against your own selves, or against parents and kindred. Whether they be rich or poor, Allah is more regardful of them than you are. Therefore, guard yourselves against being led astray by low desires, so that you may be able to act equitably. If you conceal the truth or evade it, then remember that Allah is well aware of what you do" (4:136).

Even hostility toward a people should not incite a Muslim or the Muslim community or the Muslim state to act unjustly or inequitably toward them. "O ye who believe, be steadfast in the cause of Allah, and bear witness in equity, and let not a people's enmity toward you incite you to act otherwise than with justice. Be always just, that is closest to righteousness. Fear Allah. Surely, Allah is aware of what you do" (5:9).

18

International Relations: Peace

THE WORD "ISLAM" DERIVES FROM A ROOT WHICH means "peace" and "submission." It is interpreted as meaning the attainment of peace through submission to the will of God, that is, through conformity to Divine law and guidance. In the Islamic concept, Divine law includes all law governing and regulating the universe. Peace and order are deemed essential for material, moral, and spiritual progress.

Among the attributes of God, the Quran mentions that He is "the Source of Peace and the Bestower of Security" (59:24). The establishment of peace and the maintenance of security must, therefore, be the constant objective of mankind.

The Muslim greeting in all parts of the world is: "Peace be on you, and the mercy of Allah and His blessings."

Every pursuit and activity which has a tendency to disturb the peace is severely condemned. "Do not promote disorder in the earth after peace has been established" (7:56–57). "Do not go about committing iniquity in the earth and causing disorder" (7:75; 11:86; 29:37). "They seek to create disorder, and Allah loves not those who create disorder" (5:65). "Seek not to create disorder in the earth. Verily, God loves not those who seek to create disorder" (28:78). "There are those who talk glibly and plausibly on all subjects and call God to witness as to the sincerity of their motives and intentions, and yet they constantly promote dissension by their persistence in magnifying differences and disputes, and when they happen to wield authority they run about in the land seeking to create disorder, which destroys harvests and entails severe suffering and hardship upon men. Allah loves not such conduct" (2:205–206).

The Muslims are commanded to work wholly for peace (2:209). No finer example exists than that shown by the Prophet himself.

When the Prophet announced his mission to the people of Mecca, who had known him as an honest, upright, and faithful comrade, the announcement was received with incredulity. His persistence in the assertion of his claim and in calling men to the worship of One God and to a moral and spiritual revolution in their lives at first drew only ridicule. When here and there his call began to evoke a favorable response, the ridicule turned into harassment. During ten long years the Prophet and his small but slowly increasing band of companions were subjected to cruel and merciless persecution. They bore it all with patience and dignity under the most difficult conditions. Neither abuse nor persecution could provoke them into conduct unbecoming orderly, law-abiding citizens. Except for a vehement repudiation of idol worship and persistence in proclaiming and upholding the Unity of God, neither the Prophet himself nor any member of the small Muslim community in Mecca appears ever to have attempted to defy the authority of the assembly of Elders, or the rules and conventions regulating the conduct and behavior of the citizens of Mecca. When the persecution became almost unendurable, the Prophet, rather than risk a state of civil disorder in the town, counseled that some Muslims should leave Mecca and seek asylum in the neighboring state of Ethiopia, across the Red Sea. Later, other Muslims, including the Prophet himself, migrated to Medina. The Meccan period of the Prophet's ministry is an outstanding example of the upholding of law and order by a hard-pressed and sorely persecuted group, whose membership was constantly growing and whose strength was increasing.

Though Islam has always stood uncompromisingly on the Unity of God, the Muslims were admonished not to use harsh language against the idols worshiped by Meccans lest the latter, out of spite and ignorance, be provoked into blaspheming Allah, in Whom they themselves professed belief. "Thus unto every people have We caused their doings to seem fair" (6:109). The principle stressed here is that even false doctrines and unsocial and destructive ideas, so long as they are believed in and adhered to, must be taken into account as having an appeal to those who entertain them; all conduct which is likely to cause provocation should be avoided.

In the domain of international relations, religion and interreligious relations occupy a very important position. Unfortunately, comparatively little attention is paid today to this aspect of human relations. It is assumed that religion is a private matter for each individual and, therefore, should have no direct connection with the political, social, or economic aspects of life which directly affect the relations not only of individuals, but of groups, communities, and nations with each other. This assumption is not justifiable. Religion is a vital factor in the field of human relations and there is good ground for hope that it might progressively become more effective in promoting unity and accord rather than continue to be a source of friction and conflict. It is important, therefore, to ascertain what attitude Islam adopts toward other faiths and their followers.

The Quran teaches that God has sent His revelation to all peoples from time to time and that no section of mankind has been left without Divine guidance (35:25–26). Many of the prophets of the Old Testament are mentioned by name in the Quran, and so also is Jesus, who with the other prophets is honored and revered by the Muslims (2:137). Indeed, the Quran requires belief in the truth and righteousness of all the prophets and in the revelations that were vouchsafed to them by God. The Torah and the revelation that came to Jesus are repeatedly mentioned as sources of guidance and light (5:45, 47).

Thus Islam seeks to bring about reconciliation between the followers of different faiths and to establish a basis of respect and honor among them. It holds out to them the hand of cooperation and friendship on a basis of righteousness. "Surely, those who have believed, and the Jews, and the Sabaeans, and the Christians, whoso believes in God and the Last Day, and acts righteously, on them shall come no fear nor shall they grieve" (5:70). They are all invited to unite on the basic principle which all of them profess to believe in. "Say, O people of the Book, come to an agreement on a principle common between us and you, in that we worship none but Allah and that we associate no partner with Him, and that some of us take not others for lords beside God" (3:65).

Islam stands emphatically for freedom of conscience. Everyone must make his choice, and accept or reject in absolute freedom whatever he chooses to believe in or to deny. "There is no compulsion in matters of faith, for surely guidance has been made manifest and distinct from error" (2:257). As this verse stresses, there can be no compulsion in matters of faith, because faith and belief are matters of conscience, and conscience cannot be compelled. A person could perhaps be compelled to *say* that he believes in a certain doctrine, but he cannot be compelled to believe in it. Besides, it is pointed out that no compulsion is needed. Guidance and error have been clearly set forth, and everyone must make his choice after due reflection and deliberation.

Islam bases itself upon reason and observation, and invites people to the consideration of its teachings on that basis. "The truth is from your Lord, so let him who will, believe; and let him who will, disbelieve" (18:30). "There have come to you clear proofs from your Lord, whoever will therefore see and recognize the truth, it will be for the good of his own soul and whoever will remain blind to it shall only harm himself" (6:105). The Prophet suffered keen anguish when his people appeared impervious to all reason and argument, to the various Signs set forth before them, and to every method of explanation and illustration employed in the Quran. So extreme and constant was his anguish that God repeatedly comforted him: "Haply thou wilt grieve thyself to death for sorrow after them if they believe not in this discourse" (18:7); "Haply thou wilt grieve thyself to death that they are not believers" (26:4); "Let not thy soul waste away in sighing after them. Surely Allah knows what they do" (35:9). But it is explained that complete freedom in the matter of conscience and belief is essential for the fulfillment of the Divine purpose. It would be easy for God to compel belief inasmuch as He has power even over the consciences of people, but they must be left to decide for themselves. "If thy Lord had enforced His will, surely all who are on the earth would have believed together. Wilt thou, then, force people to become believers?" (10:100).

Clear directions have been given with regard to the manner in which the message of Islam is to be conveyed to mankind. "Say, 'This is my way: I call unto Allah on the basis of understanding, I and those who follow me'" (12:109). It was the duty of the Prophet and of each one of his companions, as indeed it is the duty of every Muslim all the time, to invite people to the acceptance of the Truth, both by precept and by example, but the precept and the example must be such as to preclude the remotest suspicion of any pressure or coercion. "Call unto the way of thy Lord with wisdom and kindly exhortation, and reason with them in the way that is best. Surely thy Lord knows best who has strayed from His way; and He knows best those who are rightly guided" (16:126).

If these principles were unreservedly accepted and fully acted upon by Muslim and non-Muslim alike, inter-religious relations would be lifted from the plane of controversy, which often engenders misunderstanding and irritation, to the level of a reasoned and respectful appreciation of beneficent values wherever they may be found. Such a consummation is devoutly to be wished for and should be fervently welcomed.

Islam draws attention to factors which tend to disturb or destroy peace and order, and deprecates them. Some of these may be briefly considered.

Domination of one group by another in the domestic sphere or of one people by another in the international sphere is a potent cause of disturbance of peace, and is strongly condemned. God does not approve of the division of His creatures into groups for the purpose of domination of some by others, and whenever such an attempt is made, God's purpose works for the uplift of those who are dominated or oppressed. In this connection, the instance of Pharaoh and his treatment of the people of Israel is cited as an example. "Pharaoh behaved arrogantly in the land and divided the people thereof into sections; he sought to weaken one section, slaying their male children, and sparing their female children. Certainly he was of the workers of evil. We desired to show favor unto those who had been reduced into the position of subordinates in the land and to make them leaders and to make them inheritors of Our favors and to establish them in the land" (28:5–7). Pharaoh's end and that of his nobles and courtiers became a terrible lesson for all succeeding generations (10:91–93).

Economic exploitation of one people or country by another inevitably leads to domination by the exploiters, and develops into a threat to peace. The Quran prohibits such exploitation and points out that an economy based on the exploitation of other peoples and their resources cannot be beneficial in its consequences, nor can it endure. Only such economic development is beneficial and enduring as is based upon the exploitation of a country's own resources and on equitable sharing with others of the bounties which God has provided for each people. "Do not raise thine eyes covetously after that which We have bestowed on some groups, to enjoy for a period, of the ornaments of this life that We may try them thereby—the provision bestowed upon thee by thy Lord is better and more enduring" (20:132).

Even when a strong and powerful state avoids domination or

exploitation of weaker states or peoples, its behavior and attitude toward them, if they savor of arrogance or contempt, might cause irritation and resentment which could result in the disturbance of good relations and imperil the maintenance of peace. The Quran admonishes against such behavior, pointing out that the strength or weakness of a people is no indication or measure of its superiority or inferiority. In any case, the Quran emphasizes that, in the process of the rise and fall of nations, a people that is weak today may become strong tomorrow, and memories of conduct that occasioned resentment or engendered ill-will would rankle and lead to disturbance of good relations (49:12).

Another source of international conflict is the divergence between proclaimed intentions and policies and actual practice and conduct.

Doubts concerning motives and designs are bound to be raised by a state whose conduct is inconsistent with its undertakings and its proclaimed policies and aims. From such conduct a situation serious enough to endanger international relations can result. The Quran therefore insists on complete conformity of conduct to declarations and professions of intent. "O ye who believe, why do you say what you do not: most displeasing is it in the sight of Allah that you say what you do not" (61:3-4). On the other hand, it warns against indulgence in undue suspicion of other peoples' motives and against seeking to discover pretexts for differences and disagreements, as this might result in much harm. "O ye who believe, avoid suspicion, for suspicion in some cases might do great harm" (49:13).

Experience shows that a too ready credence of rumors, and their wide publicity, may cause grave repercussions in the sphere of international relations. These rumors may have their origin in deliberate mischief or may be the product of a too active imagination, but the harm done might sometimes be serious. The Quran warns Muslims to be extremely careful in this respect. They are told to apply a rigorous test to everything that may emanate from a source not completely dependable and trustworthy, for carelessness in this respect might not only give rise to tension but entail grave consequences. "O ye who believe, if news comes to you from an untrustworthy source, examine it carefully, lest you do harm to a people in ignorance and then be sorry for what you did" (49:7).

The tendency to broadcast all manner of news, even news that might have the effect of disturbing people's minds and agitating public opinion, is deprecated. "When there comes to them a matter of security or of fear they publish it widely: whereas if they were to refer it to the Prophet and to those in authority among them, those of them whose business it is to investigate would ascertain the truth of the matter. Were it not for the Grace of God upon you, and His Mercy, you would certainly have gone astray, except a few" (4:84). The verse does not deprecate merely the publishing of an irresponsible rumor or a piece of false news. Rather, it emphasizes that news which affects public security or is likely to disturb the public mind or agitate public opinion should be referred to the proper authorities for them to determine whether immediate publication is or is not desirable in the public interest.

The Quran is very insistent upon the due observance and performance of treaty obligations (5:2; 17:35). As everything that a Muslim does or undertakes is done and undertaken in the name of Allah, these obligations have, as it were, a sacred character. "Fulfill the covenant of Allah when you make a covenant; and break not your pledges after making them firm, while you have made Allah your surety. Certainly, Allah knows what you do" (16:92).

One element that often leads to differences and disputes concerning the meaning and the carrying into effect of treaty obligations is the type of language that may be employed in expressing the obligations undertaken by the parties. Ambiguity of language which, instead of settling differences and promoting accord, gives rise to disputes and controversies with regard to its meaning and construction should be avoided. Such language in the end leads the parties to suspect each other's sincerity and integrity of purpose. The Quran, therefore, insists that plain words and straightforward language should always be employed for giving expression to agreements that may be arrived at. It is stated that if this course is followed, God will bless the conduct of the parties with beneficence and will eliminate the consequences of their defaults. "O ye who believe, fear Allah and use the straightforward word. He will bless your works for you and cover up your defaults. Whoso obeys Allah and His Messenger shall surely attain a mighty success" (33:71-72). The insistence is upon use of language which should not be open to conflicting interpretations and thus give rise to differences and disputes.

The objective of Islam in the international sphere is an association of strong and stable states allied together in pursuance of the maintenance of peace, freedom of conscience, and promotion of human welfare. The object of all treaties, therefore, should be to further these purposes, and a treaty should not be entered into with the intent of weakening or of taking advantage of the weakness of the other party. This would weaken the whole system and ultimately disrupt it altogether. Subversive methods and exploitation of other peoples carried on under cover of treaties and covenants are therefore strongly condemned. "Be not like unto her who, after having made it strong, breaks her yarn into pieces. You make your covenants a means of deceit between you, for fear lest one people become more powerful than another. Surely Allah tries you therewith. . . . Make not your covenants a means of attaining ulterior purposes; or your foot will slip after it has been firmly established, and you will be faced with evil consequences" (16:93, 95). Treaties should bind people together in beneficent co-operation and should make them stronger. If made a means of deceit, they would divide and disrupt peoples, and all effort and labor spent on them would be wasted, resulting only in loss.

This is followed by an admonition that obligations undertaken by treaty or covenant should not be evaded or repudiated under the temptation of securing some advantage (16:96). The performance of obligations undertaken is a moral and spiritual duty which secures permanent benefits, whereas any advantage gained through evasion or a default in the performance of an obligation will be only temporary and will in the end do harm. This is reinforced with the reminder: "That which you have shall pass away, but that which is with Allah is lasting. We will certainly give those who are steadfast their reward according to the best of their works" (16:97).

It is an obligation of a Muslim state to go to the assistance of Muslims who are subjected to persecution on account of their faith. But even this obligation is subject to the strict observance of existing treaties and engagements, which must be scrupulously carried out. "If they seek your help in the matter of religion then it is your duty to help them, except against a people with whom you have a treaty. Allah sees what you do" (8:73).

Circumstances may arise, however, under which the conduct of one party to a treaty might make it difficult or impossible for the other party to continue its adherence to the terms of the treaty.

If it should be clearly established that the other party to a treaty is determined upon its repudiation or breach, a Muslim state may repudiate the treaty, but only after due notice and upon terms which would ensure that no prejudice or disadvantage would be occasioned to the other party by such repudiation. In other words, so long as an actual breach of the treaty has not taken place, one party to a treaty is not permitted to enter upon military preparations against the other party—even when bad faith is suspected— except after due notice that from a specified date the one party will no longer be bound by the treaty on account of the threatened or clearly intended contravention or breach by the other party. This would permit appropriate action for the removal of any misunderstanding that might have arisen or for the renewal of the treaty or for the conclusion of a new one if this should be found advisable and feasible. In any case, such notice would safeguard the other party against surprise and put it in a position to make the necessary adjustments consequent upon the abrogation of the treaty (8:59).

One of the obligations of a state in pursuance of its duty of preservation of peace is to maintain its defences in proper condition lest any weakness in that respect should invite aggression and a breach of international peace. Alertness and readiness is in effect a deterrent against aggression and is a direct means of promoting peace. Any sacrifices involved in that connection should be borne cheerfully because the benefits resulting therefrom are out of all proportion to the sacrifices (8:61).

The Prophet set an excellent example both with regard to the spirit in which treaties should be entered into and with which they should be carried out. The negotiations at Hudaibiyya resulted in a treaty which put an end to a state of war started by the Meccans and continued without interruption for six years, not because the Meccans were anxious for the restoration of peace, but because the Prophet was eager in that behalf. The Prophet had announced early that he would be prepared to accept any terms the Meccans might propose. All that he sought was permission to perform the circuit of the Ka'aba in peace, which was the well-recognized right of every Arab. Once the area of the Sanctuary was entered for that purpose, no molestation or hindrance could be made to the performance of what was a sacred religious duty in the eyes of the Meccans themselves. In the case of the Prophet and the Muslims, however, the Meccans threatened armed opposition. The Prophet would have been within his rights to treat this as a *casus belli*, but he was determined not to adopt any course which should involve fighting and violence. So he stayed outside the Sanctuary limits, and a course of negotiations was commenced which occupied several days.

In the end, the terms of a treaty were agreed upon, which the Muslims considered not only utterly one-sided but humiliating. Even the drawing up of the treaty in writing evoked caveats and objections from the Meccan side. Ali, the Prophet's cousin, who was chosen as the scribe for the text of the treaty, had written that one party to the treaty was "Muhammad, the Messenger of Allah." The Meccan envoy took exception to this description and insisted that the Prophet should be described as "Muhammad, son of Abdullah." The matter was referred to the Prophet, who said: "I am the Messenger of Allah, and I am the son of Abdullah. If they prefer that I should be described as son of Abdullah I would accept their suggestion." Ali was reluctant to make the change, but he had to yield.

One of the terms of the treaty was that if a Meccan youth became a Muslim and left Mecca to join the Muslims without the permission of his father or guardian, he would be returned to the Meccans. Before the treaty was signed, Abu Jandal, son of Suhail, the very Meccan envoy with whom the terms of the treaty had been finally agreed, escaped from Mecca and arrived in the Muslim camp. He had become a Muslim and therefore was being kept in strict confinement by his father; he had been severely beaten several times, to which the bruises on his body bore eloquent witness. He asked for asylum, and begged some of the Muslims to try to persuade the Prophet not to deliver him to the Meccans. The Prophet pointed out to the young man that a clause in the treaty provided that in such a case the person concerned would be sent back to the Meccans, and that the Prophet was bound by the obligation he had undertaken. Because of the young man's piteous pleadings, the Prophet agreed to speak to the father, and to ask him as a favor not to insist upon his son's returning to Mecca; but the father was adamant, and the Prophet carried out his obligation, assuring Abu Jandal that if he were patient and steadfast, God would soon provide some way of deliverance for him and other young men in a similar position in Mecca.

After the Prophet's return to Medina another young man, Abu Baseer, who also had accepted Islam, escaped from Mecca and arrived in Medina. He was soon followed by two Meccans demanding his return. The Prophet directed that Abu Baseer should be delivered to the two Meccans. Once away from Medina, Abu Baseer, convinced that nothing but torture and possibly death awaited him in Mecca, fought the two Meccans, killing one of them, and then returned to Medina. The Prophet was distressed by what had happened, and Abu Baseer was told that he must keep out of Medina, since it would be a breach of the treaty to permit him to enter. So the young man turned away from Medina, but instead of returning to Mecca he went westward, and contrived to secure some means of subsistence near the coast. He then sent a message to Abu Jandal and others in the same position in Mecca, asking that they join him.

Within a short time Abu Baseer collected a band of young Muslims around him, and he sent word to Mecca that they would bar the coastal route to Meccans traveling north. Quickly the Meccans made representation to the Prophet, asking that he restrain these young men from molestation or violence to Meccan travelers. When the Prophet explained that these young fellows were not within his jurisdiction and so not subject to his authority the Meccans suggested a compromise. If they (the Meccans) dropped the relevant term from the treaty, would the Prophet invite the young men to Medina and make himself responsible for them? This was agreed upon and carried out; and the difficulty was resolved.

In the meantime, two women who had accepted Islam escaped from Mecca and arrived in Medina. Soon their return to Mecca was demanded. The Prophet pointed out that the term of the treaty referred expressly to men and made no mention of women, and that a demand for their return was unjustified. With that the Meccans had to be content.

Later the Meccans committed a flagrant breach of the treaty by attacking a tribe in alliance with the Muslims, whereupon the Prophet advanced on Mecca and the city fell without any fighting.

It is a duty laid upon Muslims to bring about peaceful settlement and adjustment of difficulties and disputes (49:11). If two Muslim states fail to settle their differences through friendly negotiations and if the differences become acute enough to constitute a threat to the maintenance of peace between them, it becomes the duty of other Muslim states to exercise their good offices to bring about a settlement on an equitable basis. Should one of the parties to the dispute be unwilling to avail itself of the good offices of the neutral states, or, having done so, be unwilling to accept and to carry out the terms of the settlement proposed, the neutral states must all combine to consider and adopt measures to compel the submission of the recalcitrant state. For this purpose, recourse may be had to the use of force if necessary. In proposing a settlement, the intervening states should keep in view the original dispute or difference between the parties. Matters unconnected with the dispute should not be raised or discussed in connection with the settlement. When both parties are finally ready to accept the settlement, it should be carried into effect without delay. The intervening states should not raise extraneous matters, such as an indemnity or compensation for the trouble occasioned to them or for the expenses incurred by them in connection with any action necessary to procure acceptance or enforcement of the settlement; nor should the intervening states seek any advantage for themselves out of the settlement. An award made or a settlement proposed by the intervening states in such a case is described as "the command of Allah," and refusal to accept it or to carry it out is described as "transgression" (49:10).

19

International Relations: War

ISLAM REGARDS WAR AS AN ABNORMAL AND destructive activity, to which recourse should be had only as the last resort. The Quran describes war as a conflagration, and declares that it is God's purpose to put out such a conflagration whenever it erupts, meaning that when war becomes inevitable it should be waged in such a manner as to cause the least possible amount of damage to life and property; and that hostilities should be brought to a close as quickly as possible. "Whenever they kindle a fire for war, Allah extinguishes it. They strive to create disorder in the earth, and Allah loves not those who create disorder" (5:65). If aggression were not repelled by force, the earth would be filled with disorder and all beneficence would disappear (2:252).

When the Prophet left Mecca for Medina, it was hoped that the Meccans, relieved of his presence and the presence of the Muslims, would be content to leave them in peace in Medina. But this proved a vain hope. The Meccans immediately announced a reward of one hundred camels for the person who should hand over the Prophet to them, dead or alive. When they learned of his safe arrival in Medina, where he was received with honor and was in fact accepted as the chief by all sections of the people, they sent an ultimatum to the people of Medina: Expel the Prophet by force if necessary, or Medina will be invaded.

Thus was war declared upon the Muslims by the Meccans.

It was under these conditions that the Muslims were permitted to take up arms and fight against unwarranted and ruthless invasion of liberty of conscience and freedom of faith and worship. There was no other issue in dispute between the Muslims and the Meccans. It is emphatically stressed in the Quran that if permission were not to be granted to repel aggression, freedom of conscience would be utterly destroyed. The Quran states that God would assist the Muslims in the fighting which had thus been forced upon them because they were the oppressed party, but admonishes them that when God grants them security they must in their turn seek to promote righteousness and purity, faith in God, and the welfare of the people.

"Permission to fight is granted to those against whom war is made, because they have been wronged—Allah indeed has power to help them—to those who have been driven out of their homes unjustly only because they said 'Our Lord is Allah,' those who, if We establish them in the earth, will observe Prayer and pay the *Zakat*, and enjoin good and forbid evil. If Allah did not repel aggression by means of those who fight against it, there would surely have been demolished cloisters and churches and synagogues and mosques, wherein the name of Allah is oft commemorated. Allah will surely help those who help Him. Allah is indeed Powerful, Mighty. With Allah rests the final issue of all affairs" (22:40–42). Fighting is permissible only to repel or halt aggression. But even in the course of such fighting, Muslims are not permitted to adopt unduly aggressive measures. "Fight in the cause of Allah against those who fight against you, but do not transgress. Surely Allah loves not the transgressors" (2:191).

It is repeatedly stressed that the object of any fighting forced upon Muslims should be to put down persecution, "for persecution is worse than killing." But during the course of fighting, all customary restrictions and limitations must be observed except when the enemy fails to observe them; in that case Muslims may forgo them also, but only to the extent to which the enemy dispenses with them (2:192). Should the enemy desist from the fighting, the Muslims should do likewise, for "Allah is Most Forgiving, Merciful" (2:193). When freedom from persecution is secured, fighting should be brought to an end. "Fight them until there is no persecution, and religion is freely professed for Allah"; but even this is subject to the enemy continuing the fight. "If they desist, then remember that no hostility is allowed except against the aggressors" (2:194).

It is thus abundantly clear that Islam makes fighting obligatory in defense of freedom of conscience, so long as the enemy continues to fight an aggressive war with the object of depriving people of freedom of belief, profession, and worship. When freedom of conscience is secured or the enemy desists and is prepared

M

to make a just and equitable peace, fighting should stop. These are basic and fundamental directives. They permit of no refinement or deviation. There are a host of directives in the Quran with regard to war and warlike activities, but they are all subject to the conditions here laid down, and must be so construed.

It does not follow, however, that fighting is not permissible under any other circumstances. What these verses mean is that in the conditions here set out, fighting becomes obligatory and a duty which cannot be evaded. There may be a similar duty to halt aggression or to strive for the preservation of peace, and that may involve the obligation to fight; as, for instance, the obligation upon Muslim states who are seeking to bring about a settlement of a dispute between other Muslim states and who cannot secure the acceptance and implementation of a just and fair settlement without recourse to fighting against the recalcitrant state. In the same way, fighting may become obligatory for the purpose of safeguarding the security of the state. But all such fighting must comply with the condition that it be undertaken against aggression or oppression and not be carried out in an aggressive manner.

Should war become unavoidable, every effort must be made to limit its mischief and horror and to bring hostilities to a close as early as possible. Savage practices like disfiguring the enemy dead, and torturing prisoners of war, which were common in pre-Islamic Arabia, are prohibited in Islam. With regard to customs and practices in themselves not barbaric or revolting, the principle laid down is that the Muslims might extend reciprocal treatment to the enemy and might retaliate to the extent to which an injury or a wrong is inflicted upon them, but that the better part would be to endure and to forgive (16: 127).

Islam does not permit the use of weapons or devices which are calculated to cause destruction on a wide scale unless first used by the enemy. It forbids the killing or capture of noncombatants as well as molestation of ministers and teachers of religion, scholars, old men, women, and children; nor does it permit wanton destruction of property or of sources of wealth. Damage to property is permissible only if it is unavoidable in direct prosecution of a war. The directions given by the Prophet to Zaid when he was put in command of the force sent to Syria, and those given by Abu Bakr, the first Khalifa, to Zaid's son, Usamah, who was commissioned to lead an army to the northern frontiers to check a threatened invasion by the Byzantines, furnish good illustrations.

One requirement which tends to limit the horrors of war and to bring armed conflict to a speedy close is that those who are forced to have recourse to it must fight with courage and steadfastness. The Quran is very emphatic about that. One of the prayers of the righteous involved in the use of force against the enemy is that offered by the children of Israel when they were faced with fighting Goliath: "Our Lord, bestow steadfastness upon us, and make our foothold sure, and help us against the disbelieving people" (2:251).

The Quran states: "With how many prophets have there been a number of devoted men who fought beside them? They slackened not for aught that befell them in the way of Allah, nor did they weaken, nor did they humiliate themselves before the enemy. Allah loves the steadfast. The only words uttered by them were: 'Our Lord, forgive us our errors, and our excesses in our conduct and make firm our steps and help us against the disbelieving people' " (3:147–148).

The enemy must be faced with courage and steadfastness. No one should turn his back on the enemy "unless maneuvering for battle or turning to join another company." Conduct inconsistent with this brings down upon those concerned "the wrath of Allah" (8:16–17). "Allah loves those who fight in His cause arrayed in solid ranks, as though they were a strong structure cemented with molten lead" (61:5).

But even on the field of battle and in the face of the enemy, the duty owed to God is not to be neglected. The strengthening and nourishing of the spirit must be attended to at all times. Fighting may be imposed as a hard necessity, and so become a duty to be well performed, but it must always be remembered that it is only a means of securing and safeguarding suitable conditions for the pursuit and achievement of the purpose of life. It is not an end in itself. During the course of the fighting, therefore, the soul must be occupied with the constant remembrance of God, and the body should join in His worship as much as circumstances permit. Among the injunctions relating to conditions of war are the following: "When thou art among them, and leadest the Prayer for them, let a party of them stand in Prayer with thee, and let them take their arms. When they have performed their prostrations, let them go to the rear, and let another party, who have not yet prayed, come forward and pray with thee, and let them adopt their means of defense and take their arms. The enemy wish that you be neglectful of your arms and your baggage that they may fall upon you at once. It shall be no sin on you, if you are in trouble on account of rain, or if you are sick, that you lay aside your arms, but you should always adopt your means of defense. . . . When you have finished the Prayer, remember Allah, while standing, and sitting, and lying down. When you are secure from danger, then observe Prayer in the prescribed form. Verily, Prayer is enjoined on the believers to be offered at its appointed time. And slacken not in seeking the enemy. If you suffer, they too suffer, even as you suffer. But what you hope from Allah they hope not. Allah is All-Knowing, Wise" (4:103–105).

Fighting is but an incident, an expression in outward conduct of part of that which needs to be done and must be done in the pursuit of the main end. The spirit in which that end is sought is what matters. One who truly believes in God and wholeheartedly accepts as his goal the purpose which God has appointed for man must commit his all to God in return for winning God's pleasure. Such a one enters, as it were, into a covenant with God, and must endeavor to fulfill it in all the varying circumstances and exigencies in which he might find himself. "Surely, Allah has purchased of the believers their persons and their property, in return for the Garden of Allah's pleasure that they shall have (they fight in the cause of Allah and they slay and are slain) a promise that He has made incumbent upon Himself in the Torah, and the Gospel, and the Quran—and who is more faithful to his covenant than Allah? Rejoice, then, in your bargain, which you have made with Him. That indeed is the supreme triumph. Those with whom God has made His covenant are the ones who return to Him in repentance, worship Him, praise Him, go about in the land serving Him, bow down to Him, prostrate themselves before Him, enjoin good and forbid evil and watch the limits set by Him" (9:111–112).

If in the course of war any of the enemy should seek shelter with the Muslims, he must be given shelter because he would thus have an opportunity of listening to Divine revelation and of learning the wholly beneficent character of the teachings of Islam. Then should he wish to return to his people, he must be conducted back to them in security. "If any of the enemy should seek asylum with thee, grant him asylum so that he may hear the word of Allah; then convey him to his place of security. This is because they are a people who lack knowledge" (9:4).

If at any time the enemy should propose a truce or should show an inclination to agree to a cessation of hostilities, the Muslims should be ready to avail themselves of the offer so that fighting might be terminated or suspended and further damage to life and property obviated. An offer of truce or suspension of hostilities should not be declined merely on the suspicion that it may have been inspired by ulterior motives. It is expected of the Muslims that if they are forced to take up arms, they should embrace every opportunity of putting an end to fighting so that the differences between them and their enemy may be resolved through peaceful methods. "If they incline toward peace, incline thou also toward it, and put thy trust in Allah. Surely, it is He Who is All-Hearing, and All-Knowing. If they intend to deceive thee, then surely Allah is sufficient for thee. He it is Who has strengthened thee with His help and with the believers" (8:62–63).

In pre-Islamic Arabia few prisoners of war were taken. Those who surrendered themselves in the course of a battle, and for whom valuable ransom was not expected, were often killed after the battle. Those who were spared and were not ransomed were distributed among the victors as slaves, and life for them became a succession of misery and suffering. Tribal raids were often organized for the purpose of plunder and for capturing men and women who could be sold as slaves.

The difficulty with regard to prisoners of war was that in the conditions then prevailing there were no regular armies, nor any regular public establishments or institutions. For the purpose of fighting, forces were assembled on an *ad hoc* basis, and each person recruited had to look after himself for everything. Those who wished to be mounted had to provide their own mounts; the rest had to walk. Each person carried his own supplies of dried dates, roasted and ground barley, and water, which were the only provisions available and all that was needed; also, he provided his own arms. The victorious side recouped itself out of spoils gained on the field of battle, including arms, armor, camels, and horses as well as out of the ransom of prisoners of war; failing ransom, they put the captives to work. Prisoners were distributed among the victorious soldiery, the share of each being determined by his contribution in the way of arms, equipment, and the like.

With the advent of Islam, these conditions were greatly modified and everything was placed on a humane basis. No prisoners could be taken except as the result of fighting in the course of a regular war. "It does not behoove a Prophet that he should have captives except when he engages in regular fighting in the land. You desire the goods of this world, while Allah desires for you the Hereafter. Allah is Mighty, Wise" (8:68).

Prisoners taken in the course of regular warfare must not be ill-treated in any way, though proper precautions have to be taken against their escape. Once the fighting is over, prisoners should be released either as a favor or in return for ransom (47:5). If they were not ransomed, they were still distributed among those who had taken part in the fighting, but they had to be treated by those to whom they were assigned as members of their own families. The Prophet's directions were: "You must feed them as you feed yourselves, and clothe them as you clothe yourselves, and if you should set them a hard task, you must help them in it yourselves." If any person to whom a prisoner was assigned was guilty of ill-treating his captive, such conduct became the prisoner's ransom and he was entitled to his freedom. The Prophet observed a Muslim who had raised his whip to strike a prisoner in his charge. The Prophet called out to him: "What are you about to do? Do you not know that God has more power over you than you have over this prisoner?" The man's arm dropped immediately as he said: "Messenger of Allah, I set him free." The Prophet replied: "Thou dost well, or else Allah's wrath would be upon thee."

Any prisoner of war whose ransom remains unpaid is entitled to demand a written statement fixing his ransom. Once that is settled, the prisoner is free to employ himself as he chooses while making the agreed payments toward his ransom. In such cases, the person to whom he has been assigned is admonished to help him as much as possible out of his own resources to enable him to fulfill the terms of the agreement (24:34). In case a dispute arises concerning the amount of installments of the ransom to be paid by the prisoner out of his earnings, the matter is to be settled by the qazi (judge). In fact, the ransoming of captives by the Muslims themselves as a charitable act is highly commended (2:178).

As has been seen, there was a continuous state of war between the Meccans and the Muslims, beginning with the Emigration and continuing until the Treaty of Hudaibiyya established a truce. It so happened that after the battle of Uhud there was a severe famine at Mecca. The Prophet, overlooking all the suffering that the Meccans had inflicted upon him and the Muslims in

Mecca, and the war that the Meccans had started against the Muslims as soon as they had established themselves in Medina, raised a fund from the Muslims, who themselves suffered from extreme privation, and arranged to send relief to Mecca. Later the chief of a powerful tribe became a Muslim. This tribe controlled the route by which grain and other foodstuffs were transported to Mecca, and the chief threatened to put an end to this traffic. The Meccans appealed to the Prophet at Medina, requesting that the chief be dissuaded from carrying his design into effect. The Prophet sent word to the chief, directing him not to interfere with the supplies proceeding to Mecca, and the chief desisted. Thus did the Prophet, during the course of war, deal with a people who had proved themselves bitter and implacable enemies. His generous treatment of them after the fall of Mecca is unique and unmatched in history.

20

Life after Death

LIFE AFTER DEATH IS A SUBJECT ON WHICH SURE knowledge can be gained only through revelation. The Prophet has said: "The conditions of the life after death are such that the eye has not seen them, nor has the ear heard of them, nor can the mind of man conceive of their true reality." Even through revelation man can acquire knowledge of the life after death only in the language of symbol and metaphor. All illustration of the conditions of that life can be by way of similitude only.

Man's life on earth is not in itself a perfect whole: it is incomplete; it lacks fulfillment. Too often it seems to come to an end like a snapped ribbon, leaving loose ends flapping idly. If there is nothing to follow, the co-ordination of values in this life would have little meaning and, indeed, would become almost impossible. There would be no accountability and consequently no responsibility. More than that, there would be no consummation of the deepest yearnings of the human soul. Such realization as is possible in this life is only a twilight experience.

Islam insists on belief in the life after death. There are several matters of belief which Islam regards as essential, but belief in the life after death is concomitant with belief in the Existence of God (5:70). Failing belief in the life after death there is no faith at all. The absence of such belief is almost a negation of, and inconsistent with, belief in a Wise Creator.

Too often has man been apt to say: "There is no life other than our present life. We were without life and now we live; but we shall not be raised again" (23:38). "Man says: 'What! When I am dead shall I be brought forth alive?' Does not man remember that We created him before, when he was naught?" (19:67–68). Man, and indeed the whole universe, has been brought into being from a state of nothingness. It is idle to contend that inasmuch as our observation merely confirms that man dies and his *body* disintegrates, therefore his personality and his existence come to a final end with death. Man's very coming into existence is proof that there is the possibility of continuation. When the fact of man's having been brought into existence through a long process is viewed against the existence of a Wise and All-Powerful Creator, the conclusion is inevitable that man was created for a purpose, and the fulfillment of that purpose demands a continuation of life.

"They say: 'When we shall have become bones and broken particles shall we be really raised up as a new creation?' Say: 'Be ye stones or iron or some created thing which appears hardest in your minds, even then shall you be raised up.' Then will they ask: 'Who shall restore us to life?' Say: 'He Who created you the first time.' They will then shake their heads at thee and say: 'When will it be?' Say: 'Maybe it is nigh. It will be at the time when He will call you.' And then you will respond praising Him, and you will think that you have tarried but a little while" (17:50–53).

It is a misconception that a continuation of life beyond this life must involve the assembly of a dead body's bones and particles after everything has disintegrated and decomposed, so as to reconstitute the body. The body, which is developed for terrestrial existence, is fashioned for the conditions of this life. Life after death cannot and does not mean that the dead will be reassembled and reconstituted upon the earth. Even if that were possible, the earth could not hold a billionth fraction of them. Consequently, the decomposition and disintegration of the human body is completely irrelevant to the possibility of life after death.

The Quran draws attention to the phenomena of sleep and dreams to illustrate that man is capable of undergoing experiences and receiving impressions without physical participation in space and time. These experiences being part of this life, the connection between the soul and the body is no doubt maintained while the experiences last; though their physical co-relations are transformed. There is, as it were, complete realization that the total organism, body and soul, is participating in them. The Quran states: "Allah takes souls unto Himself at death, and during their sleep the souls of those who do not die. Then He retains those on which He has passed a decree of death, and sends the others back for a named period. Therein are Signs for those who reflect" (39:43). The admonition to reflect over the Signs which this phenomenon draws attention to is a clear indication that man can derive an understanding of the nature and reactions of the soul and its condition after death by pondering over his experiences during sleep.

During sleep the body reposes comfortably in bed, in a reduced state of vitality, while the soul undergoes experiences and receives impressions which leave a slight or deep impress upon it, according to the intensity of the experience. Some of these experiences are vivid enough to leave a permanent impress upon the personality. These experiences are not confined to dreams, when the functions of the body have been reduced to a minimum, and the person undergoing the experience is utterly unconscious of anything outside the dimensions of the experience itself. In many cases, people undergo similar experiences in a state of complete wakefulness, though for the moment there is, as it were, a withdrawal from other activity, mental or physical. These are generally described as visions. Dreams and visions, however, must not be confused with the effect produced upon a person's consciousness when he is under hypnotic or mesmeric control or influence. That is an altogether different kind of experience, and it is now well established that such influences and control can be acquired, developed, and exercised through concentration and practice, like any other power or skill.

The Quran invites attention to physical birth into this life for the purpose of illustrating the process of rebirth through which the soul passes after death:

"Does not man see that We have created him from a mere drop of seed? Yet behold, he is given to constant arguing. He coins similitudes for Us and forgets the process of his own creation. He says: 'Who can quicken the bones when they are decayed?' Say: 'He Who created them the first time will quicken them; and He knows every kind of creation full well, He who produces for you fire out of the green tree, and behold, you kindle from it. Has not He Who created the heavens and the earth power to create the like of them?' Yea, and He is indeed the Supreme Creator, All-Knowing" (36:78–82). Attention is here drawn to the process of man's own creation for the purpose of this life. The flesh, the bones, the muscles, the blood, the brain, and indeed all the faculties and the whole complicated and yet wonderfully co-ordinated machinery of the human body constituting a complete microcosm is all potentially contained in less than a millionth part of a drop of fluid. The Wise Creator knows what He is doing. In accord with the manifold provisions that He has already made, the drop of fluid in due course experiences a new creation at birth and matures into an intelligent human being, capable of the highest attainments in every field of life. The center of the whole process is the soul. The body is an essential part for the purpose of life in the conditions of this world. Up to a point, the soul and the body together constitute a unit and are indissoluble; then dissolution comes and that is the end of life upon earth, but that is not the end of life itself. At death the functions of the body come to an end, and except for considerations of decency and respect for the dead, it is immaterial how the body be disposed of. The soul then enters upon a process of rebirth, during the course of which it acquires a new frame, and the result is another organism for the purposes of the new life. Thus "the bones are quickened," but they are quickened out of the soul itself. "He knows every kind of creation full well" indicates that this "quickening of the bones" will be a new kind of creation. The Wise and All-Powerful Creator Who created man from an insignificant drop of fluid and created the whole universe for the fulfillment of the purpose of human life has power to endow the human soul with the capacity to develop into a new organism; and He has power to transport the soul into another universe in which it may find its complete fulfillment.

"Verily, We created man from an extract of clay; then We placed him as a drop of seed in a safe depository, then We fashioned the clot into a shapeless lump; then We fashioned bones out of this shapeless lump; then We clothed the bones with flesh; then We developed it into another creation. So blessed be Allah, the Wisest of Creators. Then after that you must surely die. Then on the day of resurrection will you be raised up" (23:13–17). "Then We developed it into another creation" refers to the stage when the body is quickened by the soul. After death, the soul undergoes the same process to be "developed into another creation." At death, with reference to the fuller life awaiting it, the soul is, so to speak, in the condition of the sperm drop. It passes through a stage which may be compared metaphorically to the womb, where it develops the faculties that may be needed in, and would be appropriate to, the conditions of the Hereafter. Its birth into a new life after passing through the process of developing its faculties to a certain degree, is the resurrection.

Even before that stage is reached, the soul is alive in the conditions of its new existence and is endowed with incipient responses, like those of an embryo in the womb.

"Does man think that he is to be left to himself, without purpose and uncontrolled? Was he not a drop of fluid emitted forth, then he became a clot, then God shaped and proportioned him, then He made of him a pair, male and female. Has not such a One the power to raise the dead to life?" (75:37–71). There can be only one answer to that question: "Yea, for He is the All-Knowing Creator."

Those who reject the life after death do so because they refuse to let reality influence their judgment. They are too arrogant to admit the possibility of even the Creator having power over them to continue their existence in the Hereafter and to call them to account for what they did in this life. "Your God is One God. As to those who do not believe in the Hereafter, their hearts are strangers to truth, and they are full of arrogance. Undoubtedly, Allah knows what they conceal and what they disclose. Surely, He loves not the arrogant. When it is said to them: 'What think ye of that which your Lord has revealed?' they say: 'Mere fables of the men of old' " (16:23–25).

He who is still hard to convince is admonished: "Man is self-destroyed: How ungrateful! From what does He create him? From a drop of seed! He creates him and proportions him; then He makes the way easy for him; then He causes him to die and assigns a grave to him; then, when He pleases, He will raise him up again" (80:18–23). The grave here does not mean the tomb in which the body is interred. Not all bodies are buried in tombs; many are cremated, some are devoured by wild beasts, some perish in a conflagration, some drown in water. The grave refers to the phase through which the soul passes after death, and in which it continues till resurrection, which corresponds to the phase through which the embryo passes in the womb while it develops the organs and faculties appropriate to its life upon earth.

That the soul is not without feeling and perception even during that stage appears from the following: "Those whom the angels cause to die while they are wronging their souls will offer submission, saying: 'We used not to do any evil.' Nay, surely Allah knows well what you used to do. Then enter the gates of hell to dwell therein. Evil indeed is the abode of the arrogant" (16:29–30). Similarly, with regard to the righteous it is said: "For those

who do good there is good in this world, and the home of the Hereafter is even better. Excellent indeed is the abode of the righteous.
. . . To those whom the angels cause to die while they are pure
they will say: 'Peace be unto you! Enter heaven because of what
you used to do" (16:31–33).

It is obvious that the conditions of the life after death, though
capable of being expressed to some degree in terms of human
speech, have not the same character as the conditions of this life.
Compared with the conditions of this life, they are purely spiritual,
and yet they are so manifested that they are felt and experienced
and realized with far greater intensity than are the conditions of
this life in the course of existence here. It is not possible with our
present faculties to realize the true nature of the conditions of the
life after death. All that is possible is to attempt some approximate,
intuitive understanding of them. As the Prophet has said, it is not
possible for the mind of man to conceive of the true reality of these
conditions. The Quran states: "No soul knows what bliss is kept
hidden for it as a reward for its good works" (32:18).

A study of the Quran reveals that each human being through
his or her conduct during this life develops certain qualities or defects in the soul which render it capable of the appreciation and
enjoyment of the conditions of the life after death or which cause
it to react painfully to those conditions. We see, for instance, that
a healthy organism reacts agreeably to the conditions of this life
and finds joy and happiness in them. A defective or diseased
organism reacts painfully to those conditions of this life which
affect it. For instance, the light of the sun, refreshing to healthy
eyes and a great source of delight on account of the facilities it
provides for human intercourse and the performance of daily tasks
and occupations, and the beauties that it reveals, becomes a source
of intense pain and discomfort to one with sore eyes, so much so
that if they are not quickly shielded from the bright rays of the
sun they may suffer permanent injury and even loss of sight. The
same applies in respect of the other senses: hearing, smell, taste,
touch, sense of heat and cold, and the muscular sense.

Similar is the case with the spiritual senses. The reactions of the
soul in the life hereafter will be governed by the condition in
which it enters upon that life. A diseased soul will react painfully,
very painfully, to the conditions of the life after death. It may
suffer indescribable tortures, according to the degree to which its
faculties have become diseased during its life on earth. A healthy

soul will react joyfully to all the conditions of the life to come.
"We call to witness the soul and its perfect proportioning. He
revealed to it what is wrong for it and what is right for it. The
one indeed will surely prosper who purifies the soul, and the one
who corrupts it will be ruined" (91:8–11).

The same concept is expressed in a different manner. "Verily,
he who comes to his Lord a sinner, for him is hell; he shall neither
die therein nor live" (20:75). This means that he who enters upon
the life after death with a diseased soul will have to face prolonged
suffering, from which he will not be able to obtain release through
complete extinction, for the soul is immortal, and does not suffer
extinction; nor will he be, during this period of suffering, in the
full enjoyment of life, for his existence will be only a series of
miseries and torments. "But he who comes to Him as a believer,
having acted righteously, for such are the highest ranks:
Gardens of Eternity, beneath which streams flow; they will abide
therein forever. That is the recompense of those who keep themselves pure" (20:76–77). Those who keep their souls pure, that is,
those who develop their spiritual faculties in this life into a state
of purity which is the state of perfect health for the soul, will
experience spiritual reactions that are blissful, the intensity of the
reactions depending upon the degree of attunement achieved by
the soul in this life.

The whole concept is well illustrated in the Quran, where the
consequences of certain types of conduct in this life are described
as defects and shortcomings that will affect the soul in the life after
death. For instance, the Quran says that he who is blind in this
life will be blind in the life after death, and will find himself even
more astray (17:73). This obviously does not mean that a person
who is physically blind in this life will be spiritually blind in the
next. Blindness here means spiritual blindness. He who has failed
to develop spiritual insight in this life will be blind in the life to
come. For instance: "How many a city have We destroyed which
was given to wrongdoing, so that it is fallen down on its roofs, and
how many a well is deserted and how many a lofty castle is in
ruins! Have they not traveled in the land, so that they may have
hearts wherewith to understand, and ears wherewith to hear?
For indeed it is not the eyes that are blind, but it is the hearts
which are in the bosoms that are blind" (22:46–47). This shows
clearly that the failure to observe, to ponder, and to take heed
gradually deprives a person of spiritual insight. He becomes

spiritually blind. Such persons, when brought face to face with
the consequences of their neglect or indifference, will exclaim:
"Had we but listened and exercised our judgment we should not
have been among the inmates of the blazing fire" (67:11). He
who develops the faculty of observation and reflects over what he
observes and draws the right conclusions therefrom, has his
spiritual insight sharpened and he will enter upon the life to come
in a state capable of experiencing the utmost delight in reaction
to the conditions of that life.

Again, it is stated that those who are placed in authority and
misuse that authority, thus creating disorder in the land instead of
strengthening and cementing human relationships, will be afflicted
with spiritual deafness and blindness (47:23–24). Persistence in
such a course deprives a person of the faculty of appreciating
good advice given to him or of drawing a lesson from his own
observations and reflections. He becomes haughty and arrogant,
and cannot tolerate any questioning of his own judgment or
any criticism of the manner in which he exercises authority.

In the same way, whoever turns away from Divine guidance
and closes his eyes to it is bound to lose his spiritual sight. He may
pride himself on his sharp perceptions and clear insight and may
even consider himself above the need of any guidance, but by
turning away from Divine guidance he is in effect destroying his
spiritual insight. "Whoso will turn away from My Reminder, his
will be a strait life, and on the Day of Resurrection We shall raise
him up blind. He will say: 'My Lord, why hast Thou raised me
up blind, while I possessed sight before?' God will say: 'Thus it
must be. Our Signs came to thee and thou dost disregard them.
In like manner will thou be disregarded this day' " (20:125–127).

The Quran explains that all human action leaves an impress
upon the soul and that the soul when it enters upon the life to
come carries the sum total of this impress with it, and reacts in
that life accordingly. The record of a person's acts and their
consequences will be presented to him, as in an open book, and he
will be told to read his book and to follow the course that it lays
down for him. His reactions will be determined by his record. He
will himself render an account of the manner in which he spent
his life on earth and that very account will constitute his reward
or his punishment. "Every man's works have We fastened to his
neck; and on the day of resurrection We shall place before him a
book which he will find wide open. It will be said to him: 'Read

thy book; sufficient is thine own soul this day as a reckoner
against thee.' He who follows the right way follows it only for the
good of his own soul; and he who goes astray, goes astray only to
his own loss. No bearer of burden shall bear the burden of
another" (17:14–16).

The state of the organs with which the soul will enter upon its
new life will correspond to the spiritual condition of its faculties
at the time of death, and their reactions to the conditions of the
new life will be manifested accordingly. These reactions will be
patent and irrefutable proof of the person's conduct and actions
in this life. A spiritually defective and diseased ear or eye or
tongue or skin shall, through its reactions to the conditions of the
new life, bear witness to the evil use to which it was put in this life.
"When they face the torment their ears, and their eyes, and their
skins will bear witness against them as to what they used to do.
They will say to their skins: 'Why bear ye witness against us?'
These will reply: 'Allah has made us to speak as He has made
everything else to speak.' He it is who created you the first time,
and unto Him have you been brought back. You did not apprehend that your ears and your eyes and your skins would bear witness against you; nay, you thought that even Allah did not know
much of what you did. That notion of yours, which you entertained concerning your Lord, has ruined you. So now you have
become of those who are the losers" (41:21–24).

It is emphasized that the consciousness of living every moment
of one's life in the sight of God is the most effective deterrent
against wrongdoing and the most potent incentive toward
righteous action. Those who live their lives in the full consciousness of being in the sight of God every moment shall enter upon
the new life in perfect spiritual health and all their reactions will
be joyful. "Those who fear their Lord will be conducted to the
Garden in groups, until, when they approach it, and its gates are
opened, its keepers will say to them: 'Peace be upon you; you
have attained to the state of bliss, so enter it, abiding therein.'
They will say: 'All praise belongs to Allah; who has fulfilled His
promise to us, and has bestowed upon us this vast region for an
inheritance, permitting us to make our abode in the Garden
wherever we please.' How excellent, then, is the reward of the
righteous workers" (39:74–75).

Heaven and hell are not separate, defined and divided regions,
but exist, as it were, coextensively. The Quran says that the extent

of heaven is equal to the whole extent of the heavens and the earth (57:22). Someone once asked the Prophet: "If heaven occupies the whole extent of the heavens and the earth, then where is hell?" He replied with another question: "When there is day, where is night?" Night, of course, means the absence of light. Hell means a state of the soul whose faculties are defective or diseased and whose reactions, consequently, are painful in contrast with the pleasant and agreeable reactions of a healthy soul. It is true that the phraseology employed constantly creates in the mind physical images, but in the conditions of human existence in this life that is inescapable. The only language that man can understand is the language to which he is accustomed. It is only by means of paraphrase and explanation that an effort can be made to bring the human mind closer to some understanding of these conditions, the reality of which is indeed beyond the ken of man.

The Quran explains that the conditions of the life after death will constitute symbolical representation of man's thoughts, designs, and actions in this life, and will be the consequences, or fruits thereof. "Give glad tidings to those who believe and act righteously, that for them are Gardens beneath which streams flow. Whenever they are given a portion of the fruits therefrom they will say: 'This is what was given us aforetime'; and upon them will be bestowed gifts in resemblance" (2:26). This shows that when the righteous are presented with the fruits of the Garden in the life to come, they will recognize them as something of which they have had enjoyment in this life also. They will be reminded of the spiritual joys experienced in this life, and they will recognize the resemblance between them and the fruits presented to them in Paradise. In the same way it is stated that in the life after death the righteous will be able to choose the kind of fruit they prefer and the kind of meat they desire. The meat referred to is "the flesh of birds" (56:21–22). Now, "bird" in the phraseology of the Quran also means "conduct" or "action" (17:14). Here again the reference to fruits and the flesh of birds clearly signifies the consequences or the fruits of righteous action.

"The similitude of the Garden promised to the righteous is: Therein are streams of water which corrupt not; and streams of milk of which the taste changes not; and streams of wine, a delight to those who drink, and streams of pure honey. In it will they have all kinds of fruit, and forgiveness from their Lord"

(47:16). The verse begins by saying that this is a similitude of the Garden promised to the righteous. The streams and their contents signify certain spiritual qualities or conditions. For instance, water signifies prosperity of every kind; milk signifies knowledge of Divine attributes; wine signifies man's love for God (which is why we often hear of a person being drunk or intoxicated with joy or with love of a person or of God); and honey signifies the Grace and Mercy of God. In connection with the mention of wine in this context, it should be remembered that this wine is not liquor. The Quran describes it as "sparkling, white, delicious to the drinkers, wherein there is no intoxication nor will they be exhausted thereby" (37:47–48). Again: "Out of a flowing spring, no headache will they get therefrom, nor will they be intoxicated" (56:19–20).

Conversely, the torments of the wicked are described as "Allah's kindled fire, which rises over the hearts," which again clearly means that these are the consequences of evil conduct which, through the operation of Divine law, assume the quality of kindled fire rising over the heart, constituting a torment for the heart (104:7–8).

The Quran states, for instance, that hell has seven gates (15:45). Hell not being a defined, physical region, "gates" in this context can only mean ways of approach or means of entrance. The words "seven" and "seventy" are often used in Arabic as meaning several or many. But even if seven be taken as having a precise significance in this context it may be said that the torments associated with the concept of hell will be experienced through seven senses: sight, hearing, smell, taste, touch, the feeling of heat and cold, and what may be called the muscular sense, or feeling of fatigue. The Quran refers to the various torments which might be experienced by a diseased soul. When the transgressors see the torment they will realize that all power belongs to God and that God is severe in punishment (2:166). They will hear its raging and roaring from afar (25:13). They will drink boiling water; they will sip it and will not be able to swallow it easily (14:17–18). They will taste neither sleep nor pleasant drink save boiling water and a fluid that stinks (78:25–26). Their food will be dry, bitter, thorny herbage; it will neither nourish nor satisfy hunger (88:7–8). Hell will be for them a bed as well as a covering, so that the torment will affect them through the sense of touch (7:42). When they are thrown into a confined place chained together, they will wish for death, but death will not come to them (25:14). Their drink will be either boiling or intensely cold, both difficult to swallow, and various kinds of other torments of a similar nature they shall endure (38:58–59). There will be chains and iron collars imposing the torment of close confinement (76:5). Some faces on that day will be downcast, lined, weary (88:3–4). But the greatest torment will be that God will not speak to them, nor look at them, nor purify them (2:175; 3:78). This will be the most terrifying and the most tormenting of their experiences. Then they will realize as never before how completely they have placed themselves at the pole opposite to the purpose of their creation, which is to become an image or a manifestation of the attributes of God (51:57).

On the other hand, the conditions in which the righteous will find themselves, and their reactions to those conditions, will be pleasant and agreeable in respect of every one of their faculties and senses. Their faces will reflect joy; they will be well pleased with their labor (88:9–10). They will hear no idle talk, nor any falsehood (78:36), nor anything vain, but only "Peace" (19:63). They will be welcomed with greetings of peace (25:76). "They will not hear therein any vain or sinful talk, except only the word of salutation, 'Peace, peace' " (56:26–27). The angels will greet them with: "Peace be on you. You have arrived at a joyful state, so enter it, and dwell therein forever" (39:74). They will not feel the unpleasant effects of heat or cold (76:14). God will provide for them a pure drink (76:22). They will dwell among gardens and springs (15:46). Fatigue and lassitude will not touch them (15:49). They will enjoy perfect comfort and the fragrance of happiness (56:90). They will ever be in rapture (76:12). Their faces will exhibit the freshness of bliss, and they will be given to drink of a pure beverage, sealed with musk (83:25–27). They will be in the midst of a vast kingdom of bliss; and they will say: "All worthiness of praise belongs to Allah, Who has fulfilled His promise to us, and has bestowed upon us this domain for an inheritance, making our abode in the Garden wherever we please" (39:75).

The supreme triumph, however, will be the realization of having won the pleasure of Allah (3:16; 57:21). "Their Lord gives them glad tidings of Mercy from Him and of His pleasure" (9:21). "Allah has promised to those who believe, men and women, Gardens beneath which streams flow, wherein they will abide, and delightful dwelling places in Gardens of Eternity, and the pleasure of Allah, which is the greatest of all. That is the supreme triumph" (9:72). "Allah is well pleased with them and they are well pleased with Him" (9:100).

One important question in connection with the conditions of the life after death is whether they will be permanent and everlasting or will come to an end. The Quran teaches that while the rewards and joys experienced in the life after death will be everlasting and ever intensifying, the pains and torments will come to an end; all mankind will ultimately find admission to the Grace and Mercy of God. We have been told that mankind has been created for the purpose of becoming the manifestations of God's attributes (51:57). That being the Divine purpose, it follows that it must be fulfilled in respect of everyone. God says: "I will inflict My punishment on whom I will; but My Mercy encompasses all things" (7:157). Indeed, mankind has been created for the fulfillment of God's Mercy (11:120). When pain, punishment, and torment will have achieved their purpose, which is curative, and is in itself a manifestation of God's Mercy, Divine Mercy will then enable each human being to react joyfully to the conditions of the life after death.

The Prophet has said that a time will come when hell will be empty, and the cool breezes of God's Mercy will blow through it. Duration in the Hereafter is within God's knowledge alone and He alone knows how long any particular condition will last. It is common experience that periods of joy and happiness seem to race by, while moments of pain and anxiety appear unending. Pain and torment will appear long, for the torment suffered under the operation of Divine law will be severely felt, and no alleviation of it may be in sight. But eternity is infinite, and in each case a stage will be reached when torment will cease, pain will disappear, and all will be joy. As the experience of pain and punishment will be corrective and reformatory, each succeeding stage will bring an amelioration, but so long as the process is incomplete, the over-all reaction will continue to be painful. The Quran states that the punishment of evildoers will appear to be unending, but it will in fact be terminated when God wills (11:108). The joys of the life after death are also subject to God's Will, but with respect to those, God's Will has been announced; they are a "gift that shall not be cut off" (11:109). For the righteous there is an "unending reward" (95:7).

Thus there will be continuous progress for all in the life after death. Those under sentence will work out their sentence, not as a penance, but as a curative process designed to cure the soul of the defects and disorders accumulated in its life upon earth and to bring it into a state of purity and health in which it can react with joy and pleasure to the conditions of the life after death. The righteous will be continuously praying for, and seeking the perfection of, their light (66:9). They will be greeted by their Lord with: "O, soul at peace, return to thy Lord; thou well pleased with Him, and He well pleased with thee. So enter thou among My chosen servants, and enter thou My Garden" (89:28–31). In these words the righteous are told that because of their unending quest for knowledge of the attributes of God—that they may become perfect manifestations of those attributes—heaven is a state of being in which there is continuous progress and continuous action. Because the attributes of God are without limit, man's seeking to become the perfect manifestation of God's attributes will be endless.

21

The Role of Islam

MANKIND HAS DEFINITELY ENTERED UPON A NEW era. Its outstanding characteristic is the rapid forward march of science and technology. Man's knowledge of, and mastery over, the forces of nature is fast expanding. The prospect ahead is instinct with eager hope, but there is also an obverse of fear and dread. All increase of knowledge is an accession of strength and should be welcomed as a Divine bounty. The fear results from doubt concerning the application of the vast knowledge to which mankind is becoming heir in daily increasing volume and from apprehension of the almost unlimited power which such knowledge could place in man's hands. Is it possible to ensure that that application will be wholly beneficent in the service of man, so that all fear of misapplication can be eliminated?

Inasmuch as man has been given free choice in these matters, there can be no guarantee, one way or the other, how knowledge and power might be used and applied. It is, however, the province of religion to provide the guidance which will foster beneficence and will at the same time eliminate or reduce to a minimum the fear and dread attendant upon the misapplication of God's bounties.

The imperative need is for moral and spiritual values to control and regulate the application of the daily increasing stores of power which science is making available to man. The alternative is disaster. For the achievement of this purpose, Islam insists upon firm faith in the Unity of God and a clear concept of man's accountability, both here and Hereafter, in respect of his conduct. This would ensure acceptance of Divine guidance, and conformity to that guidance would result in righteous action (5:70).

Belief in the Unity of God means recognition and acceptance of the truth that there is no other being worthy of man's worship and homage. He is the sole and perfect source of all Beneficence. Everything else is merely a means which He has created and provided for man's service. He has neither partner nor associate in His Being or in His attributes, and there is none like unto Him. The Quran is very emphatic on that.

"He is Allah, the One; Allah, the Independent and Besought of all. He begets not, nor is He begotten, and there is none like unto Him" (112:2–5).

There are clear indications in the Quran that mankind's repudiation in practice of the Unity, Majesty, and Power of God would convert the very bounties bestowed by God upon man for the purpose of the enrichment of human life into the instruments of man's ruin and destruction.

The Prophet has warned graphically against the trials and tribulations of our present age. When asked about the remedy for such sufferings, he said that it could be found in the opening and concluding verses of the eighteenth chapter of the Quran. The opening verses of that chapter read as follows: "All praise belongs to Allah Who has sent down the Book to His servant and has not put therein any deviation, He has made it a guardian, that it may give warning of a grievous chastisement from Him, and that it may give those who believe and act righteously the glad tidings that they shall have a good reward wherein they shall abide for ever. . . . So haply thou wilt grieve thyself to death for sorrow after them if they believe not in this discourse. Verily, We have made all that is on the earth as an adornment for it, that We may try them as to which of them is best in conduct, and We shall make all that is thereon a barren waste" (18:2–9).

The "grievous chastisement" referred to here may arrive in two stages: "Watch thou for the day when the sky will bring forth a visible smoke that will envelop the people. This will be a painful torment. Then will the people cry: 'Lord, remove from us the torment; truly we are believers'. . . . We shall remove the torment for a little while, but you will certainly revert to your evil courses. On the day when We shall seize you with the great seizure, then certainly We shall exact retribution" (44:11–13, 16–17).

In this context, attention may also be invited to the following: "An inquirer inquires concerning the chastisement which shall fall upon those who believe not, which none can repel. It is from Allah, Lord of Great Ascents. . . . They see it to be far off, but We see it to be nigh. The day when the sky will become like molten copper and the mountains will become like flakes of wool and a friend will not inquire after a friend, though they will be in sight of one another. A guilty one would fain ransom himself from the torment of that day by offering his children, and his wife, and brothers, and his kinsfolk, who might give him shelter, and all those who are on the earth, if only thus he might save himself. But no: surely, it is a flame of fire, stripping off the skin, even to the extremities of the body. It will overtake him who turned his back and retreated, and hoarded wealth and withheld it" (70:2-4, 7-19).

It is characteristic of the Quran that wherever an attribute of God is mentioned it has reference to the subject matter of the context. It is not without significance that the attribute "Lord of Great Ascents" is mentioned in connection with this warning of a severe chastisement. The nature of the chastisement is described in the succeeding verses, but the mention of this attribute shows that the chastisement will have an element of great heights, or graduated ascents, about it. The skies becoming like molten copper would indicate, among other things, the generation of intense heat. Mountains becoming like flakes of wool would signify tremendous impacts which would blow up and scatter mountains. Stripping off of the skin even to the extremities of the body would appear to point to some of the effects of radiation. The swiftness with which the horror might spread is indicated by its overtaking those who turn back and seek to escape.

The concluding verses of the eighteenth chapter, to which the Prophet drew attention, run as follows:

"On that day we shall leave some of them to surge against others, and the trumpet will be sounded. Then shall We gather them all together. On that day We shall present the torment, face to face, to those who believe not—those whose eyes are under a veil so as not to heed My warnings, and they cannot afford even to hear. Do those who believe not think that they can take My servants as protectors instead of Me? Surely, We have prepared the fire as an entertainment for those who believe not. Say: 'Shall We tell you of those who are the greatest losers in respect of their works? Those whose effort is lost in search after things pertaining to the life of this world, and they imagine they are doing great works.' Those are they who disbelieve in the Signs of their Lord, and in the meeting with Him. So their works are vain, and on the Day of Judgment We shall give them no weight. That is their reward—torment, because they disbelieved and made a jest of My Signs and My Messengers. Truly, those who believe and act righteously will have the Gardens of Eternity for an abode, wherein they will abide; they will not desire any change therefrom. Say: 'If the ocean became ink for the words of my Lord, surely the ocean would be exhausted before the words of my Lord came to an end, even though We brought the like thereof as further help.' Say: 'I am only a man like yourselves; it is revealed to me that your Lord is only One God.' So let him who hopes to meet his Lord act righteously, and let him make none sharer of the worship due unto his Lord" (18:100–111).

Here the chastisement is described as taking the form of peoples surging against each other, in consequence of which veritable hell would be let loose, and the earth would be converted into a barren waste. The spiritual cause of this conflict, of this chastisement, is described as the taking of God's servants as protectors, instead of Him. The remedy indicated is, "Your Lord is only One God. So let him who hopes to meet his Lord act righteously, and make none sharer of the worship due unto his Lord."

The true remedy, therefore, for the ills that afflict mankind to-day and that threaten to overwhelm it tomorrow is for man to turn to God with the single-minded purpose of making his peace with Him, having sincerely determined that in all matters whatsoever his guiding rule shall be: "Thy will and not mine." Truly, mankind stands again on the brink of a pit of fire. God's Grace and Mercy alone can save it. To win His Grace and Mercy, mankind must turn to Him alone, the One God, Ever Gracious, Most Merciful, discarding all and everything that may ever have been associated with Him, anything that may have displaced Him in men's minds, any being beside Him from whom mankind may at any time have besought protection. There is no other way.

Inasmuch as the indications are that the cataclysm would overtake mankind in consequence of certain causes (18:103–107), the real and effective remedy is the removal of those causes. Once this is done, mankind may be led out of the shadow of the cataclysm into the light. God's purpose is to lead mankind into His Grace and Mercy. His purpose is not to punish. Misfortunes and calamities follow upon defaults and transgressions, but the gates of God's Mercy are ever open, and everyone may enter therein through humble supplication, sincere repentance, and righteous action. Direct communion with God is the spiritual remedy.

N

"Why should Allah punish you if you make proper use of His bounties and if you believe? Surely, Allah is Appreciating, All-Knowing" (4:148). "When those who believe in Our Signs come to thee, say: 'Peace be unto you, your Lord has charged Himself with Mercy, so that whoso among you does evil in ignorance and repents thereafter and amends his conduct, then He is Most Forgiving, Merciful'" (6:55).

Here is an assurance of great comfort: "O My servants, who have committed excesses against their own souls, despair not of the Mercy of Allah; surely, Allah forgives all sins. Verily, He is Most Forgiving, Merciful. Turn ye to your Lord, and submit yourselves to Him before there comes unto you the punishment; for then shall you not be helped. And follow in the highest degree that which has been revealed to you from your Lord before the torment comes upon you unawares, while you perceive not" (39:54–56). The day will come "when some faces shall be bright and some faces shall be downcast. . . . As for those whose faces will be bright, they will be in the Mercy of Allah; therein will they abide" (3:107–108).

Once mankind turns to the One God in sincere repentance, He will lead it out of the shadows and the darknesses into the light. He will guide man along the paths of peace: "O people of the Book, there has come to you Our Messenger, who unfolds to you much of what you had hidden of the Book, and passes over much. There has come to you indeed, from Allah, a Light and a clear Book. Thereby does Allah guide those who seek His pleasure, along the paths of peace, and leads them out of every kind of darkness into the light by His will, and guides them along the right path" (5:16–17). Again: "Allah is the friend of those who believe: He brings them out of every kind of darkness into light. Those who believe not, their friends are the transgressors, who bring them out of light into every kind of darkness" (2:258).

All knowledge proceeds from God. Man encompasses only so much of it as God pleases. "He knows what is before them and what is behind them; and they encompass nothing of His knowledge save what He pleases. His knowledge extends over the heavens and the earth; and the care of them burdens Him not. He is the Most High, the Great" (2:256).

He Who has, in due order, vouchsafed to man the knowledge of the properties of the atom and of the principles of fission and fusion, surely has it in His power to bestow upon man the knowledge and comprehension of principles which would furnish adequate safeguards and full immunity against the aggressive use of nuclear power. "There is not a thing but with Us are the treasures thereof, and We send it not down except in determined measure" (15:22).

God constantly reveals Himself in a new state. All His attributes are manifested continuously. None of them ever falls into disuse. Having revealed Himself as the Creator of nuclear power, He surely could go on to reveal Himself as its guardian and controller, for all is within His power and under His control: "Of Him do beg all that are in the heavens and the earth. Every day He reveals Himself in a different state" (55:30).

It is only by turning to Him that security may be achieved. He surely has power to inspire the minds of those who are today in control of nuclear power, and are in a position to determine and direct its application, to agree upon measures which would ensure that such power shall be used only for the beneficent service of man, and shall not be employed for his destruction. He also has power to drive away from positions of authority those who continue to resist His will, and to oppose His designs. "Say, O Allah, Lord of Sovereignty, Thou bestowest sovereignty upon whomsoever Thou pleasest; and Thou takest away sovereignty from whomsoever Thou pleasest. Thou exaltest whomsoever Thou pleasest and Thou abasest whomsoever Thou pleasest. In Thy hand is all good. Thou surely hast power to do all things. Thou makest the night pass into the day, and makest the day pass into the night. Thou bringest forth the living from the dead, and bringest forth the dead from the living; and Thou bestowest upon whomsoever Thou pleasest without measure" (3:27–28). We must, therefore, turn to Him, to Him alone, the True, the Living, the One God, and humbly beseech Him to make our night pass into day, and to bring us forth alive out of death.

This imperative confronts all mankind, Muslim and non-Muslim alike. There are over four hundred million Muslims today, but they will be the first to recognize that the last few centuries have been for them a period of decline from which they are only just beginning to emerge. The decline has been particularly noticeable in the sphere of moral and spiritual values. It started with the progressive neglect of the guidance expounded in the Quran, and was intensified by an increasing proneness toward juristic hairsplitting and legal fictions, a rigid insistence upon

fanciful interpretations of the letter and a cynical disregard of the
lifegiving spirit (25:31).

Since the turn of the century, however, there have been encouraging signs of the revival of Islamic values and of a rebirth of
the true Islamic spirit. The dynamic character of the guidance
contained in the Quran is being recognized and appreciated to
an increasing degree every day, more particularly in relation
to the problems to which the astonishing advance of science
and technology during the last quarter of a century has given rise.
In a sense it may be affirmed that there has been a fresh revelation of some aspects of that guidance and of its application to the
pattern and problems of human life in the era unfolding before
our eyes. This has stimulated new yearnings and an eager reaching out toward moral and spiritual ideals. Muslim peoples every-
where feel themselves being drawn closer together through their
recognition of, and devotion to, common ideals and the spiritual
affinities that inspire and bind them. What is even more striking
and encouraging is that there is evidence in the West of eagerness
for better understanding of Islamic values and of a sympathetic
approach to the problems and difficulties facing the Muslim
peoples. An altogether new and welcome spirit of sympathy,
understanding, and appreciation, is abroad, which is a good
augury for the difficult times that lie ahead. Only through sympathetic understanding and appreciation can doubts and sus-
picions be laid at rest, trust and confidence generated, and
beneficent co-operation fostered.

The main groups of the Muslim peoples occupy, as it were, a
middle belt from the Atlantic to the Pacific. Beginning with
northwestern Africa, the indigenous populations of Morocco,
Tunisia, and Algeria are wholly Muslim. Libya, Egypt, Northern
Sudan, coastal Eritrea, and Somaliland, are almost wholly Muslim, the Coptic minority in Egypt being the only notable exception. No census has been taken in Ethiopia, where the Amharic
section of the population is in a position of dominance, but it is
estimated that the Muslims constitute nearly half the total
population. Along the west coast of Africa, Mauretania, Senegal,
Mali, and Guinea are largely Muslim; Gambia, Sierra Leone, and
Ghana have sizable Muslim populations; northern Nigeria is
largely Muslim. There is a scattering of Muslims in most of the
other neighboring countries. Syria, Jordan, Iraq, Saudi Arabia,
Yemen, Muscat, and the Arab sheikdoms along the southern and

eastern seaboard of Arabia and along the Persian Gulf are wholly Muslim. Israel has a small Muslim minority. Lebanon has, officially, a Christian majority, but no census has been taken in recent years, and the Muslims claim that owing to their higher birth rate and their lower emigration from the country as compared with the Christian population, they are now in a majority.

Turkey, Iran, Afghanistan, and West Pakistan are almost wholly Muslim. There are fifty million Muslims in India. East Pakistan is seventy-five per cent Muslim. Ceylon and Burma have small Muslim minorities. Malaya has a Muslim majority. Indonesia is ninety per cent Muslim. There is a sprinkling of Muslims in Thailand, Vietnam, Laos, and Cambodia. There is a Muslim minority in the Philippines and in the Fiji Islands.

Sinkiang and the northwest provinces of China have a majority of Muslims among their population. The southwest province of Yunnan has over a million Muslims. It is estimated that there are altogether more than forty million Muslims in China. The central Asian Soviets of the U.S.S.R. are predominantly Muslim.

The vitality and vigor of the various Muslim communities is testified to by the missionary activities being carried on in most parts of the world. The greater part of Muslim missionary activity in the past has been by way of individual effort, inasmuch as it is the duty of every Muslim to "call people to the way of the Lord." In recent years, however, organized effort for the propagation of Islam has been undertaken in addition to the missionary effort of Arab agencies, merchants, and travelers in Africa by the Ahmadiyya Movement in Islam, founded by Mirza Ghulam Ahmad in 1889 at Qadian in India, with its present headquarters at Rabwah in West Pakistan. The purpose of the Movement is to revive Islamic values drawn from the Quran and the example of the Prophet, in every sphere of life, and to carry far and wide the message of Islam, with particular emphasis on its application to the present age. The missionary activities of the movement outside Muslim countries have met with an encouraging measure of success, particularly in East and West Africa, where in several areas there is good prospect of the rapid spread of the faith in the near future. The Movement has also established missions in some countries of Europe, for instance, England, the Netherlands, the Scandinavian countries, Germany, and Switzerland.

In England several mosques and places of Muslim worship have been established in recent years. The best known are the

Shahjahan mosque in Woking, Surrey, and the London mosque in Southfields. The London mosque was built with funds contributed by the women of the Ahmadiyya Movement, and stands as a tribute to their zeal and sincerity. The mosque at the Hague was also built with funds contributed by the women of the Movement. The Movement has built mosques and established missions in Hamburg and Frankfurt in West Germany. Plans for building mosques in Zürich, Copenhagen, and Nüremberg are under consideration. Small but quite active Muslim communities have already been established in all these places, and there is a scattering of European Muslims throughout the Continent.

In the United States of America, Muslim communities have been established in more than a score of cities. They are composed in the main of colored people, but Islam is also attracting attention among the white sections of the population. The Ahmadiyya Movement established its first center in the United States, between the two world wars, in Chicago, Illinois. Its present headquarters are in Washington, D.C. The activities of the Movement in the United States fill an essential need. Its membership now runs into thousands and the results of its efforts, particularly in the sphere of moral and spiritual values, are very striking. Its members are inspired by a high sense of duty and obligation toward their fellow beings regardless of color, race, or creed, and the moral standards aimed at and achieved are indeed high. The Movement's centers are of a genuinely international character, where men and women meet each other as true brothers and sisters without any trace of distrust or discrimination. There is eagerness on all sides to cut across barriers of every description and to co-operate in utter sincerity toward the promotion of the welfare of all.

The beautiful mosque and Islamic Center on Massachusetts Avenue in Washington, D.C., established through the efforts of the embassies of Muslim states represented in Washington, is doing excellent work through meetings and lectures organized by it. The Ahmadiyya Movement also maintains a mosque at its center in Washington and has established mosques and meeting places in several other cities of the United States.

The role of Islam in the world is the same today as it has been through the centuries, namely, to help establish and foster direct communion between man and his Maker, and to bring about beneficent adjustment in the relationship between the different sections of mankind. However, the reach and pattern of human thought and life have become, and are daily becoming, vaster and more complex; life has taken on new and unfamiliar dimensions. It looks as if, in the annals of the human race, the present century will stand out as a bridge between the ancient and the modern, the old and the new. It might be designated as the Great Divide.

But truth is fundamental and eternal. It remains constant in all the changing complexities of life. Divine guidance as revealed in the Quran and proclaimed adequate for all mankind through the ages will continue to furnish not only the necessary rules, which in their essence already have been clearly recognized, but also the philosophy that lies behind them, the comprehension of which alone can satisfy reason and understanding, and generate the motive power for action. This is not to be wondered at, once the nature and function of the revelation contained in the Quran is fully grasped.

Surely God, Who has created the universe and all that is in it, including man and the phenomenon of time within which man has his being, and Who has endowed all created things with capacities appropriate to the functions which He has assigned to them (87:2–4), knows well all that may stir and agitate the mind of man from time to time: "Assuredly, We have created man and We know well what his mind whispers to him" (50:17).

He has created man as well as all science, philosophy, and learning, and He has full knowledge of all the subtleties to which the mind of man is prone: "Whether you conceal your thought or declare it openly, He knows full well what is in your minds. Does He Who has created you not know it? He is the Knower of all subtleties, the All-Aware" (67:14–15). Having that knowledge, He has provided guidance in respect of all the contingencies that man might have to face. There are numerous assurances in the Quran to that effect. It is repeatedly stressed that the guidance contained in the Quran "is a revelation from the Lord of the worlds" (26:193). As such it is comprehensive and takes into account the whole process of the evolution of the universe. There is the further assurance that it contains nothing which may be open to doubt, nor anything from which in any circumstances any harm may be apprehended (2:2), inasmuch as it is a revelation from God, Who leads the universe stage by stage toward perfection (32:3).

God is Mighty and has control and direction over the universe.

He causes beneficent results to follow upon human effort which is in accord with His laws. The assurance that the Quran "is a revelation from the Mighty, the One Who blesses human effort with beneficent results" (36:6) is a guarantee that the guidance contained therein will not only keep pace with, but will remain ahead of, man's progress in knowledge and science. This guidance proceeds from God's Wisdom and is based upon and comprises eternal truth. "The revelation of this Book is from Allah, the Mighty, the Wise. Surely it is We Who have revealed the Book to thee with all truth" (39:2-3). God's wisdom has ensured that this guidance shall, in all the contingencies that might arise, prove more than adequate. This follows from God's attributes of Perfect Power, Perfect Wisdom, and Perfect Knowledge (40:3).

God, Who has made provision for the stage-by-stage progress of man toward perfection and Who blesses man's effort with beneficent results, has provided this guidance in "a Book, the verses of which have been expounded in detail—the Quran, in clear, eloquent language—for a people who seek to acquire knowledge and to derive benefit therefrom" (41:3-4). However fast man may go forward and however far his researches into the laws governing the operations of nature and their application may lead him, the guidance provided will always prove adequate. No discoveries with regard to the past and no accession of knowledge with regard to the future shall reveal any inconsistency or deficiency in it, inasmuch as it is a revelation from the Lord of Wisdom, Who has created and devised the whole universe in such manner that all its operations can only redound to His praise. "Truly this is a mighty Book. Falsehood cannot overtake it from the past or in the future. It is a revelation from the Wise, the Praiseworthy" (41:42-43).

God has created the universe and has, out of His Power and Wisdom, bestowed upon it the quality of progress, stage by stage, toward perfection. The guidance revealed by Him takes account of that quality of the universe and keeps pace with it. "The revelation of this Book is from Allah, the Mighty, the Wise. We have not created the heavens and the earth, and all that is between them, but in accordance with the requirements of perfect truth, and for an appointed term; but those who believe not turn away from the warnings given to them" (46:3-4).

Indeed, the revelation itself draws attention to all the Signs in the heavens and in the earth, and in the creation of man and of all life, and in the various phenomena of nature, and in the provision that God has made for man's progress, and in the process of renewal of nature that is continuously in operation. "The revelation of this Book is from Allah, the Mighty, the Wise. Verily, in the heavens and the earth are Signs for those who believe. And in your own creation and in that of all creatures which He scatters in the earth are Signs for the people who possess firm faith. And in the alternation of night and day, and the provision that Allah sends down from the sky, whereby He quickens the earth after its death, and in the changes in the direction of the winds, are Signs for the people who exercise their judgment. These are the Signs of Allah which We rehearse unto thee with truth. In what discourse, then, after rejecting the guidance of Allah and His Signs will they believe?" (45:3-7).

The world is indeed in a sense vastly different today from what it was when the Quran was revealed, but the changes that have come about and those that may follow in rapid sequence, have borne and shall all bear witness to the truth that this is a revelation from the Lord of the worlds. "I call to witness all that you see and all that you see not, that it is surely the Word brought by a noble Messenger; and it is not the word of a poet; little is it that you believe! Nor is it the word of a soothsayer; little is it that you heed! It is indeed a revelation from the Lord of the worlds" (69:39-44).

Here is a direct confrontation with some of the astounding developments that portend. "I call to witness the juxtaposition of the stars—and indeed that is evidence of mighty import, if only you knew—that this is indeed a noble Quran, in a well-preserved Book, to the inner meaning of which none shall penetrate except those who are purified. It is a revelation from the Lord of the worlds. Is it this Divine discourse then that you would reject?" (56:76-82).

Having this assurance and guarantee of the accessibility to him, at all times and in all contingencies, of comprehensive Divine guidance, man has nothing to fear from the rapid advance of science and technology. These are but instruments bestowed by Divine bounty, to be availed of for the fostering of human welfare in every sphere of life. So viewed and put to beneficent use, they will continue to be multiplied as bounties and will not become the instruments of ruin and destruction. "If you will put My

bounties to proper use, I will surely multiply them unto you; but
if you misuse or abuse them, then know that My punishment is
severe indeed" (14:8). The danger does not lie in man's daily
augmenting knowledge of the laws of nature and their operation;
it resides in man's misapplication of these laws. The only effective
safeguard is the acceptance of moral and spiritual values which
lies at the root of all beneficence.

The role of Islam in the present day may be summarized as
follows: It inspires faith in, and vivid realization of, the existence
of a Beneficent Creator, without partner, associate, or equal,
Who is the sole source and fountainhead of all beneficence and
Who has created the universe and all that is in it with a purpose.
The purpose is that man shall become an image of God, a reflection and manifestation of Divine attributes, and be irradiated by
His Light. To that end man has been appointed God's vicegerent
upon earth, and the universe has been "constrained to his service."
The laws governing the universe all operate toward the fulfillment
of that Divine purpose.

Ample guidance has been vouchsafed through revelation to en-
lighten human reason and judgment, and to aid them in regulating human conduct along beneficent lines. Divine law, which
includes the law of nature, and revealed guidance proceed from
the same source; each is illustrative and explanatory of the other.
There is no possibility of conflict between the two. Islam sets
forth the intimate relationship between reason and revelation
and resolves the so-called conflict between science and religion.
It expounds and illustrates spiritual laws and truths by reference
to the operation of physical laws and the phenomena of nature,
and thus stimulates the exercise of reason and the pursuit of
knowledge of every description.

Islam teaches that each human being can and should establish
direct communion with God through faith, that is, through
acceptance of Divine guidance and through righteous conduct
which is conduct in conformity with that guidance. To bring
about and facilitate beneficent adjustment of values in all spheres
of life, and to establish a just balance, it emphasizes man's
accountability and responsibility in respect of his stewardship by
constant reminder of the transitory character of this life, and of
immortality in the life Hereafter.

On the basis of man's relationship to his fellow beings through
God, the Creator of all, it lays the foundations of a true universal

brotherhood, excluding all privilege and discrimination based on color, race, nationality, or on office, status, wealth.

By requiring faith in the truth of all Divine revelation and in the righteousness of all prophets, it seeks to bring about accord and harmony in the religious sphere, and provides a basis of mutual good will and appreciation, co-operation and respect.

In short, Islam sets forth and places at man's disposal a most effective and potent means of achieving the purpose of life. Of all God's numberless bounties bestowed upon man, it is one of the greatest and most precious, and it is indispensable for the beneficent growth of man in the epoch now unfolding before him.

Bibliography

The Holy Quran (Arabic text and English translation). Rabwah, West Pakistan: The Oriental and Religious Publishing Corporation Ltd., 1955.

Ameer Ali, *The Spirit of Islam*. London: Christophers, 1922.

Arberry, Arthur J., *The Koran Interpreted*. London: George Allen & Unwin Ltd., 1955.

Arnold, T. W., *The Preaching of Islam*. London: Constable & Company Ltd., 1913.

Arnold, T. W., and Guillaume, A., eds., *The Legacy of Islam*. Oxford: The Clarendon Press, 1931.

Asad, Muhammad (Leopold Weiss), *The Road to Mecca*. New York: Simon and Schuster, 1954.

Calverley, E. E., *Islam: An Introduction*. Cairo: The American University at Cairo, 1958.

Caselli, Aldo, trans. Veccia Vaglieri, Laura, *An Interpretation of Islam*. Washington: American Fazl Mosque, 1957.

Cragg, Kenneth, *The Call of the Minaret*. New York: Oxford University Press, 1956.

Frye, Richard N., ed., *Islam and the West*. 's Gravenhage, Netherlands: Mouton, 1957.

Gibb, H. A. R., *Mohammedanism*. London: Oxford University Press, 1949.

Guillaume, A., trans. Ishaq, *The Life of Muhammad*. London: Oxford University Press, 1955.

Pickthall, Mohammed Marmaduke, *The Meaning of the Glorious Koran*. New York: The New American Library (Mentor), 1953.

Schroeder, Eric, trans., *Muhammad's People, A Tale by Anthology*. Portland, Me.: The Bond Wheelwright Company, 1955.

Smith, William Cantwell, *Islam in Modern History*. Princeton: Princeton University Press, 1957.

Watt, W. Montgomery, *Muhammad at Mecca*. Oxford: The Clarendon Press, 1953.

Watt, W. Montgomery, *Muhammad at Medina*. Oxford: The Clarendon Press, 1956.

Yusuf Ali, Abdullah, *The Holy Quran*. New York: Harper & Brothers, 1946.

INDEX